West's Law School Advisory Board

JESSE H. CHOPER
Professor of Law,
University of California, Berkeley

JOSHUA DRESSLER
Professor of Law, Michael E. Moritz College of Law,
The Ohio State University

YALE KAMISAR
Professor of Law, University of San Diego
Professor of Law, University of Michigan

MARY KAY KANE
Professor of Law, Chancellor and Dean Emeritus,
University of California,
Hastings College of the Law

LARRY D. KRAMER
Dean and Professor of Law, Stanford Law School

JONATHAN R. MACEY
Professor of Law, Yale Law School

ARTHUR R. MILLER
University Professor, New York University
Formerly Bruce Bromley Professor of Law, Harvard University

GRANT S. NELSON
Professor of Law, Pepperdine University
Professor of Law Emeritus, University of California, Los Angeles

A. BENJAMIN SPENCER
Professor of Law,
Washington & Lee University School of Law

JAMES J. WHITE
Professor of Law, University of Michigan

Evidence in Context:

Evidentiary Problems and Exercises

■ ■ ■

By

Charles H. Rose III

Professor of Excellence in Trial Advocacy
Director, Center for Excellence in Advocacy
Stetson University College of Law

AMERICAN CASEBOOK SERIES®

A Thomson Reuters business

Mat #41060099

Thomson Reuters created this publication to provide you with accurate and authoritative information concerning the subject matter covered. However, this publication was not necessarily prepared by persons licensed to practice law in a particular jurisdiction. Thomson Reuters does not render legal or other professional advice, and this publication is not a substitute for the advice of an attorney. If you require legal or other expert advice, you should seek the services of a competent attorney or other professional.

American Casebook Series is a trademark registered in the U.S. Patent and Trademark Office.

© 2010 Thomson Reuters
    610 Opperman Drive
    St. Paul, MN 55123
    1–800–313–9378

Printed in the United States of America

ISBN: 978–0–314–26737–5

Dedication:

"For my family – my heart, my life, my joy."

"[W]e shall be better and braver and less helpless if we think that we ought to enquire, than we should have been if we indulged in the idle fancy that there was no knowing and no use in seeking to know what we do not know;– that is a theme upon which I am ready to fight, in word and deed, to the utmost of my power."

PLATO, mathematician and philosopher, (427?–347 BC)[1]

"In seeking wisdom, the first step is silence, the second listening, the third remembering, the fourth practicing, the fifth—teaching others."

IBN GABIROL, poet and philosopher (AD 1022–1058)[2]

---

[1] PLATO, *MENO* 56 (Benjamin Jowett trans., Digireads.com 2005). Plato's exact date of birth is unknown.
[2] *THE PAINTER'S KEYS*, http://www.painterskeys.com/auth_search.asp?name=Ibn+Gabirol.

CONTENTS

Chapter 1	HOW TO USE	
	A. Introduction	1
	B. Case Analysis	2
	C. Case Files	3
	D. Problems and Exercises	5
	E. Advocacy Assignments & Common Foundations	5
	F. Conclusion	5
Chapter 2	CASE ANALYSIS	
	A. Introduction	7
	B. Case Analysis	8
	1. Introduction	8
	2. The Rule of Threes	8
	C. Understand and Organize the Case File	10
	1. Beginning Case Analysis	10
	2. The Three Primary Steps	11
	3. Putting It All Together	14
	D. Case Preparation	15
	1. Closing Argument	15
	2. Case-in-Chief	16
	3. Opening Statements	17
	4. Bringing It All Together	18
	E. Case Analysis Checklist	20
	F. Conclusion	22
Chapter 3	PROBLEMS AND EXERCISES	
	A. Introduction	23
	B. Relevancy	25
	C. Relevancy & Character	29
	D. Character Evidence	33
	E. Authentication & Best Evidence	33
	F. Impeachment Problems – Bias, Interest and Ability to Perceive	39
	G. Impeachment – Reputation and Opinion	39
	H. General Impeachment	41
	I. Experts	42
	J. Hearsay & the Confrontation Clause	43
Chapter 4	STATE V. ALEXANDER	
	A. Tab A –	45

- B. Tab B – Police Investigations 63
  - Officer Report of Incident 63
  - Detective Investigative Report 66
  - Officer Incident Report 89
- C. Tab C – Witness Statements 93
  - Robert Hightower 93
  - Nikki Long 95, 102
  - Sharon Barry 97
  - Doris Presley 99
  - Billy Bob Schifflett 100
  - Anece Baxter-White 103
  - Roger Curlin 105
  - Dr. Jeremiah Jones 109
  - Brandi Alexander 113
- D. Tab D – Reports 125
  - Death Certificate 125
  - Coroner's Report 126
  - COC Documents 135
  - Lab Report and Certificate 137
  - PDQ Alarm Report 138
  - Cell Phone Record Report 139
- E. News Coverage 141
- F. Conviction Reports 151
  - Chris Alexander 151
  - Nikki Long 155, 159

Chapter 5   WASHINGTON V. HARTWELL
- A. Tab A – 163
  - Jury Instructions 170
  - Verdict Form 175
- B. Tab B – Court Filing 177
  - Summons 177
  - Complaint 179
  - Answers & Affirmative Defenses 186
  - Request for Production of Documents 192
  - Plaintiff Interrogatories 194
- C. Tab C – Police Investigations 199
  - Officer Report of Incident 199
  - Detective Investigative Report 202
- D. Tab D – News Coverage 235
- E. Tab E – Statements 237
  - Charissa Washington 237
  - Rebecca Hartwell 240
- F. Conviction Reports 243
  - Dimitri Merinov 243
  - Matt Bader 247

    Rebecca Hartwell 251
    Charissa Washington 255, 259

Chapter 6 ADVOCACY ASSIGNMENTS
   A. Introduction to Trial Advocacy 264
   B. Case Analysis 265
   C. Opening Statements 266
   D. Direct Examination 267
   E. Cross Examination 268
   F. Diagrams 269
   G. Exhibits 270
   H. Impeachment Prior Conviction 271
   I. Impeachment Character Evidence 272
   J. Impeachment Prior Inconsistent Statement 273
   K. Advanced Direct & Cross - Experts 274
   L. Refreshing Recollections 275
   M. Closing Arguments 276
   N. Voir Dire 277
   O. Pretrial Motions 278

Chapter 7 FOUNDATIONS 279

ACKNOWLEDGEMENTS
First Edition

The leadership at Stetson University College of Law creates an environment where practical academic scholarship flourishes. Dean Darby Dickerson, Associate Dean Ellen Podgor, and Associate Dean Jamie Fox, supported this project from inception to completion. Dean Dickerson's support for practical scholarly endeavors at Stetson has been a crucial component of their success, and it is just one of the many examples of the opportunities created by her leadership. My work on portions of this text was supported by Stetson's generous scholarship grant program and it would have been impossible to complete without that support.

I am fortunate to teach at a school with deep advocacy roots. The students, staff, and faculty of Stetson University College of Law made each page of this book better. Teaching at the premier advocacy institution is a gift for which I am profoundly grateful. I wish to express my particular thanks to recent Stetson students Vilma Martinez, Allana Forte, Katherine Lambrose, Chandler Irvin, and David Veenstra. Their contributions to this work have been in the best spirit of what it means to be a professional and I am fortunate to count them as both colleagues and friends. Members of the Stetson staff, particularly Bill Greiner, Beth Mills, Peggy Gordon, and Dianne Oestes, kept me on the road to sanity and completion throughout the development of this text. I could not do what I do at Stetson without the support of our excellent staff – they are the backbone of the law school.

I must also thank the folks at West Publishing for seeing the value in publishing case files and the accompanying materials that are so needed in today's law schools.

First, last, and always, I must thank my muse: Pamela, you are the song that my heart sings. I am so fortunate not to sing alone.

Finally, I must recognize the impact that my children, Laura and Charlie, have had on not only the focus of my scholarship, but more importantly my growth as a person. I found myself when I married my wife and I got to know myself through loving my children. What father could ask for more?

The mistakes within, and I am sure that there are many, are, as always, my own.

Enjoy!

Charles H. Rose III
Summer 2010

ACKNOWLEDGEMENTS
Advocacy Teachers

It is considered normal in texts such as this to identify the substantive law contained in appellate cases that are referenced in the following pages. This, however, is a book about oral advocacy and it rests primarily on the foundations of my own experiences, the substantive procedural law, and the wisdom of those from whom I have learned. The book identifies the first two well, but is woefully meager in identifying the third. The following list, incomplete though it may be, is my small attempt to identify the many excellent friends whose ideas I have used and teaching I have admired. If I left you off it was not intentional and I can only plead the advancing effects of middle age. These are the true resources for anyone who practices the art of advocacy, may your list be as long some day.

Aida Alaka
Lt Col Jan Aldykiewicz
Mr. Joseph R. Bankoff
Hon. Thomas Barber
Hon. Emmett Battles
Mr. Thomas G. Becker
Professor Chris Behan
Ms. Pamela Bell
Wendell Betts
Mr. Chris Biggs
Professor G. Robert Blakey
Mr. Joseph Bodiford
Mr. Jude Borque
Professor Brooke Bowman
Mr. George H. Brauchler
Hon. Sandy Brook
Mr. Jeffrey Brown
Colonel Robert Burrell
Mr. David Carlton
Mr. Mark Caldwell
Professor James P. Carey
Mr. Byron Cerrillo
Carol Cline
Mr. Kristopher M. Colley
Professor Lee Coppock
Mr. Nicholas Cox
Hon. Shawn Crane
Ms. Patricia L. Davis
Hon. David Demers
Professor Susan Demers
Professor Mark M. Dobson

Ms. Christine Donoghue
Professor Catherine Dunham
Lt Col Christina Ekman
Colonel Bill Eleazer
Hon. Dave Erikson
Professor Steve Everhart
Professor Kelly Feeley
Professor Roberta Flowers
Mr. Todd Foster
Mike Francis
Mr. Stuart Freeman
Melanie Freeman-Johnson
Colonel James Garrett
Hon. Christina M. Habas
Ms. Lynn Haney
Hon. George Hanks
Ms. Michelle T. Hannigan
Professor Vic Hansen
Jason Har
Colonel Tyler Harder
Lt Col Ernie Harper
Hon. Alfred C. Harrell, Jr
Master Sergeant Matt Harris
Mr. Joel Hayes
Mr. Peter A. Hedeen
Scott Hesse
Hon. Kathleen Hessinger
Todd Hiatt
Professor Peter Hoffman
Colonel Keith Hodges
Ms. Lynne M. Hufnagel
Bernard E. Hurd

Mr. William Hyland
Colonel Mackey Ives
Mr. William W. Jack
Mr. Joseph C. Jaudon
Professor Jeanne Jordan
Mr. Joshua Karton
Kimberly Knoll
Richard J. Lake
Professor Jay Leach
Hon. Lawrence Lefler
Mr. Thomas V. Linguanti
Mr. Cecil Lynn
Mr. Terrance MacCarthy
Hon. Lawrence Manzanares
Ms. Megan W. Martinez
Hon. Michael A. Martinez
Professor Tom Mauet
Michael McCulloch
Mr. James Lincoln McCrystal
Ms. Helen McKeown
Ms. Gillian More
Mr. Christian Myer
Lt Col E.J. O'Brien
Professor Eddie Ohlbaum
Captain Mark Opachan
Mr. Bill Ossmann
Professor Ellen Podgor
Professor Wes Porter

Mr. Mark Rankin
Ms. Judith Roberts
Lt Col Dave Robertson
Hon. Gilbert M. Roman
Lt Col John Saunders
Mr. David C. Schott
Hon. Daniel Sleet
Hon. Ralph Stoddard
Mr. Thomas A. Swett
Professor Jim Seckinger
Professor Hugh M. Selby
Lt Col Keith Selene
Mr. James Sheehan
Mr. Adam Shlahet
Professor Stacey-Rae Simcox
Professor Tom Singer
Ms. Rebecca Sitterly
Duston J. Slindard
Professor Reese Smith Jr.
Lt Col Mike Stahlman
Ms. Karen S. Steinhauser
Sergeant Ed Thiel
Professor Jim Underwood
Professor Stephanie Vaughan
Professor Dave Velloney
Dean Warren Wolfson

Evidence in Context: Evidentiary Problems and Exercises

Chapter 1

How to Use This Book

A. Introduction

This text is designed to create teaching opportunities in evidentiary law by presenting issues in context. This approach requires the student to learn evidence from a practical standpoint. The provided problems and exercises can only be resolved by applying a thorough understanding of evidentiary law to the real-world question concerning the presentation of evidence at trial. This recreates the context of practice and forces the student to bring policy and law to bear on an actual issue that must be solved. The text uses the case files and problems as the framework for evidentiary discussions. This creates a contextual understanding of evidentiary law that addresses how evidentiary principles relate to one another, the way in which specific goals of the litigation impact the admissibility of evidence, and the policy concerns that form the foundation for the application of the rules.

The student must first complete a thorough case analysis in order to successfully answer the problems. This book contains a review of case analysis,[1] specific evidentiary problems and exercises,[2] a criminal case file,[3] a civil case file,[4] common advocacy assignments,[5] and common foundations for admitting evidence.[6] These materials should be used in conjunction with an evidence text that focuses on substantive evidentiary law.[7] It will also serve as an excellent backdrop for understanding the deeper development of basic advocacy skills.

---

[1] Those interested in additional discussion of case analysis should refer to "Fundamental Trial Advocacy," and "Fundamental Pretrial Advocacy." Both are available through West Publishing.

[2] See Chapter 3 of this text.

[3] See *State v. Alexander* in Chapter 4 of this text.

[4] See *Washington v. Hartwell* in Chapter 5 of this text.

[5] See Chapter 6 of this text. These advocacy assignments use a defined assignment/process/outcome approach that ensures a baseline competency when used in conjunction with proper grading paradigms. Both the grading paradigms and the advocacy assignments can be found in the 2nd edition of "Fundamental Trial Advocacy (West)."

[6] See Chapter 7 of this text. This information is also available in the 2nd edition of "Fundamental Trial Advocacy (West).

[7] At Stetson University College of Law we use these case files and problems to form the core of our "tethered evidence" experience. It allows the student to learn evidence through the context of real world situations. The result

B. Case Analysis

Seven Steps to Superior Case Analysis & Preparation:
- Organize the case file
- Identify the legal issues
- Identify the factual issues
- Connect the facts to the law
- Identify the moral theme
- Plan your presentation in reverse
- Verify the evidence

The information contained in this section of the text is based upon chapters found in "Fundamental Trial Advocacy" (West), with additional information that focuses specifically on evidence-driven tasks when conducting case analysis. A thorough understanding of both the mechanics and theory behind case analysis is crucial when learning evidence in context. It is literally the first step to evidentiary mastery.

While case analysis, preparation, and investigation should occur throughout the trial, the first time you are introduced to a case is important for a number of reasons. Advocates make certain decisions during case analysis that will have a long term impact on the resolution of the case. When conducted properly, case analysis combines an understanding the law, the facts, and human nature to create a cohesive persuasive presentation. For our purposes, an understanding of the interaction between evidentiary law and case themes and theories is crucial. This understanding creates relevancy, the penultimate issue for all evidentiary questions.

Identifying which facts exist that the law will allow you to admit is a key concern. This need drives the investigative steps taken throughout the rest of the trial. Case analysis forces you to identify your factual theory - what you believe happened, your legal theory - how the law impacts the facts, and your moral theme - why your side should win. You will learn the mechanics of how to analyze a case in the next chapter. You must master this skill if you are to successfully use these materials to understand evidence.

During case analysis you review evidence, investigate issues, interview witnesses, and prepare exhibits, while continuously reevaluating the process. You rework this process until the case is complete, modifying as required based upon the portion of the trial in which you find yourself. The goal is a cohesive presentation supported by the facts that is admissible under the current legal standards.

Using case analysis will help you prepare the problems based upon identified issues that tie directly to our evidentiary code. This is impossible without a complete understanding of how evidentiary law impacts the admissibility of evidence. Case analysis is an ongoing organic process, and is particularly important when identifying what evidence is admissible, and why.

Case analysis is the structure that drives every trial advocacy decision. You cannot intelligently make these choices without understanding how evidence and advocacy relate to one another through the analytical process. Successful advocates proceed through each distinct portion of the trial in a specific fashion based upon their case analysis - you should, too.

---

is a deeper understanding of evidence and an ability to apply advocacy skills in a class that simulates the issues lawyers face every day.

C. Case Files

The scalable and adaptable case files provided here are designed to showcase the issues facing 21st century advocates. They are based on the lessons learned by Stetson's faculty, students, and alumni, reflecting the same commitment to excellence embodied in our Law School's award winning advocacy teams and its national reputation in Advocacy.

A commitment to the law, the skill, and the art of advocacy forms the foundation for persuasive advocacy. The foundation begins with *knowledge* of the process: the way we train, the way we learn, and the way we practice. This is the core of experiential learning, a preferred methodology for teaching adults. These case files focus advocates on specific advocacy skills in a simulated real world environment, allowing participants to learn the skill and the law in the context of a moment in the trial. The exercises found in chapter 6 accompanying the case file assess advocacy *skills* through the rubric of the experiential learning process. The problems found in chapter 3 address the evidentiary issues. The outcome is an approach that allows the advocate to discover the *values* of the legal profession contextually. The entire concept provides a structure that ensures a baseline of competency in the *knowledge*, *skills*, and *values* involved in becoming a better advocate through a structured approach that focuses on **assignment**, **process**, and **outcome**. The assignments contained in Chapter 6 of this text rely upon this concept of defined processes and outcomes to ensure that a baseline level of competency is produced.

The result is a well-crafted, challenging case file that promotes excellence in all facets of advocacy and evidentiary instruction. This unique multi-media product provides both academics and the practicing bar with modular course content producing varied levels of difficulty depending upon the desired teaching outcome.

The following is a brief introduction to the criminal case file:

State v. Alexander

INTRODUCTION

Brandi Alexander was accused of the shooting and killing of her husband, Chris Alexander, on the night of June 6, 20XX-2. Chris Alexander, 32, was having multiple extramarital affairs and was allegedly talking on a cell phone with one of his lovers, a woman named Nikki Long, less than two minutes before he was shot to death in his living room. The Alexander's two children, Ariel and Jasmine, were asleep in a nearby bedroom at the time of their father's murder.

A gunshot residue test was performed on Brandi the night of the shooting. It found one particle of gunshot residue on the back of her left hand. The murder weapon was a .45 caliber pistol and has not been found. One neighbor heard gunshots but did not see a car fleeing, while another said she heard the screeching wheels of a car right after the shooting. The alleged motive for the murder is jealously, vengeance, and a $250,000 insurance policy. The defendant argued at the first trial that either an intruder, or possibly another jilted lover, killed Chris. Brandi Alexander was convicted on January 9, 20XX-1, and sentenced to life in prison.

Ten months later, the circuit court threw out her conviction and ordered a new trial, citing discrimination in the jury selection process by the prosecution.

The following is a brief introduction to the civil case file:

Washington v. Hartwell

INTRODUCTION

The children were black. The driver was white. The community was outraged. It was a media circus. Was it one vehicle, two or three? A van? A dark blue Honda? A Toyota? Or was it all three? The witnesses couldn't agree. The car sped away as a horrified crowd of about 200 emptied into the street and began shouting in outrage. Children's shoes and sandals were scattered on the pavement. Next to a puddle of blood was a pillow left behind by paramedics who had treated one of the victims. Were the non-working streetlights also to blame? Did someone hide the car? Was DNA removed from the evidence? What were the unsupervised children doing in a high-traffic area at night? Who would pay? After being sought for days, a high-profile criminal defense attorney, Steve Levine, finally announced that the driver would come forward.

On March 21, 20XX-2 at approximately 7:15 p.m., Ms. Rebecca Hartwell was driving her midnight blue Toyota Echo. She was travelling north on 39th Street. It is undisputed that at some point her car hit at least two of the four children crossing the street. She also fled the scene of the accident. The hit-and-run crash killed two brothers, aged 14 and 3, and seriously injured a 2-year-old boy and a 7-year-old girl. The 3-year-old boy was caught underneath the grill of Ms. Hartwell's car and dragged approximately 150 feet before his body worked its way loose and came to final rest in the middle of 39th Street. The Toyota then fled the scene of the accident.

The criminal case has ended. Judge Jerry Parker oversaw the prosecution for negligent homicide that resulted in a hung jury on July 13, 20XX-1. The prosecution's office has indicated that they have no intention of retrying the case, citing evidentiary concerns and proof difficulties. Steve Levine contends that the nature of this trial caused the hung jury to have the effect of a dismissal with prejudice. The state's office has publically stated that they disagree with that assessment.

A civil case has been filed alleging both wrongful death and defamation. After filing answers and affirmative defenses to the Complaint, civil defense counsel moved for a change of venue. The Motion was denied.

D. Problems & Exercises

The problems and exercises contained in this text are specifically designed to identify individual evidentiary issues in a controlled environment. They build evidentiary knowledge sequentially, connecting each piece of the doctrine to the next. Topics covered include: (1) relevancy, (2) character, (3) authentication & best evidence, (4) impeachment, (5) experts, and (6) hearsay.

Each problem or exercise is presented as a moment in time during a trial or evidentiary hearing where you must marshal the evidence for, or against, the admissibility of the evidence in question. The problems increase in complexity, with later problems requiring an understanding of earlier issues in order to provide a full and complete evidentiary analysis.

E. Advocacy Assignments & Common Foundations

The advocacy exercises and common foundations found in Chapters 6 and 7 are provided for students studying in a tethered evidence course or who are looking for additional complementary methods of learning evidence. Each of the assignments focus on advocacy, but a clear understanding of evidentiary law is necessary to maximize the persuasive impact of the advocacy performance. A superior advocate should be able to look at each advocacy task and identify the potential evidentiary issues that will arise during that portion of the trial. You should use them as supplementary materials to better understand the way in which evidence permeates the trial process. Finally, the common foundations serve as an excellent tool for placing evidentiary foundations into context, particularly when dealing with authentication.

F. Conclusion

Now that we have good sense of how this text is designed to work, it is time to move on to a deeper discussion of case analysis. After reviewing the chapter on case analysis you should prepare a written case analysis for both the civil and criminal file. Conducting a proper case analysis is the key step that must be completed before beginning the problems and exercises.

-Notes-

Evidence in Context:
Evidentiary Problems and Exercises

Chapter 2

Case Analysis

A. Introduction

In this chapter we will learn how to (1) perform case analysis, (2) understand a case file, and (3) conduct case preparation. To accomplish these tasks you must choose an organizational construct that processes information, prioritizes the value of that information, and then identifies crucial legal and factual issues applicable to the case. It is truly a matter of preparation best captured in the words often attributed to Abraham Lincoln.[1] In search of the proper mechanism for case analysis and preparation advocates have relied upon many different types of organizational techniques to get a handle on this process. The way in which you conduct case analysis has long-term consequences for the clarity and persuasiveness of your position at trial.

"If I had six hours to chop down a tree, I'd spend the first four sharpening the ax."

ABRAHAM LINCOLN

A superior case analysis (1) assists jurors in understanding the relevant legal and factual issues, (2) brings clarity and focus to the issues the advocate wishes to emphasize, and (3) provides a moral theme that empowers the jury to decide the case in the client's favor. The Rule of Threes[2] provides a superior template to handle case analysis, organize case files, and prepare for trial in a way that allows an advocate to start on the right foot and be immediately successful. Every attorney must develop the ability to properly perform these tasks. While this skill is not normally taught in a law school environment, it can be learned. The use of logical constructs such as the Rule of Threes,[3] in conjunction with an attorney's heightened ability to logically

---

[1] A plethora of on-line sources attribute these words to President Lincoln but researchers and curators at the Springfield, IL, Abraham Lincoln Presidential Library were unable to verify he was actually the source. E-mail from Dr. Bryon Andreasen, Research Historian, Abraham Lincoln Presidential Lib. & Museum to David Veenstra, Student, Stetson U. College L. (copy on file with Author). Additionally, Fred Shapiro, a lecturer in legal research at Yale Law School and the editor of *The Yale Book of Quotations*, likewise concluded this reference is probably apocryphal. E-mail to David Veenstra, Student, Stetson U. College L. (copy on file with Author).

[2] Michael Eck has created the most complete internet portal on this subject. *See The Book of Threes: A Subject Reference Tricyclopedia*, http://threes.com.

[3] Mark Twain referenced trilogies in his own inimical way in *The Autobiography of Mark Twain*, see http://www.twainquotes.com/Statistics.html, stating "Figures often beguile me, particularly when I have the arranging of them myself; in which case the remark attributed to Disraeli would often apply with justice and force: There are three kinds of lies: lies, damned lies and statistics."

reason, will assist advocates in creating persuasive trial presentations through a synergistic combination of the practical and the theoretical.

B. Case Analysis

1. Introduction

Seven Steps to Superior Case Analysis & Preparation:
- Organize the case file
- Identify the legal issues
- Identify the factual issues
- Connect the facts to the law
- Identify the moral theme
- Plan your presentation in reverse
- Verify the evidence

Case analysis is the process of organizing information, applying specialized knowledge to that information, and then viewing the results of that process in light of the advocate's personal understanding of the moral values existing within the community where the case is tried. This is the point in the practice of law where an attorney melds her legal knowledge with her common sense and world experience. At times this process overwhelms a new attorney. She is not quite sure where to start, or how in-depth her initial effort should be. The advocate often wanders aimlessly through the case file, attempting to generate sufficient activity to feel as though she is accomplishing something. This is rarely, if ever, successful, and even when it is, it is not efficient.

The more successful and practical approach addresses each case by applying an overarching structure. An old chestnut often attributed to Benjamin Franklin is "to fail to plan is to plan to fail."[4] This adage definitely applies to case analysis. The only way to overcome what appears to be an overwhelming project is to begin. It is a lot like eating an elephant—you do it one spoonful at a time. The Rule of Threes provides a common sense template to assist you in "eating the elephant"[5] of case analysis. This text uses the Rule of Threes as an overarching structure for case analysis, suggests a series of common sense checklists applicable in most situations, and provides an analytical tool that explains how the three main portions of any trial are connected when analyzing a case. Before applying the Rule of Threes to case analysis it is necessary to first provide an overview of how the Rule of Threes works.

2. The Rule of Threes

The Rule of Threes is an organizational construct used to communicate ideas through the written or spoken word. It posits that when information is organized in triplets human beings are more likely to accept and internalize the messages contained within those three-pronged packages. This three-part harmony view of communication is a powerful tool if you accept its basic premise. When deciding whether or not to use the Rule of Threes you should consider examples of communications recognized and accepted as instances of superior communication. Both western civilization[6] and Asian heritage[7]

---

[4] Often Attributed to Benjamin Franklin, see JOHN MARKS TEMPLETON, *DISCOVERING THE LAWS OF LIFE* (The Continuum Publishing Company, 1995).

[5] BILL HOGAN, *HOW DO YOU EAT AN ELEPHANT? ONE BITE AT A TIME!* (Llumina Press 2004).

[6] Examples from western civilization include Greek philosophy, Judaism, and early Christianity.

[7] Classical Hinduism dates back to at least 500 B.C. with roots extending to 2000 B.C. The Hindu doctrine of divine trinity is called Trimurti (from Sanskrit "three forms") consisting of Brahma, Vishnu, and Shiva. Brahma is the Father or Supreme God;

provide many opportunities from which to choose when looking for effective examples of the Rule of Threes. The history of the United States contains many such instances where the use of the Rule of Threes delivered a message that resonated in the hearts and minds of the American people.

Consider the words of Dr. Martin Luther King, Jr.[8] Note his use of both the Rule of Threes and parallelism[9] in the two complementary triplets dealing with the twin themes of hatred and love. His message is powerful, controlled, and ultimately uplifting. Dr. King touched the emotional core of his audience by using the Rule of Threes to arrange his message in a manner that ensured acceptance by the audience. He spoke to us in a way that we could understand. The strength of his message resounded from the depths of a jail cell in Birmingham, Alabama, to the steps of the Lincoln Memorial in Washington, D.C. Advocates who use the Rule of Threes to conduct case analysis will begin to develop skills that ultimately will increase their persuasive ability at trial.

"Hatred paralyzes life;
Love releases it.
Hatred confuses life;
Love harmonizes it.
Hatred darkens life;
Love illumines it."
DR. MARTIN LUTHER KING, JR.

The Rule of Threes has been used to create belief systems and memorable phrases that are part and parcel of the tapestry that forms our daily lives. The philosophy of the ancient world focused on *logos, pathos*, and *ethos* as a way of living, understanding that who an advocate was mattered nearly as much as what they did.[10] Trilogies teaching others how to live as a member of society exist within many great written works, including The Bible, where messages such as "When I was a child, I spake as a child, I understood as a child, I thought as a child: but when I became a man, I put away childish things" are easily found.[11] As noted previously, Hinduism believes in the Trimurti form of the divine trinity reflected in the gods Brahma, Vishnu and Shiva.

The existence and use of the Rule of Threes in cultures separated by not only beliefs but time is striking from an organizational perspective and supports the argument that the Rule of Threes works because it is intrinsic to the human condition. This connection exists across cultures and evidence of it can be found in Judea-Christian traditions, the mythology of ancient Greece,[12] and the tenets of Hinduism. Beyond issues of faith however, the Rule of Threes is also

"Nature never repeats herself,
and the possibilities of one human soul,
will never be found in another.
Whatever the theories may be
of woman's dependence on man,
in the supreme moments of her life,
he can not bear her burdens."

ELIZABETH CADY STANTON

Vishnu is the incarnate Word and Creator, while Shiva is the Spirit of God. Hindus view them as inseparable unity and worship them as one deity. See "trimurti," Encyclopedia Britannica, 2006, Britannica Concise.

[8] MARTIN LUTHER KING, JR., STRENGTH TO LOVE, 122 (CollinsWorld 1977)

[9] The Catholic Encyclopedia defines parallelism to mean "The balance of verse with verse, an essential and characteristic feature in Hebrew poetry. Either by repetition or by antithesis or by some other device, thought is set over against thought, form balances form, in such wise as to bring the meaning home to one strikingly and agreeably. In the hymns of the Assyrians and Babylonians parallelism is fundamental and essential." *See* http://www.newadvent.org/cathen/ 11473a.htm.

[10] *See* ARISTOTLE, THE ART OF RHETORIC, (H.C. Lawson-Tancred trans., Penguin Books 1991).

[11] *1 Corinthians* 13:11.

[12] APOLLODORUS, LIBRARY AND EPITOME (Sir James George Frazer ed.). "[F]rom the drops of the flowing blood were born Furies, to wit, Alecto, Tisiphone, and Megaera."

grounded in our physical ability to perceive the world around us. It is part and parcel of how we think and communicate. Consider for a moment the world surrounding you. Your senses view the world from a three-dimensional perspective. These three dimensions form the boundaries of your physical world. When our world does not accurately reflect all three dimensions our physical comfort is compromised. In the same way, words and thoughts that do not reflect a Rule of Threes organizational construct ring less than true in our minds, impinging on our ability to accept as true the message being presented.

Applying the Rule of Threes creates an internal sense of believability and acceptance for the jury. Noted trial advocates have lectured on the use of this rule, including Terrence MacCarthy, a successful and famous Chicago defense attorney, and Thomas Singer, a respected member of the National Institute for Trial Advocacy and the Notre Dame Trial Advocacy faculty. When properly applied this rule serves as a template for organizing, analyzing, and presenting a case.

> **Primacy & Recency:**
> - Tell them what you are going to tell them *(opening statement)*
> - Tell them *(case-in-chief)*
> - Tell them what you told them *(closing argument)*

The doctrine of primacy and recency is an excellent common sense example of an application of the Rule of Threes. Advocates use the doctrine of primacy and recency to (1) tell the jury what they are going to tell them (opening statement), (2) tell them (case-in-chief), and (3) then tell them what they told them (closing argument). It is also used to make certain that advocates start and finish strong. They are taught to put their best facts first and last, with a filling in the middle of their weaknesses. There is persuasive power in this type of organizational structure, but advocates should be careful to not focus on "hiding" bad facts and instead work on how to either neutralize them or turn them to their advantage

You will use these tools throughout the advocacy process, including in opening statements, direct and cross examinations, and closing arguments. Before taking those next steps in your development as a successful advocate you must first learn how to understand and organize a case file. The Rule of Threes is an excellent tool for breaking case files down into their component parts, with the goal of fully answering three primary series of questions. You need to know the argument that you will make to the jury in closing arguments, the evidence you will introduce through the testimony of witnesses during your case-in-chief and the story that you will tell during your opening statement. Proper case analysis identifies and answers each of these core questions in the development and presentation of your case.

C. Understand and Organize the Case File

1. *Beginning Case Analysis*

> Knowing how a case file is supposed to be prepared empowers you to make an initial credibility determination regarding the information they do, or do not, contain.

A case file can appear in your hands in a variety of ways, depending upon the firm or government entity where you work. Regardless of the source of the file, it is important to take the time to understand the filing procedures and reporting requirements for your office and the agencies they work with before you begin to delve into the depths of a particular case file. Have someone who normally works with these reports break it down for you and explain the different parts. Once you know how a proper file is supposed to look you will be better prepared to determine when one is incomplete, poorly developed, or improperly addresses the information it is supposed to contain. This is a common sense approach to understanding documents that is crucial to your later analytical process. If you do not know how a case file is supposed to be prepared, how can you make an initial credibility determination regarding the information presented in the file? In today's legal arena much of the business of case preparation will involve documents. You must begin to develop expertise in handling them from the outset of your legal career. Assuming that you have developed the necessary practical knowledge concerning a particular case file, what should you do when you actually get one?

> **Organizing a Case File:**
>
> Gather together all relevant documents and evidence, and organize the information. Use:
>
> 1. Chronological time lines
> 2. Systems, including:
>   a. Trial notebooks
>   b. Witness folders
>   c. Computer case management software
>
> List all available information (evidence) without regard to its admissibility or whose argument it supports.
>
> Identify the relevant legal issues. Be sure to address:
>
> 1. Procedural issues (evidence and procedure)
> 2. Substantive issues (applicable statutes and the common law)
> 3. Constitutional issues (both state and federal)

Start by reading through the entire file. Take a moment after this first reading and jot down your initial impressions of the information you have just received. *What questions are in your mind? Is there something else you need to know? Have you made some initial judgments about the people involved?* These are the same types of questions that jurors will be asking when the case is presented at trial. It is at this point in the process that you are as close as you will ever be to thinking about the case the way a juror would. Once you have done this, set those observations aside in a safe place where you can later come back to them.

Your goal at this point is not to write the perfect brief or motion, but rather to get a handle on what you have before you. It is only after you gather together all of the relevant documents, legal pleadings, and other information and organize it in a systematic way, that you can see the "conceptual whole" of the case. This big picture understanding will allow you to identify strengths and weaknesses and potential moral themes and legal theories. The ability to correctly identify the underlying moral themes is crucial. Morality, right and wrong, black and white, good guys and bad guys—this is the language of the jury. It comes from our shared culture and is reflected in the societal vehicles that teach us about the law. Think in terms of the many television shows, movies, and books dealing with legal situations. The public is fascinated with the process of assigning moral blame and imposing legal judgment. If your client's story falls into an archetype the jury understands you will benefit immensely when you harness that archetype and make it part of your moral theme.

2. The Three Primary Steps

The initial step in deconstructing the case file uses the Rule of Threes to organize the information so that you can identify factual and legal issues and how they relate to one another. *Organization in a systematic fashion is the key to successfully understanding a case file.* Once you have organized the information contained in the case file you can begin to analyze the contents using the three main steps of case analysis. The three primary steps in case analysis are used

> **The Three Primary Steps in Case Analysis:**
>
> - Identify and analyze the legal issues
> - Identify and analyze the factual issues
> - Develop a moral theme and legal theory

> **Identify & Analyze the Factual Issues:**
>
> A. List the contested claims and defenses, with the burden of proof for each
> B. For each contested claim or defense identify:
>   a. The contested legal elements
>   b. The deciding questions of facts
>   c. The persuasive legal theory for each deciding question of fact
> C. Develop a plan for identifying and managing the source of facts, including:
>   a. Creating chronological time lines
>   b. Arranging documents systemically
>   c. Listing and cataloging all available exhibits
>   d. Listing all potential witnesses

for bench trials (judge alone), jury trials, arbitration panels, or any adversarial dispute resolution proceeding. A complete case analysis applies these three steps to each component part of a trial or adjudicative proceeding, ensuring the case analysis is complete. Examples of where this happens includes identifying closing argument topics, preparing direct, cross and redirect examinations, conducting discovery, deposing witnesses, creating juror profiles, choosing jurors, and selecting opening statement topics. This list is not exhaustive, but it does provide a sense of the various portions of a trial where you must apply the three main steps of case analysis.

As you perform these tasks consider the moral theme and legal theory of your case. Your theme and theory provide coherence and continuity to the facts presented at trial and connects those facts to the legal issues you chose in a way that demands victory for your side. If dissonance exists between the theme and theory and the facts or law of your case, you must adapt. Discover additional facts or law that support your position, modify your theme and theory, or settle the case. Whenever the theme and theory changes you must go back and reevaluate your case analysis in light of those changes.

A systematic approach is necessary to ensure that you cover all of the possible legal issues. To identify the appropriate legal issues you must understand not only the law, but the specific area of the law that applies to your particular case. Procedurally you should identify admissibility issues while substantively looking for strengths and weaknesses where the law intersects with the facts. Always look for both substantive and procedural legal issues because either can be case dispositive.

After identifying the important legal theories the next step is to convince the judge that your interpretation of the law applies in this particular instance. Normally this occurs during pretrial motions or motions in limine. These arguments about which law applies are normally made by counsel before the judge and outside the presence of the jury. When the issue is solely a question of law, it may be possible to argue motions without the need for evidence, but that is rarely the case. You should always remember that whenever a court is talking about evidence they are really talking about facts placed before the court through the testimony of a witness.

> **Identify & Analyze Legal Issues:**
>
> - List the legal elements for the claims and defenses
> - Analyze the legal principles and questions of law
> - Develop a legal theory for each persuasive question of fact

The first thing that a good judge will ask counsel for when arguments about the law are being made is what facts support their position and what evidence will be offered for the judge's consideration. Counsel can make a proffer of what the evidence will be, but that proffer is only counsel's opinion and not substantive evidence that the judge may rely upon when ruling. Evidence may be actual testimony, previous stipulations, or previously admitted evidence. Trial judges are not bound by the normal hearsay rules when determining most motions and can rely upon written documents or other out-of-court statements for the limited purpose of ruling on a motion.

It is imperative that you develop the skill of identifying and analyzing those facts that are case dispositive. Dispositive facts are much more easily identifiable after you have developed the appropriate legal issues presented in the case. The facts of the case will determine whether the law applied by the judge assists or hurts your theme and theory. You must fully develop the relationship between the facts and the law. *Your ability to identify the ruling legal precedent, develop case dispositive facts, and then explain their relationship to the jury using an appropriate moral theme and legal theory is the essence of trial advocacy.*

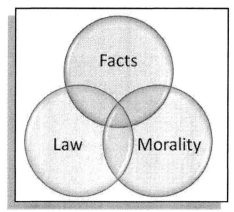

We have identified three primary areas of case analysis that continuously shift in importance depending upon who you represent and the issues at hand. You must develop the ability to sense which is most important for a particular case. Some of that ability to find the best path will develop through experience, but a great deal of it is centered in the type of person you are and in the way you personally prefer to view the world. You may have a preference for factual analysis, legal analysis, or moral issues. If you lean towards one of these areas then begin your case analysis from that perspective, taking care to ensure that you do not allow your personal predilections to prevent you from seeing issues in areas that may not be your strongest suit. Others have referred to this technique as "mind mapping," and have presented it as a conceptual tool for case analysis.[13] There is a good deal of common sense and practical wisdom in this concept.

At a minimum it is important to start from a perspective that ensures you are engaged in the process and can see relationships between categories. It is helpful to have some degree of personal introspection in order to find your best starting point. Excellent tools exist to assist advocates in this process, including the Myers-Briggs test[14] and the Kiersey Temperament Sorter.[15] The methodology you choose is not important, taking the time to know yourself before you represent others, on the other hand, is not only important but vital to a developing trial advocate, from both a competency and ethical perspective.

Once you have identified your starting point and analyzed the case you will have identified certain facts you want in or out at trial and legal rulings that will either strengthen or weaken your case. To accomplish this, advocates normally file motions with the court to identify which facts will be admissible and which law is applicable.

Motions practice at trial is an attempt by both sides to limit the admissible facts supporting the legal positions of opposing counsel while expanding the available

---

[13] HUGH SELBY & GRAEME BLANK, *WINNING ADVOCACY: PREPARATION, QUESTIONS, ARGUMENT* (formerly *Winning in Court - An Introduction to Advocacy*) (Oxford Press 2d ed. 2004).

[14] *See e.g.* NAOMI L. QUENK, *ESSENTIALS OF MYERS-BRIGGS TYPE INDICATOR ASSESSMENT (ESSENTIALS OF PSYCHOLOGICAL ASSESSMENT)* (John Wiley & Sons, Inc. 2000).

[15] *See e.g.* DAVID KIERSEY & MARILYN BATES, *PLEASE UNDERSTAND ME: CHARACTER & TEMPERAMENT TYPES*, pages (Prometheus Nemisis 1984); and *see* DAVID KIERSEY, *PLEASE UNDERSTAND ME II: TEMPERAMENT, CHARACTER, INTELLIGENCE* (Prometheus Nemisis 1992).

admissible facts that support their own legal position. Once you have identified the legal issues and facts available to you it is time to take the next step—creating a vehicle that allows you to combine the law and the facts into a persuasive whole that will convince the jury to decide in your favor. A proper case analysis assists the advocate in choosing the correct moral theme and legal theory in light of the available facts. Failure to accomplish this results in a cognitive dissonance in the minds of the fact-finder. What comes out of your mouth does not match the facts as they see them. They will conclude that you are either incompetent or lying. Either way you lose.

3. Putting It All Together

Your legal theory is the application of the relevant law to the specific facts of your case. It forms the basis for the legal or procedural reasons that you should win. The theory is how the jury goes about deciding the case your way and is derived from a complete case analysis discussed above. Considering each legal element of offenses and potential defenses will quickly identify possible legal theories. A case based solely on legal theories can be difficult from a persuasive standpoint. The shipwrecked crew adrift in a lifeboat that kills and eats the weakest member of their group and is then later rescued is a classic example[16] of the difficulties with a purely legal defense. A murder occurred, but a potential defense of necessity exists. That legal defense however, may not have a moral theme that supports it. In the shipwreck case a good argument could be made that the strongest members of the party had a duty to protect the weaker ones, not a duty to eat them. Conversely, it could be argued that the weakest member was going to die anyway, and killing him saved the lives of the others.

It is often possible for valid legal theories to run into a lack of credibility when they require the jury to adopt an unpopular moral theme or to reject a cherished community belief. In either instance you may find yourself with an excellent legal theory that will never carry the persuasive burden. Jurors are not lawyers and most advocates would do well to remember that fact. ***Legal theories must be combined with a solid moral theme to succeed.***

Do the Math:

$$\frac{\text{Good Legal Theory}}{\text{Poor Moral Theme}} = \text{Bad Result}$$

The theme is the moral reason that you should win. It is why the jury wants to decide the case your way. A good moral theme identifies an injustice that is being committed against your client and empowers the jury to right that wrong. Themes are as varied as the people, places, and situations they are designed to capture and represent. The theme provides the moral force that brings the case to life. A good theme not only gets the jury on your side, it creates a feeling of comfort within them about deciding things your way.

If you cannot find a theme within your case that will resonate with the jury, try to determine what sense of injustice exists in the case. Is there a wrong that has been committed against your client that you can use to energize the jury to decide for you? Perhaps the government rushed to judgment because your client is a minority. Or the man who committed the crime is walking around free while your client's exemplary life has been destroyed through the incompetence, stupidity, carelessness, or malfeasance of the opposing side. Other examples include the destruction of a way of life or the health of an individual

---

[16] *See R. v. Dudley and Stephens* [1884] 14 QBD 273 DC. The sketch on this page comes from a party to that case.

through the greed of a soulless corporation. The storylines are as varied and complex as the tales of humanity that surround us each day. They exist in your shared experiences as a member of the collective society that is represented by the fact-finder. Stay in touch with these perennial themes of life. They are the vehicle through which you can persuasively explain your case to others.

D. Case Preparation

Now that you have thoroughly analyzed the case you are ready to prepare for trial. Go back and review the initial impressions you wrote down after you read through the case file for the first time. Does the theme and theory you have chosen answer the questions you first wrote down? Do the facts that you will rely upon at trial reflect your earlier understanding of the case? If so, you are ready to proceed with case preparation. If not, you should take a long, hard look at the choices you made during your case analysis. It may be that you have done the best that you could as not all sides are equally arrayed in an adversarial proceeding. While it is your ethical duty to try as best you can to represent your client based upon the facts and the law available, bad facts rarely make for good cases, but they sometimes create excellent advocacy opportunities.

Regardless of the strength of your case, once you are convinced that you have fully and completely addressed all legal, factual, and thematic issues, it is time to put it all together. We will use the Rule of Threes to set the stage for accomplishing this task. The trial is broken down into three primary sections: closing argument, case-in-chief, and opening statement. I have not listed them chronologically because cases are not prepared chronologically, but rather in a logical fashion based upon the desired endpoint. Once we have "set up" our case from this perspective we will then use proof worksheets to further develop the testimony of individual witnesses based upon the case analysis conducted.

1. Closing Argument

When taking a trip, the first thing you do is pick your destination. You then plan backwards from that point, all the way back to the time of departure. Your closing argument is your destination. The case-in-chief is the route you will take and the opening statement is your departure point. The closing argument contains the words that empower the jury to decide the case in your favor. It melds the facts and the law of the case, casting them in a moral light.

A good closing argument demands, sometimes loudly, sometimes quietly, sometimes reluctantly, but demands nonetheless, that the jury do nothing other than what you ask. How can you take a jury to that place if you yourself do not know where it is that you are going? It is imperative that you begin with your closing argument—from that destination all other decisions must flow.

If you have properly identified the legal and factual issues and have chosen the right theme and theory, the closing argument will come to you as an organic expression of what your hard work has shown you to be true. If you have not properly analyzed the case, you will struggle to find a closing argument that makes sense and fits the facts and the law of the case. There is great danger in choosing a closing argument that does not organically spring from the facts and the law. You may sound wonderful delivering it, but the jury will be left cold in the end and will turn to the side whose argument makes the most sense, both rationally and emotionally. We will discuss formulating superior closing arguments later. For now, understand and internalize the belief that you start at the end with your closing argument.

If you cannot see yourself standing before the jury in that moment, with those words, then you have not done your job during case analysis and you are not yet ready to prepare the case for trial.

2. Case-in-Chief

Once you have decided on your final destination, you must choose your route. The testimony of witnesses is the primary means available to introduce evidence at trial. For every fact that you intend to argue in your closing argument, you must have a witness to introduce that fact. What you need to support your legal theory and moral theme determines which witnesses you will call to testify.

Each witness is a piece of the puzzle that you are building for the jury. This includes not only your witnesses, but your opponent's, and you should plan for both. By connecting expected testimony to the closing argument, you increase not only your persuasive ability but, more importantly, the believability of your theme and theory.

This process is double edged. Not only should you identify those issues your witnesses will testify about, but you should also identify issues you can either introduce or buttress through the cross examination of opposing counsel's witnesses. By taking the time to do this, you are testing the validity of your theme and theory and also identifying crucial testimony you must get out of witnesses on direct and cross. This type of case analysis produces a template that guides you in selecting, questioning, and preparing witnesses. The jury does not realize you have done this and instead merely hears the witnesses saying those things that support your legal theory and moral theme. You set yourself up to accomplish this by using proof analysis worksheets during case analysis to further refine the presentation of witness testimony during the trial. You use them to combine your legal and factual theories so that you can find the themes that actually work. A proof analysis worksheet is a mechanical construct that allows you to cross reference the law the must be proven, the method of proof, and potential issues. They look something like this:

PROOF ANALYSIS Worksheet:		
Charge/Cause of Action:		
Elements	Method of Proof	Defect or Attack

The use of this process is not limited to factual issues for the case-in-chief. The judge will rule upon motions and objections during the trial. Your ability to produce questions that support the admissibility or suppression of testimony or physical evidence is critical. Knowing that you want certain instructions from the judge before jury deliberations empowers you to make certain that your witnesses testify in a manner that supports the instructions on the law and the facts that you will request from the judge. By properly developing this, you can foreshadow the judge's instructions during your closing argument. The jury hears you say that the law is a certain way, and then the judge confirms your prediction and increases your credibility in the eyes of the jury by instructing the jury on the law in accordance with your argument during closing. As a consequence, you appear fair, impartial, and correct.

This makes you trustworthy in the eyes of the jury. A famous Florida trial lawyer[17] is known to say "I'll give the other side the judge, if you give me the jury." Using instructions in this fashion can help you get both.

Consider the following scenario based upon the timeless bedtime story of Little Red Riding Hood. You are defending the woodsman charged with the murder of the wolf that tried to eat Little Red Riding Hood. You would begin to prepare a proof analysis worksheet.

PROOF ANALYSIS Worksheet: *State v. Woodsman*		
Charge: Premeditated Murder		
Elements	**Method of Proof**	**Defect or Attack**
1. That a certain named or described person is dead;	Coroner – will testify that the wolf died as a result of axe wounds	Defense has potential necessity/defense of others. If the necessity defense is not valid may still be able to raise mistake of fact as to belief of the threat by wolf
2. That the death resulted from the act or omission of the accused;	Red Riding Hood will testify that wolf was in the closet when Woodsman slew it	Little Red Riding Hood – can testify that she was in immediate fear of her life at time wolf was killed, that she screamed for help and was afraid for her grandmother's life*
3. That the killing was unlawful; and	Grandmother will testify that wolf did not eat her when he had the chance	Woodsman – if he testifies can explain his State fo Mind at time of assault
4. That, at the time of the killing, the accused had a premeditated design to kill	Mother of wolf will testify that wolf was a vegetarian. Will also testify he was a pacifist (if defense opens door to character)	*Review and prepare appropriate case law on self defense and defense of others, draft appropriate instructions for judge to give

3. Opening Statements

Opening statements are the *first* thing you do once the trial starts but the *last* thing you plan for. This is the beginning point in your journey with the jury. Think of yourself as a tour guide telling your fellow passengers where you are taking them. You will identify the final destination and explain the route that all of you must travel to reach that destination. This allows you to tell the story of what happened and then forecast the relevant law in light of the legal issues that you know will be relevant when it arrives at the final destination – a verdict in favor of your client.

If you analyze your case properly the opening statement will be persuasive but not argumentative. Most advocates either descend into argument during their opening statement or spend a great deal of time explaining the process of what the jury can expect throughout the course of the trial. They do this because they have not connected the three main sections of trial together as described here.

This text takes a very fact-heavy approach to opening statements that avoids the argumentative objection for a very good reason – it doesn't help your case to argue about facts that the jury doesn't yet know or believe during opening statements. This is the time to tell the story of what happened so that the jury can begin to decide whose story makes sense. Opening statements are concerned with what

---

[17] Lee Coppock, J.D., Stetson University College of Law, National Trial Team Champion and current coach of the Stetson University College of Law Trial Team, is a legal legend in Florida. This quote is one of his favorites and it captures a great degree of practical wisdom.

happened – you will get a chance during closing arguments to tell the jury why it matters. Openings are your best chance to set the stage for the testimony and arguments that will follow. It makes no sense to argue about facts that no one else is yet aware of. An advocate that argues about facts out of context looks like someone walking down the street while talking to themselves – it is not a very persuasive picture.

4. *Bringing It All Together*

The following series of diagrams explain how to cohesively prepare your case, regardless of its relative complexity or simplicity. It is a simple concept that builds off of the earlier work that you have done using proof analysis worksheets by combining that work with an application of the rule of threes. Before you can perform this process you must first complete a proof analysis for each factual or legal issue you intend to address in your case. That proof analysis worksheet must have identified the relevant evidence you will produce and the source of that evidence. This foundational work is crucial if you are to properly prepare for trial. Oftentimes that additional work uncovers new legal theories or facts that were not available when the case first became your responsibility. The completed proof analysis worksheets connect with the following explanation to provide a cohesive graphical method that assists in preparing your case for trial.

The concept is deceptively easy, allowing for additional layers of complexity as needed. This type of analysis can be done with nothing more than a piece of paper and a pencil by drawing three columns and labeling them as follows:

Opening Statement	**Case-in-Chief**	**Closing Argument**

Think about your final destination. What do you need to bring the jury to the conclusions that require them to find in your favor? How will the facts that you must present connect to the law and the sense of injustice captured by your moral theme? Once you have this clearly in mind list those items in the Closing Argument column:

Opening Statement	**Case-in-Chief**	**Closing Argument**
		Moral Theme Factual Theory 　(evidence) 　　facts 1, 2, & 3 Legal Theory 　(law) 　　facts 4, 5, & 6

Now that you know where you are going you have to choose the route to reach your destination. This guides your approach to both direct and cross examination. This allows you to identify the subject matter of each direct and cross examination you need to conduct based upon what you must be able to say during closing arguments. Each witness connects to a fact that will be discussed during the case-in-chief. Failure to identify evidence in this fashion can directly impact on your ability to prove to your case. The beauty of this approach is that it provides you with a context for everything you do. In our diagram you could lay that out as follows:

Opening Statement	Case-in-Chief	Closing Argument
	Direct Witness (DW) DW 1: facts (1) & (6) DW 2: facts (2) & (5) Cross Witness (CW) CW 1: supporting fact CW 1: credibility CW 2: facts (3) & (4)	Moral Theme Factual Theory (evidence) facts 1, 2, & 3 Legal Theory (law) facts 4, 5, & 6

The connection between your moral theme, factual theory, and legal theory becomes obvious when you use this tool. If you want to talk about a fact or get a legal instruction from the judge in closing, you have to produce that fact through either your own witness or opposing counsel's. The same holds true for most persuasive facts and necessary legal rulings. If you lay out your case preparation in this manner, you will identify substantive weaknesses in your case based upon a lack of legal precedent, a dearth of facts, or a moral theme that simply does not comport with the facts and the law. This is a warning bell to perform additional investigation until you resolve these dichotomies. If you cannot do so, it is time to settle this particular case if it is a civil matter, or plead it out if a criminal one.

The last step in using this diagram is to list what you need in your opening statement. Opening statements serve as the bookend for the closing argument. Openings and closings contain the same strands of law, facts and morality. The emphasis is different depending upon which portion of the trial you are in, but the core value remains the same throughout the trial. Analyzing the case in this fashion allows you to use persuasive teaching techniques that both science and experience tell us work.

Opening Statement	Case-in-Chief	Closing Argument
Moral Theme (hook) Tell the story (facts) facts 1, 2, 3 Foreshadow the law (instructions) facts 4, 5, 6	Direct Witness (DW) DW 1: facts (1) & (6) DW 2: facts (2) & (5) Cross Witness (CW) CW 1: supporting fact CW 1: credibility CW 2: facts (3) & (4)	Moral Theme Factual Theory (evidence) facts 1, 2, & 3 Legal Theory (law) facts 4, 5, & 6

Consider the relationships between the three basic portions of a trial created above. By viewing them in a connected way you create a coherent message for the jury. Although you planned it in reverse by beginning at the end, it plays forward when presented. The jury hears you tell them where they are going and how they will get there in the opening statement. You then transport them to the final destination through the testimony and remind them of where they are and what that means in closing argument. To the juror, you have told them what you are going to do, done it, and then reminded them you did it and explained what it all means. You have credibility now. The jury will view you as an ethical, straight-shooter who they can trust. More importantly, you will actually be an ethical advocate that has done the ground work to ensure success. The following checklist contains the major concepts we have covered in this chapter.

E. Case Analysis Checklist

The following checklist summarizes the information presented in this chapter on conducting a superior case analysis. You should use it as a starting point as you analyze and prepare to present the cases. Over time you will add different sections to this checklist based upon the specific type of cases in your practice. For now it is a good place to begin.

I. Organize the Case File

    a. Gather and organize all relevant documents and evidence. Use:

        i. Chronological time lines

        ii. Develop Systems, including:

            1. Trial notebooks

            2. Witness folders

            3. Computer case management software

II. List all available Information (evidence) - without regard to its admissibility or whose argument it supports

III. Identify, Analyze, and Apply the Law

    a. Procedural issues (evidence and procedure)

    b. Substantive issues (applicable statutes and the common law)

    c. Constitutional issues (both state and federal)

    d. Analyze the law:

        i. List legal elements for claims and defenses

        ii. Analyze legal principles and questions of law

        iii. Develop a legal theory for each question of fact

    e. Practical legal impact:

        i. Proper claims and defenses?

        ii. Prepare and Respond to discovery

        iii. Develop Motions in Limine

        iv. Identify Potential Trial Objections

        v. Consider their impact on witness testimony

| Chapter 2 | Case Analysis | Page 21 |

        vi. Identify Potential Appellate Issues

IV. Identify, Analyze & Manage the Factual Issues

    a. Identify and Analyze - list the contested claims and defenses, with the burden of proof for each. For each claim or defense identify:

        i. The contested legal elements

        ii. The deciding questions of facts

        iii. The persuasive legal theory for each deciding question of fact

    b. Manage - identify and organize sources of facts by:

        i. Creating chronological time lines

        ii. Arranging documents systemically

        iii. Listing and cataloging all available exhibits

        iv. Listing all potential witnesses

V. Identify, Develop & Apply the Moral Theme

    a. Develop the essence of the moral theme

        i. Sense of Injustice

        ii. The Most Appalling Thing

        iii. One Liner

        iv. Grabber

    b. Consider how the moral theme is reflected in the facts and the law

    c. Combine the moral theme with the facts and law to create a persuasive story of what happened, and why it matters

VI. Plan Your Presentation in Reverse

    a. The Rule of Threes

    b. Primacy and Recency

        i. Tell them what you are going to tell them (opening statement)

        ii. Tell them (case-in-chief)

        iii. Tell them what you told them *(closing argument)*

    c. Standards of Proof

VII. Verify the Evidence

    a. Consider procedural rules to procure the evidence

    b. Consider the evidentiary rules applicable

        i. Relevancy

        ii. Character

        iii. Hearsay

        iv. Privileges

v. Foundation

    1. Authenticity

    2. Relevancy

    3. Personal knowledge

F. CONCLUSION

We have spent a great deal of time in this chapter learning case analysis and preparation. The goal has been to identify the "what." Case analysis and preparation identifies what evidence must be admitted under the law to win. While best done systemically, it remains a process that is subject to both logical thought and creativity. The final product is capable of being objectively tested to ensure that the core concepts of the law, persuasion and professionalism have been met. At the same time to methods used to perform case analysis are individual in nature. Each advocate must, to a certain extent, discover through practice the way that works best for them.

I have focused on certain overarching themes in case analysis that relate back to the concepts of pathos, ethos and logos that I have found helpful in my development. You should try them but not feel tied to them. The important thing is that you analyze from a moral, factual, and legal perspective in light of the issues the fact-finder must decide. We will apply these lessons of case analysis in this text, with specific emphasis on how the facts and evidentiary law intertwine. Relevancy is driven by case analysis, and the story you "can" tell at trial, as opposed to the one you "want" to tell, is circumscribed by all of the evidentiary rules affecting admissibility. Your next step is to practice the lessons in this chapter by performing case analysis on *State v. Alexander* and *Washington v. Hartwell*. Once you have accomplished that goal you can delve into the problems and exercises found in Chapter 3.

Evidence in Context:
Evidentiary Problems and Exercises

Chapter 3
Problems & Exercises

A. Introduction

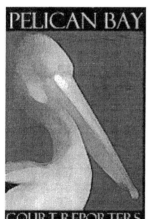

The following problems and exercise are based upon the world of Calusa County. They deal primarily with issues arising from two case files: *State v. Alexander* and *Washington v. Hartwell*. They are designed to immerse the class in the law of evidence by using the framework of client representation as a vehicle to create evidentiary discussion.

The goal is to create a learning experience where students and professors apply the evidentiary rules while immersed in the substantive law. The problems are designed to ensure that students are confronted with the seminal cases, overarching evidentiary themes, and ambiguous areas of evidentiary law.

This approach allows the student to learn evidence in context. That context includes the application of the individual rule(s) and the relationship of the rules with one another. There are certain advantages to learning evidence through this format.

Imagine for a moment that you have been given a new board game as a gift. One of the first things you do is take the pieces out of the box. You look at them, touch them, and place them on the board. You begin to imagine in your head how the game will work with these pieces. Next you read the rules to identify how you are supposed to use the pieces on the board. Then you play – it is in the playing that you actually learn how the pieces work and the connections that exist between the different parts of the game.

Now imagine that you are given another game and you are not allowed to see the game pieces and board. Instead, someone hands you a written copy of the rules from the back of the box and asks you to properly describe how the game is played and how the pieces work with one another. Difficult? Absolutely — and ineffective.

The approach in this text is designed to use the natural learning processes people employ in other situations to increase the understanding of evidentiary law, its application and processes.

We will begin the discussion of each problem by applying the law as though you are representing a party in court. Most of these problems are taken from the assigned case files, but a few of them address the legal issues of other members of the Calusa County community. Regardless of the source of the evidentiary problem you should begin the problem by addressing the call of the question as though representing the identified client or entity.

Students will make arguments to the judge (the professor) about the admissibility or inadmissibility of various types of evidence. One student will either offer the evidence (make a proffer) or object to the admissibility of the evidence. A second student will then either object (if a proffer has been made) or respond to the objection.

Once the students and professor have fully identified the legal issues in the problem through discourse the class will shift from a courtroom-based exercise to a full class discussion about the issues contained in the proffer or objection. The professor should supplement this discussion to the extent necessary to ensure understanding. Supplementation might include problems built by modifying the facts of the current problem to tease out additional evidentiary issues.

More so than any other subject in law school, evidence must be learned in context to be understood. This approach provides context so that the students can struggle with the substance in a way that ultimately makes more sense. Let's get started.

B. RELEVANCY

1. What is the relevancy of the life insurance policy on Chris Alexander? Consider how relevancy is related to your case theme and theory – be prepared to explain the connection.

2. Is it relevant that Ms. Presley heard the screech of tires outside her window? Why or why not? What did you consider in creating a relevancy argument for admissibility? Exclusion?

3. Argue the relevancy of Mrs. Alexander calling the alarm company instead of 911 when she allegedly found her husband dead in the foyer of their home from gunshot wounds

4. Consider the importance of the prosecution's theory concerning the actions of Ms. Alexander the night of her husband's murder.

5. Argue the relevancy of Mrs. Alexander's interactions with law enforcement the night of her husband's murder.

6. What is the relevancy of the way the Alexander children were treated, as well as the way they acted, the night of their father's murder?

7. Consider the relevancy, under any theory, either defense or prosecution, of the presence of the marijuana and cocaine in the Wendy's bag found in the den of the Alexander home.

8. Argue the relevance of the photos showing the bullet holes in the Alexander home. Consider the location, nature of collection and what witness you would call to establish their relevancy

9. Argue the relevancy of the shooting range records from the week before Chris Alexander was murdered. As you consider relevancy make certain to carefully review the document. Do not focus on issues of hearsay now, but do think about how you showing that the information contained in the document is what it purports to be might affect the document's relevance.

10. What is the relevancy of Rebecca Hartwell's Letter to the Editor printed in the Pelican Bay Star? What did you consider when developing this relevancy argument?

11. What is the relevancy of Rebecca Hartwell's conviction for reckless driving? Argue for its admissibility.

12. Assume for a moment that Nikki Long would testify, if allowed, that when she was confronted by Brandi Alexander outside of her hair salon, she observed a "shiny metal object that looked like a gun" in the open purse of Brandi Alexander. Argue the admissibility of this hypothetical testimony.

13. Consider the relevance of Chris Alexander's alleged drug activity, Rebecca Hartwell's interest in dance, the family studio of the Hartwell's and the quality of the Alexander marriage.

14. Argue the relevance of Mr. Hightower's negative opinion of Chris Alexander if offered by the defense or prosecution. Put aside for now the opinion's potential admissibility under FRE 701.

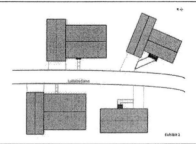

15. What is the relevance of Dimitri Merinov's relationship with Ms. Washington?

16. How is it relevant that officer Record had to arrest one individual at the accident scene for "picking up" what they described as "evidence" of the crime?

17. How relevant is the presence of the black piece of plastic with the letters T O Y O T A in the roadway?

18. Is the over the counter medicine taken by the Alexander children on the night of their father's murder relevant?

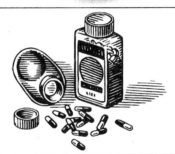

19. What is the relevance of the Honda hubcap on the road?

20. Assume that Ms. Washington has a past that includes drug use severe enough to support the Department of Children and Family Services removing the children from the home for an extended period of time – is this relevant? Why or why not?

21. Doris Presley is blind in one eye and is extremely nearsighted in her remaining functional eye. Is this relevant? If so, how?

22. Argue the relevancy of the Calusa County Courier article quoting Rebecca Hartwell.

23. Chief Willie Hightower told Officer Anece Baxter-White that he would conduct the interview of his brother, Robert Hightower. Is this decision relevant? Why or why not?

24. Rebecca Hartwell's cell phone records indicate that she was on the phone in the minutes surrounding the accident on 22nd street. Relevant?

25. The citizens of Pelican Bay that use the Community Center routinely shoot out the street lights lining that area of 22nd street in order to facilitate privacy. Relevant? Why or why not?

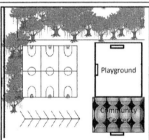

C. Relevancy & Character Problems

26. Why does the state think that Brandi Alexander killed Chris Alexander? What Direct Evidence exists supporting this position? What must the state prove to show that the direct evidence is true? How do you establish credibility?

27. What Direct Evidence shows that Rebecca Hartwell's car was the first car to strike the Washington children? What must be accepted in order to believe that direct evidence is true? How can credibility of that evidence be established?

Evidence in Context: Evidentiary Problems & Exercises   Page 29

28. .What is the relevance of Ms. Presley saying that "They were always such a nice couple....They were such a nice family." Should she be allowed to testify as to the nature of their relationship? Why?

29. What is the relevance of Robert Hightower's opinion that Chris Alexander was a "bad influence" in the neighborhood and a known small time drug dealer? What direct evidence exists? What method of proof exists?

30. Why are the diagrams depicting the Alexander home relevant? What factors must you consider when establishing relevancy and admissibility?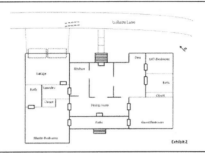

31. Consider the relevancy, under any theory, either defense What is the relevancy of the overhead pictures of the accident scene? Argue admissibility. How would you lay foundation?

32. What is the relevancy of the photo of the eldest Washington child? Argue admissibility.

33. Argue for the admissibility of the actual insurance policy on Chris Alexander. Relevancy? If the insurance policy is relevant, what about the disposition of the proceeds. Does it matter who requested the policy or the circumstances surrounding the manner in which the policy was taken out?

34. Argue the relevancy, or lack thereof of the actions of Brandi Alexander immediately after her husband was found shot. Consider in this discussion the status of the Alexander children, and the location of the bullet holes and any other relevant evidence available.

35. What is the relevance, or lack thereof, of the Chris Alexander's past involvement in drug activity? What about his nickname or tattoos?

36. Ms. Sarah James is suing Police Officer Jerry Jones for violating her sons' civil rights when he shot and killed them while they were leaving a convenience store in Calusa county after robbing it during the early morning hours of November 1st. Officer Jones was getting out of his cruiser to enter the convenience store in order to fill his thermos with coffee. He had a history with the James boys and recognized them when they came running out of the front door of the store. Officer Jones shot and killed both brothers in the convenience store parking lot. At the civil trial officer Jones' defense attorney is attempting to admit evidence of the James boys' propensity for misusing guns under the theory that Jones' choice to use deadly force when dealing the with the James boys was justified because he had a reasonable belief that the brothers posed a serious threat to his safety. In support of this theory the defense wishes to offer three different pieces of evidence:

The first piece of evidence the defense wishes to offer is a cross-burning the James brothers conducted in an African-American community. According to one of the boys who allegedly participated in the burning, the James brothers fired a .44 Magnum into the air six times after the cross had been lit. After the cross began to burn, the brothers ran back to a white area of town and hid with guns in anticipation of retaliatory acts from the African-American community. Although no weapons charges were filed against the brothers, one of them was charged with disorderly conduct. This incident was investigated by a Lieutenant Record, who reported directly to Jones during that time.

The second piece of evident arose from an accidental shooting where Jimmy Collins shot himself in the leg. Although there was no evidence that the gun belonged to the James brothers, they were present at the shooting. Jones worked that case, and testified that the shooting was an accident.

The third piece of evidence came from an investigation of an armed robbery at a restaurant. While Jones was investigating the robbery he learned that the girlfriend of one of the James Boys had been bragging about how he was involved in the robbery. No charges were brought against the James brothers as a result of Jones' investigation of that case.

The plaintiff's attorney for Ms. James objects to the use of the evidence.

a. What are the best arguments for admissibility of each piece of evidence?
b. What are the best arguments for excluding each piece of evidence?
c. How should the judge rule?
d. Why?

37. Does it matter that Ms. Washington was having trouble with a boyfriend and DCF? If relevant, can it be proved through character evidence? How?

38. What is the relevancy of the conversation that Brandi Alexander has outside of the beauty salon with Nikki Long?

Evidence in Context: Evidentiary Problems & Exercises — Page 31

39. What is the relevancy of the fact that the Hartwell's own a dance studio? Their immigrant background? Family structure and workings? What are the arguments for and against admissibility?

40. Why should the trial judge be given the authority to decide issues of logical and legal relevance? Why not just give each side a time limit and let them choose what evidence to admit in the time that they have?

41. You are the prosecutor in *State v. Alexander*. Your investigator has uncovered evidence that 15 years ago the defendant, Brandi Alexander, was involved in a serious relationship with a young man. He cheated on her. After she learned about his cheating she confronted him at his home. She kicked him in the genital area multiple times, causing massive hematomas to his body. He refused to press charges. You have extrinsic evidence of these events.

    Are these events admissible?

    a. Identify the theory of admissibility.
    b. How will the defense respond?
    c. What will be your counter response?
    d. How will the judge rule?
    e. Why will the judge rule that way?

D. Character Evidence

42. You are the plaintiff attorney in the civil case of *Washington v. Hartwell*. Assume for the purposes of this problem that your investigator has returned the following factual summary concerning the Reckless Driving offense for which Rebecca Hartwell was convicted on January 21, 20XX-10:

    On March 16, 20XX-11 Rebecca Hartwell was driving home from dance class. She was a senior in high school and kept a very busy schedule, beginning classes and outside activities at 6:00 a.m. every day and ending her extracurricular activities around 7:00 p.m.. Around 8 p.m. that night she was heading south on 53rd Street when she approached a light that was turning yellow. She chose to increase her speed to make it through the light. She continued to increase speed until she was going approximately 10 mph over the speed limit. Three blocks later she attempted to pass a car and lost control of her vehicle, running off the road and hitting a tree. She gave a statement describing these events to the police officer who responded to the scene.

    Are these events admissible?

    a. What are the arguments for admissibility?
    b. What are the arguments against admissibility?
    c. Identify the theory of admissibility and the manner in which you will admit this evidence if allowed.

43. You are the plaintiff attorney in the civil case of *Washington v. Hartwell*. Assume for the purposes of this problem that your assigned investigator has returned the following factual summary concerning the Reckless Driving offense for which Rebecca Hartwell was convicted on January 21, 20XX-10:

> On July 4, 20XX-11 Rebecca Hartwell was driving home from a party she had attended celebrating the 4th of July. At the party she drank three wine coolers. She drove to the party and also drove home. While driving home late that night, around 11 p.m. she was driving north on 87th Street when a homeless man stepped out in front of vehicle. She struck the man, injuring him severely. She stopped her car immediately and went out to help the homeless man. While she was assisting him the police arrived. Smelling alcohol on Ms. Hartwell they conducted Field Sobriety Test which she failed. She later gave a breathalyzer sample that registered .016, twice the legal limit. She was charged with DUI which she pleads down to the offense of Reckless Driving.

Are these events admissible?

   a. What are the arguments for admissibility?
   b. What are the arguments against admissibility?
   c. Identify the theory of admissibility and the manner in which you will admit this evidence if allowed.

44. You are the defense attorney in the civil case of *Washington v. Hartwell*. Assume for the purposes of this problem that your investigator has discovered a case file at the Department of Children and Family Services that indicates Ms. Washington lost the custody of her children based upon a neglect allegation that occurred during the time of her drug use. They were placed in foster care for 9 months. Ms. Washington entered into a voluntary drug treatment program and upon completion of the program was reunited with her children.

Are these events admissible?

   a. What are the arguments for admissibility?
   b. What are the arguments against admissibility?
   c. Identify the theory of admissibility and the manner in which you will admit this evidence if allowed.

Evidence in Context: Evidentiary Problems & Exercises   Page 33

45. You are the plaintiff attorney in the civil case of *Washington v. Hartwell*. Assume for the purposes of this problem that your private investigator has uncovered the following actions by Ms. Hartwell: (1) She has presented over 30 bad checks to the bank for payment over the last two years; (2) She told her principal at the school where she works that she was sick for the end of the week when in fact she took a "sick days" vacation; and (3) She routinely takes five dollars from the coffee fund she runs for the teachers' lounge. You have extrinsic evidence (both witnesses and documents) to prove these actions.

   Are these events admissible?

   a. What are the arguments for admissibility?
   b. What are the arguments against admissibility?
   c. Identify the theory of admissibility and the manner in which you will admit this evidence if allowed.

46. You are the prosecutor in *State v. Alexander*. Your investigator has uncovered evidence that 15 years ago the defendant was involved in a serious relationship with a young man. He cheated on her. After she learned about his cheating she confronted him at his home. She kicked him in the genital area multiple times, causing massive hematomas to his body. He refused to press charges. You have extrinsic evidence of these events.

   Are these events admissible?

   a. What are the arguments for admissibility?
   b. What are the arguments against admissibility?
   c. Identify the theory of admissibility and the manner in which you will admit this evidence if allowed.

47. Mr. Bader is on trial for assaulting his roommate, Mr. Adams. On direct Adams claimed that he and Bader were arguing about who left the cap off the toothpaste when Bader viciously attacked him. On cross-examination, the defense counsel gets Adams to admit that he falsified a receipt for a laptop computer in order to rip off Wal Mart for several hundred dollars. The state now wants to introduce testimony from Adam's former boss that Adams is a gentle and peaceful person.

   What evidence is admissible? Why? Why not?

48. At her trial for possession with intent to distribute and use of cocaine, the accused, Ms. Nikki Long, presented a mistake of fact defense. She also testified that when she was a member of the city council she was "death" on drugs and would not tolerate drug use or sale. On cross-examination, the prosecution wants to question Ms. Long about a police report that contained information from a confidential informant that he sold crack cocaine to Ms. Long twice while she was a city council member.

   Can he do so? What basis? Potential objections?

49. Prior to her second trial for murder Brandi Alexander's attorney meets with the prosecutor to work out a possible deal. The prosecutor agrees to consider a plea to negligent homicide but wants to hear the story of what really happened directly from Ms. Alexander. Ms. Alexander and her attorney meet with the state and the prosecution tapes her story. After negotiations on the plea break down they proceed to trial. At trial the state seeks to offer her statements.

Admissible? Why or why not?

50. Mr. Hightower is on trial for poorly managing the accounts of the Calusa County Board of Education. His alleged malfeasance resulted in the county losing 12.8 million dollars of revenue. As a result the athletic programs were shut down. During his defense he calls Mr. Michael Alexander who testifies that in his opinion, Mr. Hightower is the best school accountant the school board has used in the last 30 years. Mr. Alexander then stated that he worked with Mr. Hightower for five years. He readily cites several examples of Hightower's numerous achievements to support his opinion that Hightower was an excellent accountant who never made mistakes. These examples include the immaculate books Hightower kept, the way the office looked and the immense amount of time Hightower spent volunteering in the local soup kitchen.

Objections? Why? Ruling?

51. The prosecutor was so busy reading over his closing argument during Alexander's direct examination that he failed to make any objections to any of the testimony. On cross-examination he asks Alexander if he is aware that Hightower videotaped a sexual encounter he had with a married employee and that he threatened to show the video to her husband if she did not pay him $50,000. The Prosecutor also asks Alexander about a Letter of Reprimand (LOR) Hightower received for failing an internal audit. He then asks Alexander about a memorandum of concern Alexander received for misusing the county road grader for personal use on his farm.

Objections? Ruling? Why?

52. Alexander says he knows nothing about either of the first two incidents. In his rebuttal case, the prosecutor wants to introduce a copy of the LOR and the videotape into evidence. Afterwards the defense counsel attempts to introduce a letter of apology from the Board of Directors to Alexander concerning the false allegations about the Lear Jet.

Objections? Ruling? Why?

53. Dimitri Merinov is on trial for molesting his daughter. At trial, the prosecutor introduces evidence from a neighbor that she caught the accused in her back yard exposing his genital area to the neighborhood children. This incident was not part of the charged offenses. In his closing argument, the prosecutor tells the jury that since the accused exposed his genitals to the neighborhood kids it is more likely that he also molested his daughter.

Objections? Rulings? Basis?

54. Betty Joe Alexander is charged with assaulting Brandi Alexander with a bookend in the elementary school library on March 2nd. The state's first witness is Sally Waters, the school librarian, who testifies that she saw the assault and eventually broke up the fight by informing them their copy privileges would be suspended if they didn't stop. On cross, the defense counsel elicits evidence that Brandi had apparently pulled a chair from under Betty Joe, called her "ignorant" and came after her with a copy of the cumbersome and heavy copy of the M volume of the Encyclopedia Britannica. Ms. Pressler, the state's next witness, testifies that in her opinion Brandi Alexander is a peaceful person. In fact, she has seen her provoked several times in the last year by members of the community incensed over the verdict in her first murder trial and she has backed down each time. The defense counsel objects on the basis that this line of questioning is improper character evidence.

Ruling?

55. The state then calls Mr. Greiner. Mr. Greiner is familiar with Brandi Alexander's reputation within the elementary school community and she is known as being a violent and aggressive person. The defense counsel again objects on the basis this is improper character evidence.

Objections? Rulings? Basis?

E. Authentication & Best Evidence Rule

56. Argue the admissibility of the three photos and four diagrams of the accident scene in *Washington v. Hartwell*.

57. Argue the admissibility of the diagram that does not show the trees beside the basketball courts by the community center.

58. Argue the admissibility of the black piece of debris with the letters T O Y O T A found by Officer Record at the scene of the accident.

59. Argue the admissibility of the hubcap from a Honda Accord found by Officer Record at the accident scene.

60. Argue the admissibility of Nikki Long's handwritten notes to Chris Alexander.

61. Argue the admissibility of the business card found in Chris's wallet.

62. Argue the admissibility of the Lab Report.

63. Argue the admissibility of the Cell Phone Record.

64. Argue the admissibility of the Calusa County Courier article dated March 27, 20XX-2.

65. Argue the admissibility of the photos of the marijuana and cocaine found in the Alexander home.

Evidence in Context: Evidentiary Problems & Exercises   Page 37

F. Impeachment Problems - Bias, Interest and Ability to Perceive

66. Consider the admissibility of Officer Record's testimony in *Hartwell* concerning his ability to see the location where the children were struck while he was interviewing Johnny Broadsides by the basketball courts.

67. In *Hartwell* argue the admissibility of Matt Bader's eyewitness testimony concerning the speed of the vehicle that hit the children.

68. Argue the admissibility of the conversation between Nikki Long and Brandi Alexander outside the hair salon.

69. Assume that Mrs. Presley testified in favor of Brandi Alexander on direct. Argue the admissibility of cross examination questions designed to show that Brandi Alexander routinely brings Mrs. Presley home baked goodies

70. Assume that on direct examination Demitri Merinov testifies favorably for Charissa Washington. Argue the admissibility of questions during cross examination concerning his relationship with Ms. Washington.

G. Impeachment - Reputation and Opinion

71. Bill Hartwell has testified on direct examination for the defense. On rebuttal the plaintiff calls Jamie O'Brien, Gina's boyfriend, to testify that Mr. Hartwell is "more than a bit of a liar." Argue admissibility.

72. Argue the admissibility of Robert Hightower's testimony on direct examination that Brandi Alexander had a reputation of woman who was reaching her breaking point.

73. While preparing for trial the defense discovers that when Nikki Long was pregnant with Chris Alexander's baby she went to the doctor and had an abortion. Argue the logical and legal relevance in *Alexander* of questions by the defense if:

    a. On cross examination of Ms. Long.
    b. If, after Ms. Long denies the abortion on cross, defense seeks to call the doctor who performed the procedure.
    c. Without questioning her on cross, calling her best friend whom she told about the procedure.

74. Marian Hartwell testifies that her daughter Rebecca has been a very safe driver for the last ten years. May the plaintiff cross examine using the Rebecca's conviction for reckless driving? May they also cross examine about the facts behind that conviction?

75. During cross examination of Nikki Long defense seeks to offer evidence that: (1) Ms. Long was on the phone with Mr. Alexander immediately before he died, (2) Ms. Long uses drugs, (3) Ms. Long hates Brandi Alexander, (4) Ms. Long has a violent temper, and (5) Ms. Long's last boyfriend disappeared under "mysterious" circumstances.

H. General Impeachment

76. The accused, Mr. Broadsides is charged with larceny and conspiracy to commit larceny. The prosecutor grants immunity to a co-conspirator, Mr. Saunders, and calls Saunders to prove up the conspiracy charge. Just prior to his testimony, the prosecutor gets word that Mr. Saunders is going to deny any knowledge of or involvement in the larceny. The Prosecutor calls Mr. Saunders anyway in order to impeach him with prior statements he made to detectives detailing his and Broadsides' involvement in the larceny.

    Defense counsel objects. What is the issue? What factors does the judge need to know before she rules?

77. The Accused, Mr. William Hartwell, is on trial for sexual harassment of several employees. He wants to impeach a state eyewitness about their prior drug use at work.

    Is this a valid area of character impeachment? Why or why not?

78. Jimmy Jones is on trial for murder. He presents an alibi witness, Bubba Schifflett, who testifies that Jimmy Jones was at the Fat Friar Club playing pool at the time of the murder. On cross-examination, the prosecutor asks Mr. Schifflett if he ever forged his roommate's checks. Bubba denies the allegation. The prosecutor then wants to call Clarence, Bubba's roommate, to testify that Bubba did forge several of his checks.

    Is Clarence's testimony admissible? Why or why not?

79. Jimmy Jones is still on trial for murder, except now the prosecutor asks Bubba Schifflett if he owes Mr. Jones any money because he lost a bet on a pool game. Bubba denies owing Jones any money. The prosecutor now wants to call Sharkey to testify that Bubba does owe Jones money because of a gambling debt.

   Is Sharkey's testimony admissible?

80. Jones is still on trial for murder; except now the prosecutor wants to introduce evidence that Bubba has a misdemeanor conviction (last year) for forging his roommate's checks. Bubba denied ever being convicted.

   Can the prosecutor prove the misdemeanor with extrinsic evidence? Does the judge have any discretion to exclude this evidence under FRE 403?

81. Johnny Broadsides is charged with the June 20XX robbery of the Pelican Bay Bank of America. He is denied bail. At Mr. Broadside's jury trial the prosecutor calls an eyewitness, Ms. Nicole Con. Instead of identifying Broadsides, Ms. Con testifies that Mr. Broadsides was not in the bank during the robbery. After regaining consciousness, the prosecutor seeks to impeach Ms. Con with the following: (1) a sworn statement made by Ms. Con at the police station two days after the robbery in which she placed Mr. Broadsides in the bank; and (2) deposition testimony in which Ms. Con identified Mr. Broadsides as one of the robbers.

   Which of the statements, if any, should the prosecutor be able to use to impeach Ms. Con? If admitted, for what purpose should the statement(s) be considered?

82. Mr. Broadsides is still on trial for bank robbery. During their case in chief the defense calls Mr. Kyle MacGregor, who testifies that he and Mr. Broadsides were playing basketball outside of the community center at the time of the robbery. To impeach Mr. MacGregor's credibility, the prosecutor asks him if he had been convicted of a misdemeanor for assaulting another person in a bar, whether he forged a sick slip to avoid work, whether he had been arrested by the IRS in 2002 for conspiracy to commit fraud. Mr. MacGregor denies each of these allegations.

   What may the prosecutor do now?

83. Mr. Broadsides is apparently indebted to Ms. Washington to the tune of $7,500. Is this relevant to the Hartwell case? If relevant, is it admissible? If so, how? Would it matter if Mr. Broadsides denied the debt during cross examination by defense counsel?

I. EXPERTS

84. Expert Exercise – "Luck be a Lady Tonight"

The accused, Roger Curlin is pending trial for filing false tax returns in violation of 26 U.S.C. § 7206(1). It seems that after Mr. Curlin won a free trip to Vegas he developed an uncontrollable urge to gamble. Over a three-year period, he would fly out to Vegas almost every weekend and gamble day and night, squandering vast sums of money. Mr. Curlin is a pathological gambler. In his free time he works full-time as a law enforcement agent. Roger Curlin never reported any of his gambling winnings or losses on his income tax returns as required by law. Further, whenever Curlin won money he would make sure that he never deposited more than $9,000 in any one account in order to avoid Treasury reporting requirements.

The defense is considering whether to call Dr. Nick Lucky (Dr. Nick) as an expert witness at trial. Dr. Nick has a Masters Degree in psychology. He has been living on the French Riviera for the last 10 years and he has developed an interest in compulsive gamblers. (He is a reformed gambler). In fact, a few years ago he and a few of his colleagues began studying compulsive gamblers who come to the Riviera to gamble. These gamblers come to France and blow their life savings on various games of chance. Dr. Nick's primary study group was composed of 5 men, all from Eastern Europe, who came to the Riviera in hopes of winning enough money to retire from their welding jobs.

Based on his studies, Dr. Nick would testify that some of these pathological gamblers, like Mr. Curlin, have distortions in their thinking, which can have various impacts. For example, according to Dr. Nick, pathological gamblers do not want to keep records because that would force them to confront the reality of their losses, which would create emotional upheaval. Pathological gambling is a recognized disorder under the *Diagnostic and Statistical Manual of Mental Disorders*, (DSM-IV). However, Dr. Nick is the first expert in the field to assert that poor record keeping is a symptom related to compulsive gambling. Dr. Nick has reviewed Mr. Curlin's case file and he believes that these distortions in thinking may negate the knowing and willfulness of Curlin's conduct. Dr. Nick published an article about his theory in *Gambler's Monthly*. He has also appeared on Nightline and testified once in a Nevada district court about his theories.

You are the Defense Counsel for Mr. Curlin, and the senior partner in your criminal defense firm wants you to prepare a memo about this expert witness. Specifically, she wants to know three things. First, what factors should the judge use to evaluate the admissibility of this expert? Second, how should those factors apply to the facts of this case? Third, what are the tactical considerations for calling or not calling this expert?

J. Hearsay & THE Confrontation Clause

85. Mr. Bader is on trial for the robbery of a local convenience store on 24th Street. Ms. Amanda Jones was working in the store filling out the nightly deposit slip for the cash in the drawer. She testifies that when she saw Mr. Bader approach her with a gun in his hand she dropped the deposit bag and screamed, "Oh dear Lord, I'm a dead girl." Objection - hearsay. Ruling?

86. Ms. Washington is on trial for possession of cocaine. At trial, the prosecutor calls a police officer to testify that when he went to Ms. Washington's home to talk to her about what happened to her children his K9 partner Rex alerted on Ms. Washington's pocket book. The defense objects on the basis of hearsay. Ruling?

Evidence in Context: Evidentiary Problems & Exercises   Page 41

87. Jamie O'Brien is charged with receiving stolen goods (two diamond earrings) from Dimitri Merinov. During the criminal trial the state makes out a prima facie case and rests. O'Brien wants to testify that Merinov gave him the diamond earrings, told him he had bought them as an anniversary present for his live-in girlfriend Charissa Washington, and asked O'Brien to keep them until their anniversary. O'Brien further testifies that he believed Merinov. State objects – hearsay. Admissible?

88. The defense seeks to admit the testimony of Willie Alexander that Mr. Hightower appeared angry and combative when Alexander told him he couldn't find "Frosty." The state makes a hearsay objection. Argue admissibility.

89. The defense offers the testimony of Officer Baxter-White that when she attempted to speak with the defendant at the scene the defendant was "incredibly upset, weeping, screaming, almost howling." The State objects. Argue admissibility.

90. The State seeks to offer the testimony of Nikki Long that when Brandi said "Sorry to hear about your loss, but good things never happened to bad people," she also took her hand, made it into the shape of a gun and pointed it at Nikki's head. She then mimed pulling the trigger and smiled in an evil fashion. Argue admissibility.

91. Charissa Washington is asked to state her name for the court and the defense objects on hearsay grounds. Defense then offers to voir dire the witness to establish that the witness is relying upon hearsay from her mother to answer this question. Respond for the plaintiff's counsel.

92. Mrs. Presley attempts to testify that Brandi Alexander never complained about Chris' time away from home or "extra-curricular" activities. Argue admissibility.

93. Defense seeks to offer the letter written by Nikki Long found at page 13 of the *Alexander* case file. Specifically they want to cross examine Ms. Long about the following:

    "Babe!

    I wish I could see you some mo. It has been too long since we been together. I'm startin' to think you might not be leaving her – better not be so. I love you so much and I want us to have a baby together. Please kick that ho to the curb!"

    Argue admissibility.

94. Billy Bob Bass is the next door neighbor of the Alexander's. He attempts to testify on direct examination that while trimming the hedges on his side of the fence in the backyard he heard the following argument.

    - *Brandi*: Baby please stay home tonight. Please. That guy keeps coming by and I'm scared. I miss you, don't you still love me at all? *Slight sobbing.*

    - *Chris*: You better get it through your thick head; I love her – not you. You are a cold hearted bitch and I'm not staying with you anymore. It's like sleeping with a dead fish. She makes me feel alive, you don't have any passion at all and I need more.

    - *Brandi*: You son-of-a-bitch – if I see you with that whore again I'll give you cold fish!

    - *Chris*: You don't have the balls. That's the whole problem; you don't live life you just exist. I need more and I'm going to get it!

    - *Brandi*: You're going to get it all right, just wait and see. And you won't be getting it from me! You stupid drug-dealing ass!

    - *Sounds of a slap, a blood-curdling scream, clothes ripping. Quickly followed by the sounds of a struggle and then indistinct words and noises. Billy Bob continues to clip the hedges while all this is going on. Eventually it becomes quiet. He hears a door close in the Alexander's back yard. Then he hears the following.*

    - *Brandi*: Don't have any passion? Well that was passion. I love him so – he will always be my man!

95. Tracie Johnson works with Nikki Long at the Salon "Where girls get their hair did." The defense seeks to offer testimony by Tracie concerning a "rumor" that Nikki was dating two bad dudes at the same time. Both of them had a reputation of being part-time gangsters and local drug dealers. Argue admissibility.

96. Plaintiff offers Ms. Hartwell's Letter to the Editor on page E-1 of the Calusa County Courier. Argue admissibility.

97. The plaintiff's attorney seeks to admit evidence from the breathalyzer that Ms. Hartwell took immediately after her reckless driving incident in 20XX-11. The defense objects – hearsay. **Ruling?**

98. During the Hartwell trial the plaintiff's attorney calls Johnny Broadsides to testify that on March 21st immediately before the children were struck he heard the oldest Washington boy yelling at the other children to "run faster, we need to get home or mom is going to be so mad at us." He then heard the middle child scream "Watch out for that white van!" Admissible?

Evidence in Context: Evidentiary Problems & Exercises

99. Reggie Harris is stopped for a minor traffic violation in Pelican Bay. During the traffic stop the police lawfully discover over 10 kilos of cocaine in the trunk of the Reggie's car. After his arrest Reggie asks what he can do to help his case; he eventually tells the state that he knew he was transporting cocaine, but he received the cocaine from Brandi Alexander as payment for murdering her husband Chris. At Brandi's trial the state wants to introduce Harris's statement implicating Brandi. The defense objects - hearsay. Admissible?

100. Nikki Long testifies on direct examination that she loved Chris and he loved her and that they were going to be together forever. Defense attempts to offer the letter written by Nikki dated June 1, 20XX-2. Argue admissibility.

101. In the week before her husband is murdered Brandi Alexander begins acting strangely at work. She tells the students they must now refer to her as "She Who Must Be Obeyed." She forces them to stand on their head in the corner of the classroom when they fail to comply with her requests (these are third graders). She tells the school principal in a staff meeting that she has recently been promoted to "Queen of the Universe" and that her first act as Queen is to fire the principal. At trial she raises a defense based on a lack of mental responsibility. She wishes to offer her statements to the students and principal? Hearsay?

102. Mr. Alonzo lives next door to Mr. Hightower. While sitting in the front porch swing with his wife Sally he sees Mr. Hightower walking across the street with an "object" in his hands the night that Chris Alexander is murdered. He immediately writes down what happened on a beer napkin. At trial Mr. Alonzo attempts to testify about what he saw that night. He ends up reading his notes on the beer napkin to the jury since his memory of the event was incomplete. Is this hearsay? Admissible?

103. Nikki Long is suspected of dealing in drugs and possessing cocaine. At Brandi Alexander's trial the defense counsel calls a cop to testify that during a routine traffic stop a drug dog alerted on Nikki's car trunk. The state objects on the basis of hearsay. Admissible or not? Why?

104. Ms. Washington testifies that after she saw the children dead and dying in the street she ran back home where she took a lethal dose of sleeping pills in order to kill herself. Defense objects claiming hearsay, what ruling?

105. Ms. Johnson works at Nikki's Salon. She testifies at Brandi's trial that she heard Nikki Long tell Brandi that she would "get her." The State objects, hearsay. Ruling?

106. Ms. Alexander is on trial for assaulting Ms. Long. She takes the stand and testifies that just prior to hitting Ms. Long, Ms. Long ran towards her yelling, "I'm going to kick your ass." State objects, hearsay. Ruling?

107. Mr. Merinov is on trial for molesting his girlfriend's daughter. During the cross-examination of the victim, the defense counsel attempts to show the victim's bias against Mr. Merinov because he grounded her several months ago. The defense believes that this bias is one reason that she made allegations of abuse. In cross-examination the defense counsel also tries to show that the victim's in-court testimony was the product of overly suggestive interview techniques used by detectives. To rebut the charge of suggestible interview techniques, the prosecutor calls a school counselor to testify about a report of abuse the victim made to her before the detectives interviewed the victim. The statement she made to the school counselor is consistent with her in-court testimony. Defense counsel objects, claiming that her statement to the school counselor occurred after Mr. Merinov grounded the victim and is inadmissible hearsay. Is this statement to the counselor hearsay under FRE 801?

108. Mr. Bader is charged with assault and indecent assault of his girlfriend, Ms. Waffle. On the night of the incident, Ms. Waffle called 911 to report that Mr. Bader had tied her to a bed and physically and sexually abused her. The police went to the scene and took a statement from Ms. Waffle. In order to document her injuries, the police also took Ms. Waffle to the hospital where a doctor and a social worker examined her. During her examination, Ms. Waffle told the doctor and the social worker what Mr. Bader had done to her. A few weeks before trial, Ms. Waffle reconciles with Mr. Bader and refuses to cooperate with the government. She also claims that the entire incident was consensual sexual activity. The government wants to introduce the statements Ms. Waffle made to the doctor and social worker as hearsay exceptions under FRE 803(4). The defense objects. What factors should the court consider to determine the admissibility of these statements?

109. Same facts as above, but before Ms. Waffle recanted, she provided a second statement to the police a week after the charged incident and right after Mr. Bader called her and threatened to kill her. Ms. Waffle immediately contacted the police. They came to her house and she provided the most detailed account of the assault available. Prosecution wants to admit this statement as residual hearsay under FRE 807. Defense objects. What factors should you use to determine the admissibility of this statement?

110. At Ms. Alexander's trial the state produces a new eyewitness named Delia Banks. Delia testifies she saw the accused running from her house carrying a pistol shortly after she heard shots. During the defense case-in-chief, Alexander's attorney calls Phillip Sparks, Delia's next door neighbor. Sparks testifies that he talked with Delia the day after the murder and she told him that she did not see anybody because she was watching Wheel of Fortune. State objects - hearsay. Ruling?

Fundamental Trial Advocacy:
The Law, the Skill & the Art

State v. Alexander
Cases and Materials

Charles H. Rose, III
Professor of Excellence in Trial Advocacy
Director, Center for Excellence in Advocacy
Stetson University College of Law

Notes

STATE V. ALEXANDER

PROFESSOR CHARLES H. ROSE III
Director, Center for Excellence in Advocacy
Stetson University College of Law[1]

"We empower students to find within themselves their unique voices – to become the best possible advocates they can be."[2]

The following student at Stetson University College of Law gave of their time, expertise and creativity to assist in producing this case file. Without their help this project would still be an idea that was less than half way to completion. Each embodies the Stetson Spirit and I gratefully acknowledge their contributions. They are:

Center for Excellence in Advocacy Fellows

Vilma Martinez Allana Forté
Christian Radley Katherine Lambrose

Case File Project Volunteers

Jessica Austin Nichole Bibicoff
Jonathan Johnston Lindsey Mack
Ashley Mortimore Joseph Murray
Jason Rice

I wish to express my gratitude to the leadership at Stetson - Dean Darby Dickerson, Associate Dean Ellen Podgor, and Associate Dean Jamie Fox. They helped make this text possible through their unfailing support of creative scholarship.

The ideas behind using case files to teach are grounded in concepts of experiential learning. It is in doing that true education occurs.[3] These files are designed to create optimal "learning by doing" opportunities – the foundation upon which advocacy instruction, if not all learning, rests.

---

[1] This work would not have been possible without the generous support of Stetson University College of Law's scholarship grant program for faculty.

[2] Professor Charles H. Rose III, Director, Center for Excellence in Advocacy, www.law.stetson.edu/excellence/advocacy

[3] Myles Horton, the co-founder of the Highlander Folk School, referred to this with a phrase from a Spanish song that translated reads "We make the road by walking." This is one of the best captured thoughts about experiential learning I have ever read.

– Introduction –

These case files are scalable, adaptable, and relevant to the issues facing 21st century advocates. They are based on the lessons learned by Stetson's faculty, students and alumni, reflecting the same commitment to excellence embodied in our Law School's award winning advocacy teams and national reputation in Advocacy.

A commitment to the law, the skill and the art of advocacy creates persuasive advocacy. The foundation begins with the **process**: it's the way we train, the way we learn, and the way we practice. This is experiential learning. These case files focus the advocates on specific advocacy skills in a simulated real world environment, allowing participants to learn the skill and the law in the context of a moment in the trial. The exercises accompanying the case file develop advocacy **skills** through the rubric of the experiential learning process. This approach allows the advocate to develop **values** that contextually reflect the legal profession. These case files provide a structure for the **process**, **skills** and **values** involved in becoming a better advocate.

The goal of this effort is to design a well-crafted, challenging case file that promotes excellence in all facets of advocacy instruction. The way in which a case file is organized, presented and supported is a balancing act that either increases or decreases its effectiveness. The result of this balancing act is a unique, multi-media product that provides both academics and the practicing bar with modular course content producing varied levels of difficulty (novice, intermediate, and advanced), that is developed for, and measured by, quantifiable outcome assessments.

State v. Alexander

CASE FILE CONTENTS

Tab A: Introduction..48
- Introduction to the Case
- Indictment
- Jury Instructions
- Verdict Form

Tab B: Police Investigations..63
- Officer Report of Incident – Alexander Murder
- Detective Investigative Report – Alexander Murder
    - Diagram of Alexander Neighborhood. Prepared by ABW
    - Diagram of Alexander home. Prepared by ABW
    - Diagram of Alexander home foyer. Prepared by ABW
    - Letter dated 5/15/20XX-2. Taken from jacket of Chris Alexander
    - Letter dates 6/1/20XX-2. Taken from jacket of Chris Alexander
    - Business Card taken from Chris Alexander's wallet
    - Photo of Wendy's bag of food. Taken by EM
    - Photo of bag found in Wendy's bag in Alexander home. Taken by ABW
    - Photo of baggie found in Wendy's bag in Alexander home. Taken by ABW
    - Photo of .45 pistol. Found in Alexander home by ABW
    - Photo of 9mm pistol. Produced by EM
    - Photo of exterior door of Alexander home. Taken by EM
    - Photo 1 of interior door of Alexander home. Taken by EM
    - Photo 2of interior door of Alexander home. Taken by EM
    - Photo 3 of interior door of Alexander home. Taken by EM
    - Photo 4 of interior door of Alexander home. Taken by EM
    - Photo of slugs removed from door frame by ABW
    - Photo of slugs taken from concrete floor by EM

- o Photo of .45 ammo found in Alexander home. Taken by ABW
- o Photo of skid marks outside of Alexander home. Taken by EM
- o Shooting Club sign in sheet
- Officer Incident Report – Drug Activity

Tab C: Witness Statements..93
- Statement of Robert Hightower
- Statement of Nikki Long
- Statement of Sharon Barry
- Statement of Doris Presley
- Statement of Billy Bob Schifflett
- 2nd Statement of Nikki Long
- Statement of Anece Baxter-White
- Deposition of Roger Curlin
- Deposition of Dr. Jeremiah Jones
- Testimony of Brandi Alexander

Tab D: Reports & Certificates..125
- Chris Alexander Death Certificate
- Coroner's Report
- Chain of Custody documents
- Lab Report and Certificate
- PDQ Alarm System Report
- Cell Phone Record Report

Tab E: News Coverage..141
- Pelican Bay Star, Nov. 3, 20XX-2 "Doctor Horrible"
- Pelican Bay Star, Dec. 7, 20XX-2 "DA Argues Infidelity, Money Motivated Killing"

- Pelican Bay Star, Dec. 9, 20XX-2 "Detective: Suspect Lied Night of Husband's Death"
- Pelican Bay Star, Dec. 13, 20XX-2 "Teacher's Attorney Blasts Investigation: Defense Claims Detective Left Details Out of Report"
- Pelican Bay Star, Jan. 1, 20XX-1 "Teacher's Murder Trial Resumes"
- Pelican Bay Star, Jan. 4, 20XX-1 "Juror Dismissed in Ex-Teacher's Murder Trial"
- Pelican Bay Star, Jan. 9, 20XX-1 "Teacher Guilty!"
- Pelican Bay Star, Nov. 15, 20XX-1 "Retrial Set For Teacher Charged with Murder"

Tab F: Conviction Reports..151
- Chris Alexander Drug Conviction Record
- Nikki Long Filing False Police Report Conviction Record
- Nikki Long Possession Conviction Record

Notes

State v. Alexander

INTRODUCTION

Brandi Alexander was accused of the shooting and killing of her husband, Chris Alexander, on the night of June 6, 20XX-2. Chris Alexander, 32, was having multiple extramarital affairs and was allegedly talking on a cell phone with one of his lovers, a woman named Nikki Long, less than two minutes before he was shot to death in his living room. The Alexander's two children, Ariel and Jasmine, were asleep in a nearby bedroom at the time of their father's murder.

A gunshot residue test was performed on Brandi the night of the shooting. It found one particle of gunshot residue on the back of her left hand. The murder weapon was a .45 caliber pistol and has not been found. One neighbor heard gunshots but did not see a car fleeing, while another said she heard the screeching wheels of a car right after the shooting. The alleged motive for the murder is jealously, vengeance, and a $250,000 insurance policy. The defendant argued at the first trial that either an intruder, or possibly another jilted lover, killed Chris. Brandi Alexander was convicted on January 9, 20XX-1 and sentenced to life in prison.

Ten months later, the circuit court threw out her conviction and ordered a new trial, citing discrimination in the jury selection process by the prosecution.

IN THE CIRCUIT COURT OF THE FIRST JUDICIAL DISTRICT OF
CALUSA COUNTY, XXXXX

STATE OF XXXXX,

v.

BRANDI ALEXANDER,

Defendant.

CASE NO.: 0318-20XX

INDICTMENT

I. MURDER FIRST DEGREE

IN THE NAME AND BY THE AUTHORITY OF THE STATE OF XXXXX:
The Grand Jurors of the State of XXXXX, duly called, impaneled, and sworn to inquire and true presentment make, in and for the body of the County of Calusa, upon their oaths, present that on or about the 3rd day of June, 20XX-2, within the County of Calusa, State of XXXXX, BRANDI ALEXANDER did unlawfully from a premeditated design to effect the death of a human being, kill and murder CHRISTOPHER ALEXANDER, a human being, by shooting him multiple times with a firearm, in violation of XXXXX Statute 118.01, to the evil example of all others in like cases offending and against the peace and dignity of the State of XXXXX.

A TRUE BILL:

George Peabody Smalley
Foreperson of the Grand Jury

I, Prosecutor for the Circuit Court in the First Judicial District, in and for Calusa County, XXXXX, do hereby aver, as authorized and required by law, that I have acted in an advisory capacity to the Grand Jurors of Calusa County previous to their returning the above indictment in the above-styled case.

Nick Cox
PROSECUTOR
FIRST JUDICIAL DISTRICT
CALUSA COUNTY

Presented before: the Honorable Jerry Parker, 1st Judicial Circuit, Calusa County, XXXXX

IN THE CIRCUIT COURT OF THE FIRST JUDICIAL DISTRICT OF CALUSA COUNTY, XXXXX

STATE OF XXXXX,

v.

DEFENDANT

JURY INTRUCTION NO.: 1

Plea of Not Guilty; Reasonable Doubt; and Burden of Proof

The defendant has entered a plea of not guilty. This means you must presume or believe the defendant is innocent. The presumption stays with the defendant as to each material allegation in the [information] [indictment] through each stage of the trial unless it has been overcome by the evidence to the exclusion of and beyond a reasonable doubt.

To overcome the defendant's presumption of innocence, the State has the burden of proving the crime with which the defendant is charged was committed and the defendant is the person who committed the crime.

The defendant is not required to present evidence or prove anything.

Whenever the words "reasonable doubt" are used you must consider the following:

A reasonable doubt is not a mere possible doubt, a speculative, imaginary or forced doubt. Such a doubt must not influence you to return a verdict of not guilty if you have an abiding conviction of guilt. On the other hand, if, after carefully considering, comparing and weighing all the evidence, there is not an abiding conviction of guilt, or, if, having a conviction, it is one which is not stable but one which wavers and vacillates, then the charge is not proved beyond every reasonable doubt and you must find the defendant not guilty because the doubt is reasonable.

It is to the evidence introduced in this trial, and to it alone, that you are to look for that proof.

A reasonable doubt as to the guilt of the defendant may arise from the evidence, conflict in the evidence, or the lack of evidence.

If you have a reasonable doubt, you should find the defendant not guilty. If you have no reasonable doubt, you should find the defendant guilty.

IN THE CIRCUIT COURT OF THE FIRST JUDICIAL DISTRICT OF CALUSA COUNTY, XXXXX

STATE OF XXXXX,

v.

DEFENDANT

JURY INTRUCTION NO.: 2

Murder — First Degree
§ 782.04(1)(A), Stat.

To prove the crime of First Degree Premeditated Murder, the State must prove the following three elements beyond a reasonable doubt:

1. (Victim) is dead.

2. The death was caused by the criminal act of (defendant).

3. There was a premeditated killing of (victim).

An "act" includes a series of related actions arising from and performed pursuant to a single design or purpose.

"Killing with premeditation" is killing after consciously deciding to do so. The decision must be present in the mind at the time of the killing. The law does not fix the exact period of time that must pass between the formation of the premeditated intent to kill and the killing. The period of time must be long enough to allow reflection by the defendant. The premeditated intent to kill must be formed before the killing.

The question of premeditation is a question of fact to be determined by you from the evidence. It will be sufficient proof of premeditation if the circumstances of the killing and the conduct of the accused convince you beyond a reasonable doubt of the existence of premeditation at the time of the killing.

State v. Alexander

IN THE CIRCUIT COURT OF THE FIRST JUDICIAL DISTRICT OF CALUSA COUNTY, XXXXX

STATE OF XXXXX,

v.

DEFENDANT

JURY INTRUCTION NO.: 3

Murder — Second Degree
§ 782.04(2), Stat.

To prove the crime of Second Degree Murder, the State must prove the following three elements beyond a reasonable doubt:

1. (Victim) is dead.

2. The death was caused by the criminal act of (defendant).

3. There was an unlawful killing of (victim) by an act imminently dangerous to another and demonstrating a depraved mind without regard for human life.

An "act" includes a series of related actions arising from and performed pursuant to a single design or purpose.

An act is "imminently dangerous to another and demonstrating a depraved mind" if it is an act or series of acts that:

1. a person of ordinary judgment would know is reasonably certain to kill or do serious bodily injury to another, and

2. is done from ill will, hatred, spite, or an evil intent, and

3. is of such a nature that the act itself indicates an indifference to human life.

In order to convict of Second Degree Murder, it is not necessary for the State to prove the defendant had an intent to cause death.

State v. Alexander

IN THE CIRCUIT COURT OF THE FIRST JUDICIAL DISTRICT OF CALUSA COUNTY, XXXXX

STATE OF XXXXX,

v.

DEFENDANT

JURY INTRUCTION NO.: 4

Weighing the Evidence

It is up to you to decide what evidence is reliable. You should use your common sense in deciding which is the best evidence, and which evidence should not be relied upon in considering your verdict. You may find some of the evidence not reliable, or less reliable than other evidence.

You should consider how the witnesses acted, as well as what they said. Some things you should consider are:

1. Did the witness seem to have an opportunity to see and know the things about which the witness testified?

2. Did the witness seem to have an accurate memory?

3. Was the witness honest and straightforward in answering the attorneys' questions?

4. Did the witness have some interest in how the case should be decided?

5. Does the witness's testimony agree with the other testimony and other evidence in the case?

State v. Alexander

IN THE CIRCUIT COURT OF THE FIRST JUDICIAL DISTRICT OF CALUSA COUNTY, XXXXX

STATE OF XXXXX,

v.

DEFENDANT

JURY INTRUCTION NO.: 5

Rules for Deliberation

These are some general rules that apply to your discussion. You must follow these rules in order to return a lawful verdict:

1. You must follow the law as it is set out in these instructions. If you fail to follow the law, your verdict will be a miscarriage of justice. There is no reason for failing to follow the law in this case. All of us are depending upon you to make a wise and legal decision in this matter.

2. This case must be decided only upon the evidence that you have heard from the testimony of the witnesses [and have seen in the form of the exhibits in evidence] and these instructions.

3. This case must not be decided for or against anyone because you feel sorry for anyone, or are angry at anyone.

4. Remember, the lawyers are not on trial. Your feelings about them should not influence your decision in this case.

5. Your verdict should not be influenced by feelings of prejudice, bias, or sympathy. Your verdict must be based on the evidence, and on the law contained in these instructions.

In closing, let me remind you that it is important that you follow the law spelled out in these instructions in deciding your verdict. There are no other laws that apply to this case. Even if you do not like the laws that must be applied, you must use them. For two centuries we have lived by the constitution and the law. No juror has the right to violate rules we all share.

IN THE CIRCUIT COURT OF TWENTIETH JUDICIAL DISTRICT
CALUSA COUNTY, XXXXX
CRIMINAL DIVISION
VERDICT FORM

State   )
)
) CASE NO.: 20XX-**2-183**
)
v.   )
) DIVISION:
)
Alexander.   )
)

We, the Jury, return the following verdict, and each of us concerns in this verdict:
(Choose the appropriate verdict)

I.   NOT GUILTY

We, the jury, find the defendant, Christopher Alexander, NOT GUILTY.

_____
Foreperson

II. FIRST DEGREE MURDER

To prove the crime of First Degree Premeditated Murder, the State must prove the following three elements beyond a reasonable doubt:

1. (Victim) is dead.

2. The death was caused by the criminal act of (defendant).

3. There was a premeditated killing of (victim).

We, the jury, find the defendant, Christopher Alexander, GUILTY of Murder in the First Degree.

_____
Foreperson

III. SECOND DEGREE MURDER

To prove the crime of Second Degree Murder, the State must prove the following three elements beyond a reasonable doubt:

1. (Victim) is dead.

2. The death was caused by the criminal act of (defendant).

3. There was an unlawful killing of (victim) by an act imminently dangerous to another and demonstrating a depraved mind without regard for human life.

We, the jury, find the defendant, Christopher Alexander, GUILTY of Murder in the Second Degree.

_____
Foreperson

-Notes-

CALUSA POLICE DEPARTMENT
CALUSA COUNTY

INCIDENT REPORT
PAGE 1 OF 3

OFFICER'S NAME:	DATE:	TIME:	LOCATION:
A B-White	6-6-20XX-2	2301 hours	West Calusa Hills

COMPLAINANT'S NAME:	DOB:	ADDRESS:	CITY/STATE ZIP
PDQ Alarm Systems		6731 Lullaby Lane	Pelican Bay, XX 33707

HOME PHONE NUMBER:	WORK PHONE NUMBER:	MOBILE/PAGER NUMBER:
		n/a

ALLEGED SUSPECT'S NAME:	DOB:	ADDRESS:	CITY/STATE ZIP
Brandi Alexander		6731 Lullaby Lane	Pelican Bay, XX 33707

HOME PHONE NUMBER:	WORK PHONE NUMBER:	MOBILE/PAGER NUMBER:
555-5172	555-6382	555-3327

(W1) WITNESS'S NAME:	DOB:	ADDRESS:	CITY/STATE ZIP
Doris Presley	2-4-51	Lullaby Lane	Pelican Bay, XX 33707

HOME PHONE NUMBER:	WORK PHONE NUMBER:	MOBILE/PAGER NUMBER:

(W2) WITNESS'S NAME:	DOB:	ADDRESS:	CITY/STATE ZIP
Robert Hightower	10/31-64	Lullaby lance	Pelican Bay, XX 33707

HOME PHONE NUMBER:	WORK PHONE NUMBER:	MOBILE/PAGER NUMBER:
555-8442	555-0997	555-3997

WRITE COMPLETE DETAILED REPORT:

The department received a call at the station from an alarm service that was reporting a shooting at a home on Lullaby lane. I proceeded directly to the home, arriving in approximately 10 minutes. Upon arrival I observed that the front door was open with light on inside the home. Neighbors were gathered at the homes on both sides of the house in question, as well as in the front yards across the street. Upon approaching the house I noticed the smell of burning rubber and noted that there were skid marks that appeared to be fresh in front of the home on Lullaby lane, on the road itself.

OFFICER'S SIGNATURE	PRINTED NAME / RANK / BADGE NUMBER
Anece Baxter-White	Anece Baxter-White Patrolman #4613

State v. Alexander

Report Continued from Page 1:

Lights were on in the home and the front door appeared open. I proceeded to the front door, identifying myself as a police officer. Upon arriving in the home I noticed shell casings on the ground outside and inside the front door. A woman was weeping uncontrollably while kneeling next to the body of a man — she appeared to be trying to wake him up.

    I inspected the body laying in the foyer. It was clear that several shots had been fired into the body, specifically two shots or more to the groin. I noticed that there were several bullet holes in the floor underneath the body, and I found at least one bullet lodged in the door frame of the foyer. I also found two notes that are attached to this incident report in the pocket of the dead man, as well as a business card in his wallet.

    Looking around the house I noted that the television was on very loud in the den next to the foyer. Upon entering the den I noted the presence of a Wendy's food bag. Inside the bag was a cheeseburger and fries. Underneath the cheeseburger I found 1 plastic bag of what appeared to be marijuana and an additional small bag of white powder. I conducted field tests and results indicated that the powder contained cocaine and the green leafy substance was marijuana. After speaking with the wife it was determined that a GSR test of her hands was not necessary. My team and I left after questioning the wife.

Upon arriving at the station instructed to return to the Alexander home to assist in additional investigation.

OFFICER'S SIGNATURE	PRINTED NAME / RANK / BADGE NUMBER
Anece Baxter-White	Anece Baxter-White/officer/#4613

INITIALS

ABW

Report Continued from Page 2:

Returned to the home. Retrieved 6 remnants of slugs, 2 from the door jamb and 4 from the floor. Retrieved box of .45 caliber ammunition provided by Ms. Alexander. All evidence gathered was taken to the evidence room. Photos were forward to detective Edwin Morris, along with diagrams of the area.

------------------------------Nothing Follows------------------------------

OFFICER'S SIGNATURE	PRINTED NAME / RANK / BADGE NUMBER
Anece Baxter-White	Anece Baxter-White/officer/#4613

REPORTING OFFICER: Anece Baxter-White
DATE REPORTED: 6/6/20XX-2

REPORTING OFFICER
SIGNATURE: Anece Baxter-White
OFFICER BADGE: #4613
DATE: 6/7/20XX-2

REVIEWING SUPERVISOR
SIGNATURE: Willie Hightower
OFFICER BADGE: #1240
DATE: 6/7/20XX-2

CALUSA POLICE DEPARTMENT
CALUSA COUNTY

REPORT OF INVESTIGATION

Report No	Date:	Complaining Witness:
20XX-206060321	6/8/20XX-02	PDQ Alarm Systems
Investigating Officer:		**Suspect:**
Detective Edwin Morris		Brandi Alexander (wife of decedent)
Division:		**Address:**
Homicide		6731 Lullabye Lane, Pelican Bay, XX 33707
Victim(s):	**Age:**	**General Description:**
Christopher Alexander	32	Male, 72", 195 lbs, Tattoo - Frostie

Investigator's Notes, June 8, 20XX-2:

Case assigned to Homicide division. Opened case file, began investigation.

On June 6, 20XX:-2 Officer Baxter-White and Chief Willie Hightower responded to a PDQ alarm system 911 call indicating an attack at the Alexander residence. Canvassed neighborhood for witnesses. Identified potential individuals to interview. She Prepared diagrams of neighborhood (exhibit 1), Alexander home (exhibit 2), and Interior of Alexander home (exhibit 3). Officer Baxter-White collected two letters from the coat pocket of the deceased (exhibit 4 & 5), and a business card from the deceased's wallet (exhibit 6).

June 7, 20XX-2.
Developed diagrams of the relevant areas of Lullaby Lane (exhibit 1, 2 and 3 of this report)
Catalogued & Photographed the following evidence seized from the Alexander Home:

- Bag of Wendy's food (exhibit 7)
- Bag of green leafy substance (probable marijuana)(exhibit 8)
- Bag of white powder (probable cocaine) (exhibit 9)
- Photograph of a .45 pistol (note this is a photograph found in the home on the writing desk of Ms. Alexander) (exhibit 10)
- Photograph of a 9mm pistol matching description of that owned by Chris Alexander (exhibit 11)
- Photographs of the bullet holes in the home (exhibits 12, 13, 14, 15, 16)
- Photographs of slugs and ammunition retrieved from Alexander home (exhibits 17, 18, 19)
- Photograph of tire marks on Lullaby Lane (exhibit 20)

June 18, 20XX-2.
Received Coroner's Report, inserted into case file

June 23, 20XX-2.
Visited "From My Cold Dead Hands" Gun Club. Retrieved Sign In Roster for May 25, 20XX-2 and inserted into case file.

July 4, 20XX-2.
Statement of Robert Hightower taken by Edwin Morris

State v. Alexander

CALUSA POLICE DEPARTMENT
CALUSA COUNTY

REPORT OF INVESTIGATION
PAGE 2 OF 2

July 8, 20XX-2
Statement of Ms. Nikki Long taken by Edwin Morris

August 12, 20XX-2.
Statement of Ms. Sharon Barry taken. Inserted into case file.
Received statement of Ms. Doris Presley taken by Investigator Stubbs. Inserted into case file.

August 14, 20XX-2.
Received statement of Billy Bob Schifflet taken by Investigator Stubbs. Inserted into case file.

August 15, 20XX-2
Received death certificate from coroner's office, inserted into file

September 23, 20XX-2
Inserted photo of 9mm pistol matching the description of the one owned by Chris Alexander (based upon the firearm registration records for said firearm)

October 10, 20XX-2.
Received results of drug testing. Inserted Lab report and chain of custody document into the file.

October 14, 20XX-2.
Recovered PDQ Alarm Report for month of June 20XX-2. Inserted into case file

Subsequent investigation revealed that Brandi Alexander shot and killed her husband, Chris Alexander, using a .45 caliber weapon. Investigative efforts included interviewing all identified witnesses, recovered evidence and searching for potential weapons registered to the Alexander's. Two weapons were registered to Chris Alexander, a .45 caliber pistol and a 9mm Beretta. I recovered a picture of the .45 registered to Chris Alexander. This picture was provided by Ms. Alexander in accordance with my request. Neither weapon was recovered at the scene. Through proper investigative steps I was able to ascertain that Ms. Alexander was familiar with the .45 caliber weapon, having fired it at the gun range approximately one week prior to the murder. Probable cause clearly exists Brandi Alexander murdered Chris Alexander. Forwarded contents of case file to state prosecutor on October 15, 20XX-2.

Investigation continues.
July 13, 20XX-1. Received affidavit of Officer Anece Baxter-White.
July 19, 20XX-1. Statement of Nikki Long taken by Edwin Morris at Ms. Long's request.

Investigation continues.

Sworn and subscribed in my presence, June 12, 2005.	I swear and affirm that the report above and the attached files are true and correct to the best of my Belief and Knowledge.
Signature: *Edwin Morris*	
Supervisor: Robert Burrell	
Supervisor's Signature *Robert Burrell*	Signature: *Edwin Morris*

State v. Alexander

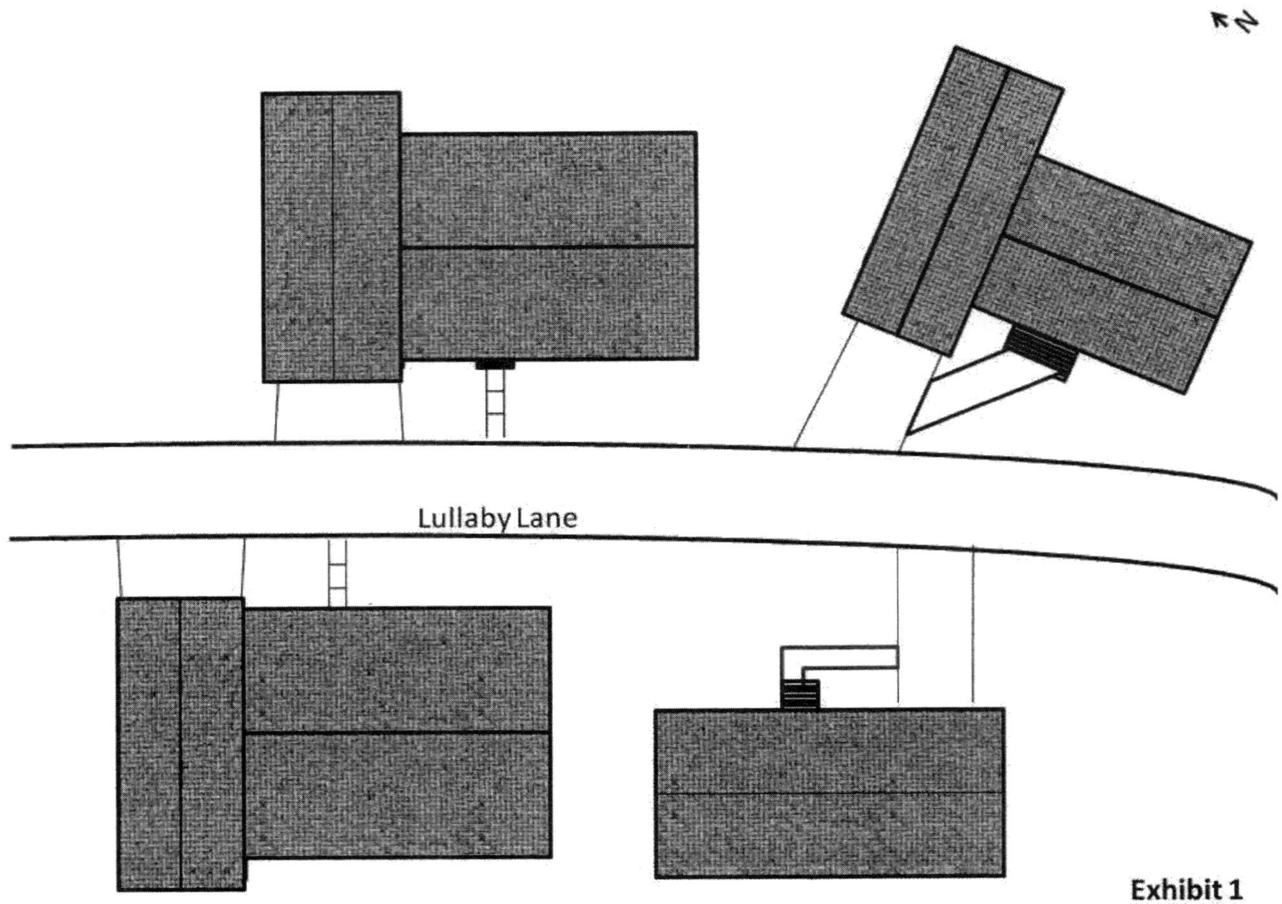

Lullaby Lane

Exhibit 1

State v. Alexander

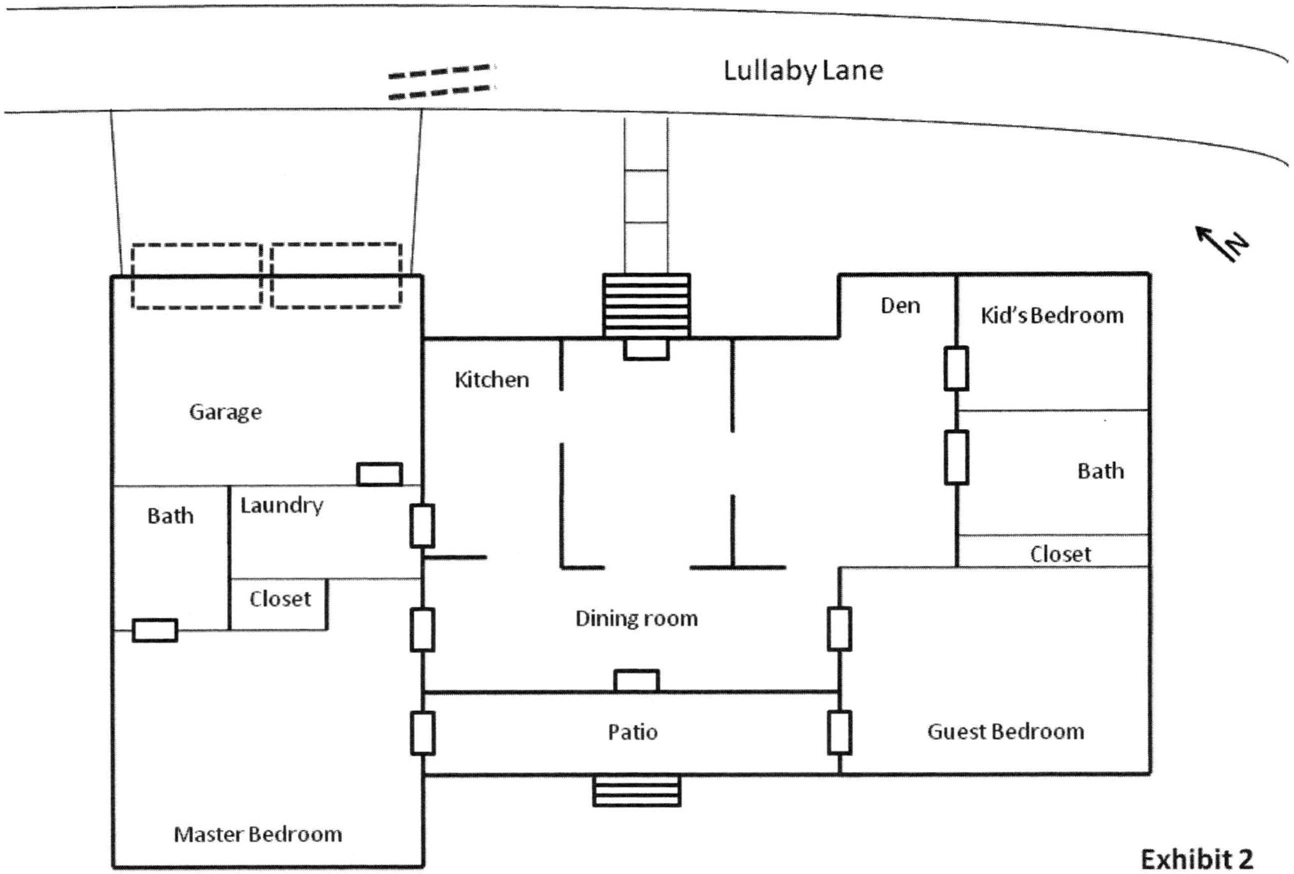

Exhibit 2

State v. Alexander

Tab B Page 69

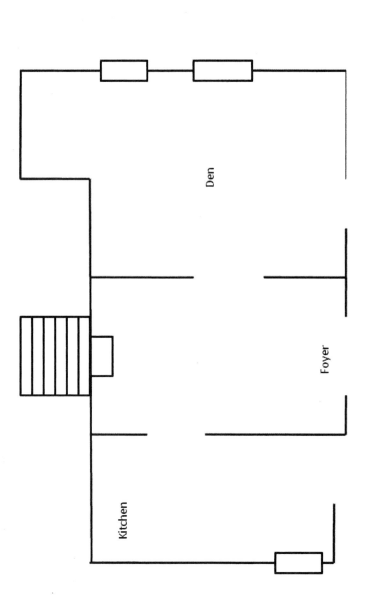

Hey Baby!

I was thinking of you tonight and my mind was wandering to when we will finally be together.

That wife of yours is such a bitch! I cannot wait to see her get hers. I will so make you happy. See you tonight!

TS
5/15/20XX-2
XXOOXOO

Babe!

I wish I could see you some mo. It has been too long since we been together. I'm startin' to think you might not be leaving her — better not be so.

I love you so much and I want us to have a baby together. Please kick that ho to the curb!

NS
6/1/20XX-2
Call ME or else.....

Nikki's
where girls get their hair did ™

Can't wait to see you!

xxx ooo

Exhibit 7

Tab B Page 74

State v. Alexander

Exhibit 8

Exhibit 9

Tab B Page 76

State v. Alexander

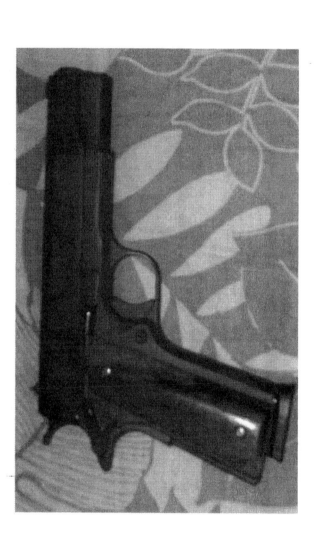

Exhibit 10

State v. Alexander Tab B Page 77

Exhibit 11

Exhibit 16

Tab B Page 83

State v. Alexander

2 slugs retrieved from door jamb of Alexander home by ABW. Unable to conduct ballistics testing without a potential murder weapon.

Edwin Morris   Jan 7, 20XX-2

Exhibit 17

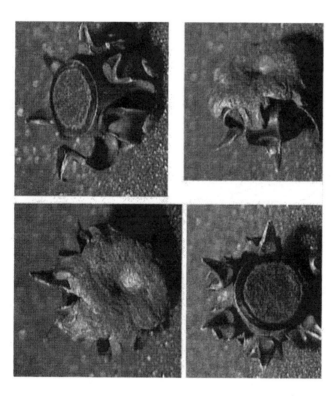

4 slugs I retrieved from concrete floor of Alexander home. Unable to conduct testing without a potential murder weapon, but do match type of ammunition seized from the home..

Edwin Morris   Jun 7, 20XX-2

Exhibit 18

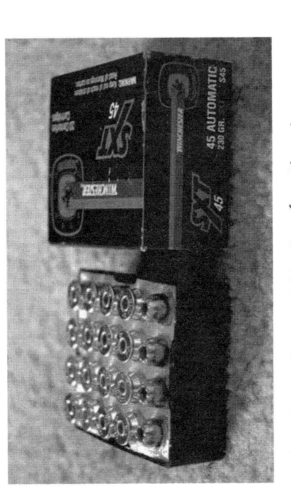

.45 caliber rounds retrieved by ABW from Alexander home on June 6, 20XX-2.

Edwin Morris Jun 7, 20XX-2

Exhibit 19

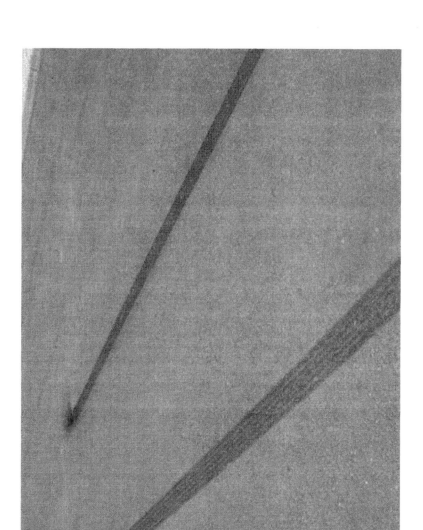

Exhibit 20

Tab B Page 87

State v. Alexander

From My Cold Dead Hands
Pelican Bay Shooting Club

Sign In Roster

Name (Print & Sign)	Date/Time	Weapon	Range
Donald Sutherland	May 25, 20XX-2 0900 hours	9 MM Glock	2
Tyler Harder	May 25, 20XX-2 0945 hours	.22 caliber rifle	1
Wild Bill Osmann	May 25, 20XX-2 10:13 AM	M1 Carbine	1
Brandi Alexander	May 25, 20XX-2	.45 Pistol	3
Chris Alexander	May 25, 20XX-2 11:25 AM	9 mm	4
Wild Bill Osmann	May 25, 20XX-2 11:45 AM	.38	4
Norm Pearson	May 25, 20XX-2 1145 hours	.22 target pistol	3
Range closed for maintenance.	1400 hours	B.B.S.	

CALUSA POLICE DEPARTMENT
CALUSA COUNTY

INCIDENT REPORT
PAGE 1 OF 3

OFFICER'S NAME: Willie Alexander	DATE: 1-6-200x-2	TIME: 1442	LOCATION: West Calusa Hills
COMPLAINANT'S NAME: Robert Hightower	DOB:	ADDRESS: 6732 Lullaby Lane	CITY/STATE ZIP: Pelican Bay, XX 33707
HOME PHONE NUMBER: 727-555-3461	WORK PHONE NUMBER: 727-555-3465	MOBILE/PAGER NUMBER: n/a	
ALLEGED SUSPECT'S NAME: Alias – Frosty	DOB: Unknown	ADDRESS: Unknown	CITY/STATE ZIP: unknown
HOME PHONE NUMBER: n/a	WORK PHONE NUMBER: n/a	MOBILE/PAGER NUMBER: n/a	
(W1) WITNESS'S NAME: Juanita Hightower	DOB:	ADDRESS: 6732 Lullaby Lane	CITY/STATE ZIP: Pelican Bay, XX 33707
HOME PHONE NUMBER:	WORK PHONE NUMBER:	MOBILE/PAGER NUMBER:	
(W2) WITNESS'S NAME:	DOB:	ADDRESS:	CITY/STATE ZIP:
HOME PHONE NUMBER:	WORK PHONE NUMBER:	MOBILE/PAGER NUMBER:	

WRITE COMPLETE DETAILED REPORT:

Mr. Hightower called the Calusa County Sherrif's Department with a complaint that some unknown guy going by the name of Frosty was selling drugs in the neighborhood. He complained that he watched the traffic in the neighborhood and he had noticed a lot of low rider type cars going by his house and parking on the street. Calusa County referred to PBPD. He also complained because he had called the Pelican Bay police department about gunfire in the neighborhood from some "hoodlums" down the street and nothing had been done. I canvassed the neighborhood but was unable to verify Mr. Hightower's allegations as to Frosty. Will refer to crime stoppers program for additional investigation.

OFFICER'S SIGNATURE	PRINTED NAME / RANK / BADGE NUMBER
Willie Alexander	Willie Hightower/SGT/7031D

State v. Alexander

Report Continued from Page 1:

Mr. Hightower appeared combative and irritable when I told him I couldn't fine "Frosty." I smelled incense burning in the Hightower home, but did not observe any improper activity. I did find a group of gang members down the street that I ran off — they were just hanging out and I observed no illegal activity.

---------------------------------Nothing Follows---------------------------------

OFFICER'S SIGNATURE	PRINTED NAME / RANK / BADGE NUMBER
Willie Alexander	Willie Alexander/SGT/7031D

INITIALS
WA

Report Continued from Page 2:	

---------------- This Page Not Used ----------------

OFFICER'S SIGNATURE	PRINTED NAME / RANK / BADGE NUMBER
Willie Alexander	Willie Alexander/SGT/7031D

REPORTING OFFICER: Willie Alexander DATE REPORTED: 1-6-200x-2

REPORTING OFFICER SIGNATURE: Willie Alexander OFFICER BADGE: #7031D DATE: 1-6-200x-2

REVIEWING SUPERVISOR SIGNATURE: Willie Hightower OFFICER BADGE: #1240 DATE: 1/6/200X-2

State v. Alexander

-Notes-

Sworn Statement of Robert Hightower   July 4, 20XX-2

RH page 1 of 2

My name is Bob Hightower. I am 44 years old. I was born and raised here in Pelican Bay. After high school, I went away to college at the University of Florida, where I received my B.S. in Physics and my Masters degree in Civil Engineering. After college, I decided to move back to Pelican Bay to get a job and start a family. Although I was offered a much higher-paying job in Biloxi, I just couldn't see myself living anywhere other than Pelican Bay. My entire family lives here and I love this city. I've been working at the same civil engineering firm for the past 15 years.

I have two older brothers. My oldest brother, Eric, is the commander of the Pelican Bay Police Department. He was actually the one assigned to investigate Chris Alexander's murder. Well, maybe not the murder itself, but I know he was the one who investigated the crime scene. I love Eric and would do anything for him. I think he is the best cop in the state. He would never lie for any reason and he always does his job perfectly.

My other brother is Ricky. He is the one we do not like to talk about much. You see, he never seemed to care about the consequences of his actions. He was in trouble with the law throughout high school and well into his adult life. Just a few years ago he finally got what was coming to him and was sentenced to twenty-five years for the attempted murder of his live-in girlfriend. He is still in jail and that is where he deserves to stay. He has been nothing but a disgrace to our entire family.

One of the main reasons I don't like Ricky is because he got me caught up in some of his criminal problems a few years back. He approached me around ten years ago to drive him around for work and such because his car broke down. I decided to help him because he had some recent problems with the law and I wanted to help him get his life back in order. Anyway, after I picked him up one day from a friend's house, a police officer pulled me over because I had a broken taillight. My brother told me just to "play it cool." I had no idea what he was talking about. The cop noticed that something was off and asked both of us to step out of the car. They ultimately found marijuana on him and a small bag underneath the seat. Because they were charging me with felony possession, I accepted the prosecutor's plea deal and testified against Ricky. Because I testified, they only gave me six months probation.

The only other legal trouble I had was with the IRS back in the early '90s. It happened because I forgot to include $10,000 worth of investment income on my tax return. The IRS brought charges of fraud and tax evasion against me. However, they eventually dropped the charges because I was very compliant and quickly paid all the taxes, plus penalties, and interest.

Although I have lived across the street from the Alexanders for several years, I really didn't talk much to either Brandi or Chris. Chris knew my brother, Ricky. So, I guess the adage is true—you know—the company you keep and all. Anyway, I didn't know Brandi or Chris, really. However, I do know a little bit about each of their reputations around town.

State v. Alexander

Sworn Statement of Robert Hightower   July 4, 20XX-2

With Brandi, I think it is common knowledge that Brandi knew her husband was cheating on her with at least two women. She had the reputation as being a woman who was reaching her breaking point. One of my friends saw her at the grocery store the day of the murder and told me that she looked angry and ready to pop. I just think she could not tolerate the cheating and lies anymore. Brandi also had a reputation of being a hothead. I had a dispute with her about her children hitting a baseball through my window and she just would not listen to me. I tried to talk to her calmly and explain to her that I only wanted her to pay for the window. Instead of talking, she screamed and yelled at me. She told me not to lecture her on how to raise her children. I think that is exactly what happened when she shot Chris. My guess is that she just would not listen to her husband's excuses and snapped.

I think it is common knowledge that Chris had issues with drugs, but nothing serious, just marijuana. I have seen some very disreputable people come by his house a few times when I was up late reading on my porch, especially in the last year or so. They would go in his house for only one or two minutes and then leave holding something in their hands. Everyone knew he liked to buy and sell small amounts of marijuana. I don't know if it means anything, but I found a very odd note in my car one day that stated, "Hey, if you need more to sell, let me know. C.A." I am positive the note fell out of Ricky's pocket because I just dropped him off at work, and it wasn't in my car when I picked him up. Also, although I don't know for sure, I think it was Chris Alexander's handwriting on the note.

On the night of Chris's murder, I was sound asleep in my bedroom when I heard what sounded like gunfire. It was so loud that I thought it was coming from my front yard. Concerned for my family's safety, I grabbed my .45 caliber gun and ran towards the window to see what was going on. I looked out the front window and didn't see anything in my yard or the Alexanders' yard across the street. I didn't hear anyone's house alarm going off. I certainly didn't see any car speeding away. The cops, including my brother Eric, came to my house to ask me questions about forty-five minutes after I heard the shots. I was completely truthful to them and told them everything I knew. I made sure to tell them about Chris and Brandi's reputations. In the end, I am positive that Brandi shot Chris. I just have this feeling about it that will not go away. I am normally never wrong about these things.

RH page 2 of 2

Signed: *Robert Hightower*

July 4, 20XX-2

Witnessed by: Detective Edwin Morris

Signed, *Edwin Morris*

July 8, 20XX-2

Sworn Statement of Nikki Long　　　　　　　　　　　　　　　　　　　　July 8, 20XX-2

NL page 1 of 2

1. My name is Nikki Long. I hereby swear under penalty of perjury that the following is a true and
2. accurate recounting of all relevant events that I can remember concerning my relationship with
3. Chris Alexander and the time leading up to his death. I believe this statement to be a true and
4. complete version of events as I remember them. I told my story to Detective Morris who then
5. typed it up and let me review it.

6. My name is Nikki Long. I'm 25 years old. I own Nikki's Beauty Shop. I have been working
7. there since I was 19. I actually met Chris, two years ago, while I was at the Salon. The day I
8. met Chris is a day I will never forget. It was love at first sight. I was outside of the salon taking
9. my 15 minute break, when all the sudden this fine, dark, tall, handsome man pulled up in the
10. parking lot. He was on his way to Pro Style. Pro Style is a barber shop for men that's next door
11. to Nikki's. When he walked by me he asked me for the time, and since I knew I had to make an
12. impression I told him it was time for him to meet the girl of his dreams. Of course he laughed,
13. and he actually missed that appointment he had for his hair cut. We sat outside and talked for
14. about 2 hours. After that day Chris and I were inseparable. Well almost, the only time we spent
15. apart was when he had to go home to Brandi and the kids.

16. Brandi was jealous of me. Jealous that I'm younger, jealous that I'm prettier and thinner, jealous
17. that her man loved and wanted me. It started to go downhill really bad with Chris and Brandi
18. when she found out I was pregnant. When I found out I was going to have Chris's baby I
19. couldn't keep it a secret. I told everyone at the salon that they were going to have to start
20. planning my baby shower because I was about to be a mommy! I knew Brandi was going to find
21. out about the baby because she was friends with people who came to Nikki's, and she got her
22. hair done there a few times as well.

23. I ended up losing that baby and when that happened I didn't go to work for, like, 3 weeks. I was
24. miserable, I was sad because Chris and I were finally going to have a child, we were going to be
25. a family and I lost all that when I lost the baby. I didn't know if he would leave "her" once I lost
26. the baby and worrying about that nearly broke my heart. When I finally decided to come back to
27. work, Brandi was there getting her hair done. When she saw me, she said "sorry to hear about
28. your loss, but good things never happen to bad people." I couldn't believe she said that to me. If
29. I didn't love Chris so much, and have so much respect for his family, I would have slapped her
30. right then and there. I did swear at her, calling her a bad word and promised her that she would
31. "get" hers someday.

32. 　　*very NL*
33. Chris's family is ^*very* important in our town. His family is respected, and I would never want to do
34. anything that would cause drama for them so I calmed down after I yelled at her. I just smirked
35. at her and went to my station to get ready for the day. I felt like I shouldn't waste any more
36. breath on Brandi, I had what she wanted. I had her man
37. *And I was keeping him too!*
38. *NL*

Sworn Statement of Nikki Long July 8, 20XX-2

I told Chris about what Brandi said to me at my job, and he assured me not to worry about her. He said that Brandi did this to herself. He told me that Brandi did not have feelings for him anymore, and all she cared about was her own self-image. They weren't even sleeping in the same room. He would sleep on the couch, and the only reason he had not left her was because of the kids. And he promised me that it wouldn't be long until he left her for good and would marry me.

Chris and I were going to get married, and Brandi knew it. That's why she did what she did. On the night of Chris's murder, Chris went out with his brother. I was going to go out with them that evening, but I had 3 perms, and 2 press and curls that day and I was exhausted. I told Chris, to just call me on his way home so I knew he made it home safe. Chris always called to kiss me goodnight, so I waited by the phone. Chris called me while he was on his way home. He told me that he had stopped at Wendy's for a burger. Chris always got a burger and a drink before he went home. He seemed to have a lot of friends at the Wendy's. He told me that you should never go to sleep on an empty stomach, especially after drinking.

While we were on the phone, Chris told me that he wanted us to move in together. He said that he and Brandi got into an argument earlier that day, and he told her it was over. He said that he told her he would be leaving by the end of the week. I was so excited that Chris was finally leaving Brandi. I had been sharing Chris for two years, and finally he would be all mine. My conversation with Chris lasted around 35 minutes. I heard him use his keys to open the door, and I heard him reset the alarm to his house. I also heard him turn on the TV, and then he complained that his order was wrong. They put onions on his burger, and Chris hates onions. All of a sudden Chris then said "I'll call you back". I asked him is she in front of you, and he said yes. Whenever Chris would say I'll call you back, especially when he says it suddenly, then, that's my signal to just hang up, and I know he will call me back when Brandi leaves the room.

My Chris did not call me back that night. I never got my goodnight kiss from him. I learned that two minutes after we hung up he was killed. I guess she figured if she couldn't have him, then neither could I.

NL page 2 of 2

Nikki Long
Nikki Long
July 8, 200x-2

Witnessed by: Detective Edwin Morris

Signed, *Edwin Morris*
July 8, 200x-2

Sworn Statement of Sharon Barry   August 12, 20XX-1

S.B page 1 of 2

1. My name is Sharon Barry. I hereby swear under penalty of perjury that the following is a true
2. and accurate recounting of all relevant events that I can remember concerning my interactions
3. with Brandi and Chris Alexander.

4. I first met the defendant, Brandi Alexander about six months before Chris Alexander passed
5. away. According to the insurance policy the date that we met was January 5, 20XX-2.

6. At the time I worked for Friends Helping Friends (FHF) Insurance as an insurance agent.
7. Currently, I am no longer employed with FHF Insurance. I work for another insurance company,
8. as a supervising agent.

9. According to my notes, I was contacted by Chris Alexander in mid-December of 20XX-3 to
10. meet with him and his wife. They were looking to purchase an insurance policy for Chris
11. Alexander in the event that he passed away, so that he could make sure that his wife and children
12. were taken care of financially. I specifically remember that it was Chris who called because I
13. thought it was such a responsible thing for a husband and father to do.

14. The meeting on January 5, 20XX-2 took place at the Alexander' home. The meeting took place
15. at 6 pm after both Brandi and Chris were home from work. The meeting was routine. I received
16. personal information from both Brandi and Chris regarding their ages, health, family history, and
17. other insurance policies or health coverage. At that time, I was made aware that Chris had
18. another insurance policy, which was issued by Chris's employer for roughly $80,000. We talked
19. about all of their options, and I remember filling out a worksheet with them establishing that
20. Chris was underinsured – not uncommon for folks his age by the way.

21. After completing all the relevant insurance forms, Brandi and Chris obtained coverage for Chris
22. at $250,000. This insurance amount was based on the monthly cost of the policy. A higher
23. insurance amount would have cost them more money each month, and they were unable to afford
24. any higher coverage. The premium is based on all the personal information that was provided to
25. me at the time. The premium amounts are pre-set based on the personal information. I followed
26. the proper procedures outlined by FHF Insurance when providing the coverage amount and
27. monthly cost.

28. At that time Brandi declined to insure herself. It was my understanding that Brandi and Chris
29. made this decision after talking over the monthly cost of life insurance for either both of them, or
30. just for one. I am unaware how or why this decision was reached. After providing them with an
31. insurance quote, I allowed Brandi and Chris to talk about their decision in private. I went
32. outside while they were talking in private, and they called me back into the house when they had
33. made a decision. Chris signed the paperwork that day.

34. Chris listed Brandi, his wife, as his sole beneficiary.

35. I had no further contact with either Brandi or Chris until after Chris was killed. About 4 days
36. after Chris died, Brandi called me. Brandi told me that Chris was murdered and that she needed

State v. Alexander

Sworn Statement of Sharon Barry August 12, 20XX-1

1 to claim his life insurance. She qualified her desire for the life insurance collection in such a
2 short period of time after his death, because she needed the money to help cover funeral
3 expenses. This was not unusual, since funeral homes expect payment when services are
4 rendered.

5 I immediately put the claim through to my superiors at FHF Insurance, and a check was ready
6 within a few days. I called Brandi back that same day and told her that the claim was
7 processing. We talked a long time. Brandi seemed so terribly distraught and in need of
8 sympathy and attention. I asked Brandi if it was okay for me to come by and pay my respects.
9 She told me where she was staying, since Chris died in her home, she said she was staying at her
10 mother's house. Brandi told me she could not bear to go back into her house, the place where
11 the love of her life was brutally murdered.

12 I took the next few days off of work and stayed by Brandi's side, along with her other friends
13 and family. We became instantly close, and, as sad as this is, we bonded during her time of
14 mourning. To this day we remain friends. We talk on the phone at least twice a week; we go to
15 dinner and movies together.

16 I enjoy Brandi's company. She is such an honest, sweet, and caring person. It was devastating
17 when she was charged with Chris's murder. There is no way she could have killed Chris. She
18 only spoke fondly of him, regardless of his affairs. She knew that Chris loved her more than any
19 other woman. She told me over and over again how she refused to leave her. Brandi is a
20 wonderful mother too. Her children are well-behaved, polite and adorable. This is because
21 Brandi has raised them properly, like a good-hearted woman would.

SB page 2 of 2

Sharon Barry
Sharon Barry
August 12, 20XX-1

Witnessed by: Detective Edwin Morris

Signed, *Edwin Morris*

August 12, 20XX-1

Witness Name: Doris Presley
Date Statement taken: August 12, 20xx-2
Investigator: Dana Stubbs

1. I remember the night Chris Alexander was killed. I don't remember the exact date,
2. but I clearly remember what happened that night.. How could I forget? I've been Mr. and
3. Mrs. Alexander' neighbor for about fifteen years. They were always such a nice couple. We
4. would say hello in passing and Mr. Alexander sometimes mowed my lawn for me. Their children
5. were always so polite. They where such a nice family... That's why it was such a shock to me
6. when he was killed.

7. On the night Mr. Alexander was murdered I was on the phone with my aunt. My mom's
8. 65th birthday was that coming weekend and my aunt and I were talking about the surprise
9. party we were planning on throwing for her. Aunt Nancy is a bit old and hard of hearing so we
10. were talking pretty loud. No matter though, I sure heard those gunshots. They were very
11. loud. Scared me half to death they did. At first I didn't know what it was exactly. I
12. thought it might have been a car backfiring, but they came so close together I knew it
13. couldn't be that. It's just so unusual to hear gun shots in my neighborhood I didn't know what
14. to do. That neighbor Mr. Hightower has fired his pistol in the neighborhood a time or two and
15. it sounded a lot like that.

16. Next thing I know, I heard a car screeching out of the driveway next door. I was
17. too afraid to go to the window and look, but I heard the car pull out of the driveway and
18. head east away from my home. I would say the screeching happened only seconds later — it
19. all happened so fast. I didn't go outside because I don't like to go out after dark. The
20. cops never came by to talk with me about it and I thought they knew about the car. I
21. called the DA's office to offer my help but they never came by either. As God is my witness
22. this is my memory of the events that evening.

Signed: Doris Presley

Witness Name: Billy Bob Schifflett
Date Statement taken: August 14, 20xx-2
Investigator: Dana Stubbs

1. My name is Billy Bob Schifflett and I own the "From My
2. Cold Dead Hands" Shootin' club in Pelican Bay. Well, actually
3. we sit outside the city limits in Calusa County. We are really
4. part of Gulfport, a small unincorporated place where folks can do
5. what they like without the government interfering in our business.
6. Gulfport has a long history of folks that like on the outskirts of
7. society and we like it that way – for good reason.

8. I've owned the club for about 5 years now, I won it in a poker
9. game from a fellow that ain't around here no more. I pay my taxes,
10. high though they are, and I don't cause nobody no trouble and I
11. intends to keep it that way.

12. I don't remember who actually came into the Shooting club
13. to use the range on the 25th of May, 20XX-2, but we do have
14. specific procedures that the federal government requires us to
15. follow and I've been following them since 911.

16. Whenever anyone comes in I make them take a short safety
17. test, we give them a briefing and then check their ID to make
18. certain that they are who they claim to be. They go downstairs to
19. the shooting range to use it. We don't go downstairs with them,
20. but we do control access to the

State v. Alexander

Witness Name: Billy Bob Schifflett
Date Statement taken: August 14, 20xx-2
Investigator: Dana Stubbs

1 shooting range area. All of our ranges, and we got 4 of them, are
2 downstairs. Range 1 is a rifle range and the other three are for
3 pistols. They are underground for safety reasons.

4   Once shooters get downstairs they have to sign in on our
5 sign in sheet. I don't watch them do that, and they are on their
6 own honor to do it. Gun owners are usually sticklers for following
7 rules – it's a safety thing.

8   I know both Chris and Brandi Alexander. I went to school
9 with them and Chris has bought quite a few guns from me over the
10 years. He's bought pistols and rifles. I sold him a .45 caliber
11 pistol about a year ago that was Army surplus. Brandi's come
12 here with him once or twice, but I don't specifically remember
13 seeing her anytime in the club in the last 6 months.

14   I have provided you guys with a copy of our sign in roster like
15 you asked. I did close the range around 2 on the 25th of May
16 20XX-2. I waited till no one was using it. I don't remember how
17 much brass we cleaned up that day and what type of guns were
18 fired. You'd have to check the roster and talk to the folks on it.

Signed: Billy Bob Schifflett

State v. Alexander

Sworn Statement of Nikki Long   July 19, 20XX-1

NL page 1 of 1

1   My name is Nikki Long. I have thought a long time about what happened that awful
2   night and I have more information that I need to tell you. I've been racking my brains
3   trying to remember exactly what it was I heard and last night in a dream it came to me.

4   When Chris said "I'll call you back" I got angry at him. I'm ashamed to admit it but I had
5   really been pissed at him for not leaving Brandi yet and I yelled at him. Yes, I know, I'm
6   so ashamed to admit it but I yelled at my darling Chris in those last moments before he
7   died. He started to say something and then I heard Brandi through the phone. She was
8   yelling. I heard her say "Are you talking to that whore Nikki Long? I told you to stay
9   away from that slut!"

10 Then I heard a door slam. Chris said to me "look baby I gotta...." And then all of a
11 sudden I heard these loud banging sounds. Right after that I heard a gun go off several
12 times and then I heard someone pick up the cell phone and the line went dead.

13 I hope she burns in Hell for taking Chris away from me that night.

NL page 2 of 2

Nikki Long
Nikki Long
July 19, 20xx-1

Witnessed by: Detective Edwin Morris

Signed, *Edwin Morris*

July 19, 20XX-1

State v. Alexander

Affidavit - Officer Anece Baxter-White   July 13, 20XX-1

ABW Page 1 of 2

My name is Anece Baxter-White. I hereby swear under penalty of perjury that the following is a true and accurate recounting of all relevant events related to my involvement in this case. I have prepared this affidavit at the request of the prosecuting attorney in the case of *State v. Alexander*. I was the officer on the scene the night of Chris Alexander's murder. I have been a police officer for Calusa County for the past 15 years. During this time, I have investigated about 50 shootings, as well as numerous other violent crimes. I have been trained in the collection of evidence by the Calusa County Police Department.

On the night of June 3, 20XX-2, our department received a 911 call at 11:16 pm from the defendant's PDQ alarm service reporting a shooting. Myself and other officers were sent to the scene by our dispatch office. To my knowledge we did not receive a 911 call from the defendant herself. I arrived at the scene at some point after the call. I wrote in my report that I arrived at 11:01pm, but I know that this is incorrect, because we didn't receive the 911 call until 11:16pm. I was about 10 minutes away from the neighborhood when I received the call.

Outside of the home, I observed skid marks on the road in front of the defendant's driveway. The front of the home had nice landscaping, with several trees and rose bushes. It seemed like a nice upper-middle class neighborhood. A few neighbors were standing on their front lawns observing the situation. I directed another officer to interview some of the neighbors to search for leads. The defendant's front windows were closed, but the front drapes were open. When I approached the front door, I noticed several shell casings on the ground and heard the defendant crying. She appeared to be in distress; she was in the living room kneeling beside her husband's body, shaking him, and yelling at him to wake up. The paramedics had to pull her away from the body.

The body was located in the living room. The deceased was lying on his back, but it was unclear whether he had been standing or sitting when he was shot. Further inspection of the body revealed that the decedent had sustained multiple gun wounds, including two (2) shots to the groin area, which usually indicates a crime of passion. There were also two (2) bullets found in the concrete underneath the body, which could indicate that the gun was fired after the decedent had already fallen. The only blood present at the scene was that underneath the decedent, which lead me to believe he was not moved after death, and was shot and killed in the room he was found in. The bullets came from a .45 caliber gun. We turned the bullets over to ballistics for testing.

Besides the bullets in the body, I also observed a bullet lodged in the doorway to the foyer. The positioning of the bullet indicated that the shooter was probably standing near the front door when they fired the gun. There were multiple bullet holes in the home. We retrieved several slugs, but the rounds fired were hollow points that broke apart on impact. I also discovered bullets in the interior walls of the living room and the foyer inside the home. No viable samples for ballistics testing could be located and I cannot state with any degree of certainty the weapon that fired these rounds.

State v. Alexander

Affidavit - Officer Anece Baxter-White July 13, 20XX-1

ABW Page 2 of 2

Upon further investigation of the house, I noticed the decedent's shirt and shoes in the living room. The television was turned on, and there was a bag of Wendy's food on the table. There was a small bag of marijuana and another of cocaine inside the takeout bag. It appeared that the decedent had been watching TV in the living room, was drawn to the foyer for some reason, then was shot. I also walked through out the house prior to speaking with Ms. Alexander. I looked at all of the windows and none appeared to have been broken or tampered with. I noted that the alarm system was activated and currently functioning. I then attempted to talk to Ms. Alexander but she was incredibly upset, weeping, screaming, almost howling.

When the defendant finally calmed down, I asked her what had happened. She told me she was asleep in her bed, and was awaken by a sound which she thought was her air conditioning. She smelt smoke and got up to investigate. She then observed the front door open, and saw her husband lying on the ground. She determined he was dead. She stated her PDQ alarm company called her, and they called 911 for her. I then asked her if she had a gun. She replied that she did not. However, when I searched the defendant's bedroom, I found an empty gun holster, belonging to a 9 mm gun, underneath the bed. I asked her again if she had a gun. This time she replied she did, and led me to a 9mm gun she kept high on a shelf in the laundry room. This gun used to shoot the decedent, a .45 caliber revolver, was not recovered.

The defendant's children were also home. They slept through the shooting, and did not wake up when myself and the detectives arrived. I found this to be unusual, because gun shots are loud, and the children's bedroom was in very close proximity to the living room. However, there was no evidence found at the scene to indicate that the children had been drugged. There did appear to be 8 empty Benadryl cellophane packets on the kitchen table but Ms. Alexander stated, and the parents of Chris Alexander verified, that the children had been sick with colds.

After about 3 hours of searching the home and interviewing the defendant, my team and I left. Once I got back to the station it was determined that a GSR test of the defendant's hands would be necessary. The test was conducted after the time we had left the home. We did not maintain constant supervision with the defendant between the time we left the scene and when the GSR test was conducted.

Anece Baxter-White

Anece Baxter-White
July 13, 20XX-1

State v. Alexander

IN THE CIRCUIT COURT OF THE FIRST JUDICIAL DISTRICT
CALUSA COUNTY
CRIMINAL DIVISION

State)
)
)
)
)
v.) CASE NO.: 0318-20XX
)
)
)
Brandi Alexander)
)

DEPOSITION OF: Roger Curlin

TAKEN BY: State

BEFORE: COURT REPORTER Vilma Rodriquez
PELICAN BAY COURT REPORTERS
2113 Veritas Way
PELICAN BAY, XX 33707

DATE: September 11, 20XX-2

LOCATION: Criminal Justice Center
6745 49th Avenue South
Pelican Bay, XX 33707

State Attorney Questioning Begins:

1 Q: Please state your name and Profession.

2 A: My name is Roger Curlin and I am a Forensic Scientist with
3   the State Bureau of Investigation. I have held that
4   position for the last fifteen years.

5 Q: What is your educational background?

6 A: I graduated from University of Phoenix with a Bachelor of
7   Science in Biochemistry and received my Masters degree from
8   the University of Phoenix.

State v. Alexander

1 Q: Do you have a doctorate?
2 A: No, I was working on my doctorate when I had some family
3   issues, so I have not completed my dissertation in order to
4   obtain my doctorate degree. I have done all the course
5   work.
6 Q: What types of forensic science do you specialize in?
7 A: I do not specialize in any type of forensic science because
8   I find that too restricting, instead I am broadly trained
9   and skilled in a variety of forensic specialties.
10 Q: What investigative steps did you take involving the
11   Alexander murder?
12 A: On June 3, 200x-2, I was summoned by the Pelican Bay Police
13   Department to the home of Chris and Brandi Alexander. I
14   conducted an initial examination of the crime scene and
15   determined that the shooter in this case should have
16   gunshot residue on their person and hands.
17 Q: What is a gunshot residue test?
18 A: A GSR test is the most common test performed to determine
19   if a person was in the presence of gunshot residue within a
20   limited time period after a weapon is discharged.
21 Q: How do you test for gunshot residue?
22 A: The test is pretty simple and the procedure is performed
23   all over the United States and is admitted as evidence in
24   many criminal cases. Like I said, the test is fairly
25   simple. When someone fires a gun, the gun releases a

1   pattern of particles that leave a residue. This residue is
2   comprised of a combination of lead, barium, and antimony
3   particles that are fused together. The same explosion that
4   forces the bullet out of the gun also releases these
5   particles into an invisible cloud that leaves traces of
6   residue on the shooter's hand, surrounding area, and the
7   victim's body. In order to determine if a person has fired
8   a gun, the procedure is to swab the area of the suspect's
9   hand to collect any residue present. Then, we analyze the
10 swabs with a GSR machine that determines if the swab
11 samples are positive for traces of GSR and, if so, to what
12 extent.
13 Q: When do you test someone for GSR?
14 A: I test the individual or individuals the detective on the
15   scene wishes to have tested. In this case, that would be
16   the defendant, Brandi Alexander.
17 Q: Where was this test conducted?
18 A: At the Alexanders' residence. I tested Mrs. Alexander at
19   her home. I swabbed both hands and placed the cotton swabs
20   into two sterile bags; one for the left hand and one for
21   the right hand. I noted that Mrs. Alexander's dominant hand
22   was her right. I later performed the analysis, and I
23   determined that there was at least one particle of GSR from
24   the left hand swab taken from Mrs. Alexander.
25 Q: What do you need to ensure the most accurate results?

1 A: For the most accurate results, a GSR sample should be taken
2   within five (5) hours of the initial gunshot. I performed
3   the test on Mrs. Alexander within three (3) hours of the
4   shooting, but if Mrs. Alexander washed her hands or had
5   substantial contact with anything, the amount of GSR on her
6   hands at the time of the swab would be reduced.
7 Q: Does the fact that you are not specifically trained in GSR
8   testing affect the validity of your test results?
9 A: No. Although I do not have extensive expertise or education
10   in the analysis or methodology of GSR, I did take the
11   course that was offered by the manufacturer of the GSR
12   machine we use to analyze the swabs. I do not think there
13   is a need for any additional training, in fact, there is
14   not really that much to know. Either there is GSR on the
15   suspect or there is not, it is as simple as that. In my
16   mind, <u>if there is GSR present then the person must have
17   fired a weapon recently.</u> I am not aware of any studies
18   that have dealt with other ways in which GSR might
19   contaminate a scene, and I have not studied the predicted
20   GSR patterns for types of weapons.
21 Q: You are qualified to conduct the test and record results?
22 A: Yes, that is a fair and accurate description of what I do.
23 Q: I have no further questions.
24   //Defense Counsel declined to question the witness during
25   the deposition//

State v. Alexander

IN THE CIRCUIT COURT OF THE FIRST JUDICIAL DISTRICT
CALUSA COUNTY
CRIMINAL DIVISION

State)
)
)
)
)
v.) CASE NO.: 0318-20XX
)
)
)
Brandi Alexander)
)

DEPOSITION OF: Dr. Jeremiah Jones

TAKEN BY: State

BEFORE: COURT REPORTER Vilma Rodriquez
PELICAN BAY COURT REPORTERS
2113 Veritas Way
PELICAN BAY, XX 33707

DATE: September 12, 20XX-2

LOCATION: Criminal Justice Center
6745 49th Avenue South
Pelican Bay, XX 33707

State Attorney Questioning Begins:

1 Q: Please state your name and Profession.

2 A: My name is Dr. Jeremiah Jones, and I am both the County
3 Coroner and Medical Examiner for Calusa County. I have held
4 that position for the last twenty years.

5 Q: What is your educational background?

6 A: I graduated from State University with a Bachelor of
7 Science in chemistry and attended medical school in
8 Grenada. I completed my residency in 20XX-24. For the

State v. Alexander

1 first four years I worked in the emergency room of Calusa
2 County Hospital and then became the county coroner in 20XX-
3 20.
4 Q: Do you have any specializations?
5 A: Yes. I have conducted advanced studies in medical examiner
6 training. I have also been on Court TV many times. They
7 affectionately refer to me as Dr. Death on that show. I
8 try to share my years of expertise with the audience.
9 Q: What types of forensic science do you specialize in?
10 A: I specialize in cause of death investigations. I am
11 particularly adept at event reconstruction as determined by
12 the placement, angle, velocity and burn mark patterns
13 associated with gunshot wounds.
14 Q: What investigative steps did you take involving the
15 Alexander murder?
16 A: I conducted the initial examination to determine the cause
17 of death.
18 Q: How did you accomplish this?
19 A: I conducted an initial examination of Mr. Alexander's body
20 when it was first brought into the county morgue. It was
21 immediately obvious that he died from gunshot wounds to
22 both the groin and chest. I determined that the manner of
23 death was homicide and that the cause of death was by
24 gunshot.
25 Q: What happened after you conducted this initial examination?

State v. Alexander

1 A: I put on my M.E. hat and got down to work. I performed an
2 autopsy of Mr. Alexander in order to determine why he died.
3 Q: What did you determine?
4 A: I determined that Mr. Alexander was shot twice in the chest
5 of 4 times in the groin. Based upon the pattern of blood
6 splatter it was evident that the groin injuries occurred
7 first.
8 Q: Is it really possible to determine that?
9 A: Absolutely. The flow of blood internally, when combined
10 with the information provided by the investigating police
11 officers made it clear. I don't even need to see any
12 alleged blood splatter patterns to make this determination.
13 The wounds in the body are the controlling factor when
14 analyzing cause of death here.
15 Q: Which shots caused the death of Mr. Alexander?
16 A: Clearly the groin shots. It appears that he was shot in
17 the groin, severing at least one femoral artery. He was
18 then allowed to bleed for approximately 10 minutes,
19 probably while being held at gunpoint. Once he had "bled
20 out" a great deal the coup de grace was administered by
21 shooting him twice in the chest.
22 Q: Doctor, to what degree of medical certainty can you state
23 this opinion as to the cause of death?
24 A: I am completely certain of it. I would stake my reputation
25 on it.

State v. Alexander

1 Q: I have no further Questions.
2   //Defense Counsel declined to question the witness during
3   the deposition//

Excerpts from Prior Sworn Testimony of Brandi Alexander
1st Criminal Trial

DIRECT EXAMINATION

Defense Counsel Begins

1 Q: Mrs. Alexander, please introduce yourself to the jury.
2 A: My name is Brandi Alexander, and I am the defendant in this
3   case.
4 Q: Tell us about yourself.
5 A: I am the youngest of three children. My parents always
6   jokingly referred to me as their "little Einstein." I was
7   really bookish and nerdy as a kid. Unlike most teens, I
8   didn't really rebel, do drugs, or get into alcohol. I liked
9   school and put my energies into doing well. My brother and
10   sister always gave me a hard time about it. They used to joke
11   that I was "old before my time."
12 Q: When did you first meet your husband?
13 A: I first met Chris in high school in 20XX-14. He was a year
14   behind me in school.
15 Q: What do you remember about him then?
16 A: I remember he was popular, athletic, and liked girls and
17   cars. Girls liked him, too, but the rumor was that he liked
18   to love girls and then leave them. So, of course, I was a
19   little worried when he started to date one of my girlfriends,
20   Cynthia. They dated only for a short while during my senior
21   year.

State v. Alexander

1	Q: What interaction did you have with him back then?
2	A: Chris and Cynthia had gone together to the senior prom. I
3	remember that night pretty well, partially because my date
4	had broken his leg that very same day and couldn't make it,
5	and partly because Cynthia was angry with Chris because he
6	wanted to stop by Wendy's before the dance. I laughed when
7	she told me the story and she stormed off saying that I was
8	naive and "didn't know anything" leaving Chris and me alone
9	at the punch bowl.
10	Q: What happened then?
11	A: Chris seemed embarrassed and made some small talk. When he
12	learned I didn't have a date for the evening, he didn't make
13	me feel bad about not having a date and went out of his way
14	to include me without hurting Cynthia's feelings. He was
15	very nice to me. I remember thinking he was handsome, smart,
16	and funny. He had a nice smile. Cynthia and I made up later
17	that night. The three of us had a great time at the prom.
18	Q: When was the next time you got together with Chris?
19	A: Oh it was years later. Chris and I met again --oh, I think
20	it was in May of 20XX-11. It was right before my college
21	graduation. I had just had my hair done at the hair salon
22	when I ran into him. He recognized me first. He told me he
23	was going in to the barber shop next door to get a shave and
24	a haircut. Other than a well-kept a goatee, Chris looked the
25	same as he did in high school—he had that same easy smile.

State v. Alexander

1	Q: What did you two talk about?
2	A: We made some small talk and laughed about prom night. I told
3	Chris that Cynthia had died last year from breast cancer.
4	Chris said he knew her husband well and that he had visited
5	Cynthia at home a few times before she had passed. We
6	discussed how Cynthia had turned to medical use of marijuana
7	to ease her pain, even though it had not been prescribed for
8	her. Chris said he heard that too, and agreed that Cynthia's
9	last weeks had been sad and tragic.
10	Q: Did you see him again?
11	A: Yes. When Chris suggested we have lunch together sometime, I
12	mentioned there wasn't a Wendy's for several miles and said I
13	didn't like their Frosties. Chris laughed. He said he loved
14	Wendy's and would forgive me that. He also joked that he
15	understood now that Wendy's was off-limits for a "first
16	date"—he learned that much from prom night. Then he asked
17	for my number and promised to call me, which he did later
18	that night. We made a date for the following weekend and
19	dated for several months afterward.
20	Q: Were you working then?
21	A: No, but shortly thereafter I got a job as an elementary
22	school teacher after graduation. I taught third grade at
23	Pelican Bay Elementary School, only four blocks from my
24	parents' home.
25	Q: Did Chris work?

State v. Alexander

A: Unlike me, Chris never went to college after high school. He always told me that college wasn't his "thing." Although most of his family was in law enforcement or civil service, Chris always told me that he preferred to work with his hands and he couldn't stand the idea of being in a job where people told him what to do just because they outranked him. He said he "gave up the chance to join the Army" for that very reason and went to trade school instead. After graduating from trade school, Chris had landed a good job as a tool and die maker for Industrial Metal Fabrication (IMF) Company, less than a mile from my parents' home. He said the flexible swing-shift hours, high hourly pay, union protection, and benefits suited him well.

Q: Did your husband have a lot of contacts in the community?

A: While we were dating, Chris always ran into people he knew. Although they were friendly with Chris, none of them really seemed to know him that well. The women we ran into made me nervous—they were very forward with Chris and touched him a lot, which was not my style. Chris would tell me not to mind the other girls—that I was the one for him. He said he liked that I was "old fashioned" and looked out for him, and he never let anyone, man or woman, get too close. He said that friends were less important to him than family, and I was family. I liked that he worried about what I thought. His popularity made me feel important and proud of him.

Q: What did your family think of him?

A: My family liked Chris well enough. My mom never seemed to warm up to him, though. I just figured it was my mom being a mom—she was always protective of me and my siblings. My brother and sister lived in town, but met Chris only two times before Chris and I were married. They all got along fine. Chris and I were married on December 20, 200x-10. Chris and I never had sex before marriage—mostly because we agreed it should be that way. Chris respected who I was and I never felt otherwise.

Q: How did you get along with his family?

A: Good most of the time. Chris had a large extended family—blood relatives, distant cousins, and friends of the family made up the majority of his social network. They were very different from my own family in that they distrusted outsiders and seemed "larger than life."

Q: How did you adjust to his family?

A: Well, you know, Chris was different around them. He talked loudly and irreverently. Chris was always the center of attention and seemed to lose himself in the attention they lavished on him. They called Chris often—at home, on his cell. There seemed to be no boundaries among them, except one: Chris always insisted that people call him before they dropped by the house. This was Chris's golden rule, and no

State v. Alexander

one ever violated it. They usually called Chris on his cell, but it was not unusual for people to call the house as well.

Q: Was there anything else about Chris's behavior that seemed strange to you?

A: It was not unusual for Chris to head out in the middle of the night to have drinks, play cards, or hang out with "his family." Chris said it was just how his family was. He said if I just accepted that, his family would eventually warm up to me. They never really did though.

Q: How did you feel around his family?

A: Actually, I never really felt comfortable around Chris's family—especially around Chris's brother Willie. Willie drank too much and made me feel uncomfortable around him. One time, at a family picnic, both Willie and Chris had been drinking. They'd gone off together for a while, leaving me to help Chris's mom and cousins to clean up. When Chris and Willie returned, I smelled the faint odor of marijuana on them both. No one else seemed to notice. No one said a word. On the way home, when I asked Chris about it, he became angry with me. He left the house and did not come home for three days. When Chris returned, we never spoke about it again. In order to maintain peace in our home I accepted that I would never question Chris's behaviors around his family again, so long as Chris continued to treat me with respect.

1 Q: Did there come a time when Chris' work situation changed?
2   Tell us about that.
3 A: About two years after we married, Chris's shifts became
4   erratic at work. He was working long hours, two shifts a
5   day. Although I missed spending time with him, he said the
6   money was too good to pass up. He said it would help us save
7   money and buy a large home.
8 Q: How did all these extra hours affect your family life?
9 A: The hours began to take their toll on Chris, I guess on me,
10   too. He became resentful, and angry, he told me he had
11   changed his mind about having children. He said he didn't
12   want to feel "tied down"—I was devastated. Although we had
13   been using protection and had agreed to wait until I was
14   tenured to start a family, we had always planned to have
15   children. Around this time I accidentally got pregnant.
16   Chris became distant and angry at first, but one day, just
17   seemed to "snap out of it."
18 Q: What happened next?
19 A: We bought a spacious three-bedroom home in an upper-class
20   neighborhood in Pelican Bay, West Calusa Hills on Lullaby
21   Lane, just before our first daughter, Ariel, was born. About
22   two years later, I gave birth to our second daughter,
23   Jasmine. Chris adored them. Even though Chris still worked
24   long hours and came home late at night at least three or four

times a week, he seemed a changed man. Chris was a devoted husband and father.

Q: Why did you have an alarm system at your house?

A: Shortly after we moved into our new home, we contracted with PDQ to install a monitored alarm system. Having the system made me feel much more secure, given that Chris's work hours sometimes involved his coming home late.

Q: Were there any weapons in the home?

A: Chris had a gun. Because Chris won't buy a gun safe, I make him keep it in the laundry room—on a high shelf out of the girl's sight and reach. It's the only way I can forget it's there and not worry about it being in the home.

Q: Why did you get life insurance on your husband recently?

A: One of Chris' friends put us in contact with Sharon Barry, a Friends Helping Friends (FHF) Insurance agent. Sharon set up a meeting with us, and agreed to come to our home to accommodate Chris's schedule. Sharon recommended we purchase a $250,000 policy, based on what we could afford at the time. A part of the insurance policy was assigned to pay funeral costs in the event of one of our deaths. We felt that this policy, plus the group policy Chris had through IMF would be more than ample to cover our family's needs.

Q: I would like to draw your attention now the night your husband was murdered. Do you remember that night?

A: I remember the night Chris was killed. I remember pieces—some of it is vivid and clear in my mind. Other parts of it are fragmented.

Q: Please explain.

A: June 3, 200x-2 was a Thursday evening. School had let out for the summer a few weeks earlier. Around 10:00 PM, I received a call from my niece, Lilli Duke. We discussed our plans to meet for lunch the next day and only talked about one minute. After hanging up the phone, I went to check on the girls. They were sound asleep. The girls are like their father—they can sleep through a live marching band playing in their bedroom. Although I don't specifically remember checking the alarm before going to bed, it was usually my habit to do so. I hate being alone in the house with the girls when Chris isn't home.

Q: What did you do next?

A: I took a bath and got ready for bed. I think I was asleep by 10:30—bathing relaxes me. I have always been an early bird, but something of a light sleeper. Chris usually slept in the den when he got home late so he wouldn't wake me. Chris wasn't home by the time I fell asleep.

Q: Did you stay asleep?

A: No, something startled me awake. I am still not certain if I know exactly what it was. At first, I thought the noise might be the air conditioner outside our bedroom window. The fan and motor always makes noise when it kicks on, sort of like a clack, loud hum, and then a pop, pop, pop. It drives Chris crazy. I've learned to sleep through it or ignore it.

Q: What was the noise?

A: I don't know, but I don't think it was the air conditioner. At least I don't think so. Before I realized what was happening, I was in the living room. I saw Chris's body on the floor. The alarm was sounding. The front door was open. Chris was half dressed. He was not moving. I think I screamed. I remember yelling at him—pounding on him to wake up. I did not move from Chris's side. I think I was there when the police arrived. It felt like an eternity. Later, I learned it only took them a few minutes to arrive.

Q: What happened after the police arrived?

A: I don't really remember, I just remember questions being asked of me. After I knew the girls were safe, I just zoned out. There were police and technicians all over our home. It was noisy. I don't even know what I was thinking, other than I wanted to go somewhere safe with my girls. I remember vaguely that the police asked me about guns in the house. I think I told them there were no guns because I had forgotten about the one in the laundry room. When the police showed me a holster they found under the bed, I remembered the gun in the laundry room and took them to it.

Q: How long did this questioning by the police last?

A: I'm not real sure, but after several hours, the police allowed me, Ariel, and Jasmine to leave the house with my brother. The police didn't search me before leaving, but, later, they called me back to the house and tested my hands and arms for gunpowder. The test turned out a single speck of gunpowder on the back of my left hand. Even though I told the police I did not kill my husband and that I was right-handed, they did not seem to believe me. I was arrested for the murder of my husband, Chris Alexander. My life, as I had once known it to be, ended forever.

Q: Ms. Alexander did you kill you husband?

A: No.

Q: Well if you didn't whom do you suspect?

A: I think it might have been that "lady" Nikki Long, she was mad because Chris had broken things off with her and come back home to me and the girls. He always came back to us. She had been talking crap around town about how she was going to take my man and I know that sort of stuff embarrasses his family - you just don't want to make them mad.

Q: Nothing further, Your Honor.

-Notes-

Name	Sex	Hour of Death	Date of Death
Chris Alexander	M	2300 hours	6/6/20XX-2
Race	**Age**	**DOB**	**County of Death**
Other	36	10/22/20XX-36	Calusa
SSN	**Marital Status**	**Surviving Spouse**	**State of Death**
555-45-3244	Married	Brandi Alexander	XX
Residence-State	**Residence-County**	**Residence-City**	**Street Address**
XXXXXXX	Calusa	Pelican Bay	6731 Lullaby Lane
Father	**Mother**	**Address(es):**	
Willie Alexander	Frances Alexander	9123 South St., Pelican Bay, XX 33465	
Informant's Name	**Mailing Address:**		
Brandi Alexander	6731 Lullaby Lane, Pelican Bay, XX 33707		
Disposition:	**Cemetery/Crematorium**	**Location:**	**Medical Examiner:**
Buried	Happy Acres	Pelican Bay	*Dr. Jeremiah Jones, M.E*

Funeral Home:	Mailing Address:
Happy Acres	P.O. Box 345, Pelican Bay, XX 33902

Person who pronounced death:	Pronounced Dead on:	Location:
Dr. Jeremiah Jones County Coroner/Medical Examiner	6/6/20XX-2	Calusa County Hospital 1921 Sherman Way Pelican Bay, XX 33450

Coroner:	Mailing Address:
Dr. Jeremiah Jones	Calusa County Hospital 1921 Sherman Way, Pelican Bay, XX 33450

Cause of Death:	Signature of Coroner:
Internal injuries from gunshot wounds to the chest and groin. Victim bled to death	*Dr. Jeremiah Jones, M.E.*

Other Significant Conditions:	Autopsy:	Was Case Referred to Medical Examiner:
4 non-lethal gunshot wounds	Yes	Yes

Accident/Suicide/Homicide/Other:	Means of Death:
Homicide	Gunshot wounds, Loss of Blood

Place of Death:	Address:
Home	6731 Lullaby Lane Pelican Bay, XX 33707

OFFICE OF THE MEDICAL EXAMINER
CALUSA COUNTY

Jeremiah Jones, M.D.
Eric Kilhim, M.D.
Carol Morbid, M.D.
505 South Morte Circle
Pelican Bay, XX 33333
(505) 555-0001

NAME: Chris Alexander
SEX: Male
RACE: White
AGE: 36
DOB: 10/22/1771

AUTOPSY NO: 00XX-2-767
DATE OF AUTOPSY: Jun 8, 00XX-2
TIME OF AUTOPSY: 10:15 a.m.
PATHOLOGIST: Jeremiah Jones, M.D.
Chief Medical Examiner

FINAL PATHOLOGICAL DIAGNOSES:

I. MASSIVE HEMORHAGING FROM SEVERED RIGHT FEMORAL ARTERY

II. MASSIVE HEMORRHAGE FROM SEVERED LEFT FEMORAL ARTERY

III. HEMORRHAGE IN RIGHT ANTERIOR GROIN AREA

IV. HEMORHAGE IN LEFT ANTERIOR GROIN AREA

V. HEMORRHAGE IN LEFT CENTRAL CHEST AREA

CAUSE OF DEATH: MULTIPLE GUNSHOT WOUNDS TO THE GROIN AREA

MANNER OF DEATH: HOMICIDE

Dr. Jeremiah Jones, M.D.
Jeremiah Jones, M.D.
Chief Medical Examiner

State v. Alexander

Office of the Medical Examiner
Calusa County

Chris Alexander
00XX-2-767

CLOTHING:

The body has a pair of boxer underwear on, soaked with blood in the groin area. No other clothing items. No jewelry.

EXTERNAL EXAMINATION:

The body is that of a well-developed, well-nourished white male appearing the offered age of 38 years old. The body measures 74 feet and weighs 195 pounds.

The unembalmed body is well preserved and cool to touch due to refrigeration. Rigor mortis is developing in the major muscle groups. Liver mortis is fixed and purple posteriorly except over pressure points. During initial examination, there was no rigor and lividity was at a minimum and unfixed.

There are six gun shot wounds. All six wounds enter the body in the anterior and exit the body in the posterior. Two wounds are in the right chest area and four in the groin area. The wounds are described in detail below.

The scalp hair is black and measures up to 4 inches in length in the fontal area and up to 3 inches in the back and on top of the head. The irises are black and the pupils are dilated with redness. The teeth are natural and in good condition. The fenula are intact. The oral mucosa and tongue are free of injuries. The external ears have no injuries.

The neck is symmetrical and shows no masses or injuries. The trachea is in the midline. The shoulders are symmetrical and are free of scars.

The flat abdomen has no injuries. The back is symmetrical. The buttocks are unremarkable.

The fingernails are short and clean.

OTHER IDENTIFYING FEATURES:

There is one scar and one tattoo on the body.

SCAR:
There is ¼ inch scar on the top right arm anterior of the elbow.

TATTOOS:
There is one tattoo of the word "Frosty" on the right arm posterior of the shoulder. There is another tattoo of a marijuana leaf on the left arm posterior of the shoulder.

INTERNAL EXAMINATION:

The body was opened with the usual Y incision. The left chest and groin areas displayed significant trauma from gun shots. Otherwise, unremarkable.

BODY CAVITIES:

The muscles of the right chest were normal and the muscles of the left chest were torn and traumatized form the gun shots. The lungs were atelectatic when the pleural cavities were opened. The ribs, sternum and spine exhibit no fractures. The right pleural cavity was free of

Office of the Medical Examiner
Calusa County

Chris Alexander
00XX-2-767

fluid. The left pleural cavity contained a moderate amount of blood. The pericardial sac has a normal amount of clear yellow fluid. The diaphragm has no abnormality. The subcutaneous abdominal fat measures 5 centimeters in thickness at the umbilicus. The abdominal cavity is lined with glistening serosa and has no collections of free fluid. The organs are normally situated. The mesentery and omentum are unremarkable.

NECK:

The soft tissues and the strap muscles of the neck exhibit no abnormalities. The hyoid bone and the cartilages and the larynx and thyroid are intact and show no evidence of injury. The larynx and trachea are lined by smooth pink-tan mucosa, are patent and contain no foreign matter. The epiglottis and vocal cords are unremarkable. The cervical verbal column is intact. The carotid arteries and jugular veins are unremarkable.

CARDIOVASCULAR SYSTEM:

The heart and great vessels contain dark red liquid blood and little postmortem clots. The heart weighs 308 grams. The epicedial surface has normal amount of glistening, yellow adipose tissue. The coronary arteries are free of atherosclerosis.

The pulmonary trunk and arteries are opened in situ and there is no evidence of thromboemboli. The intimal surface of the aorta is smooth with a few scattered yellow atheromata. The ostia of the major branches are normal distribution and dimension. The inferior vena cava and tributaries have no antemortem clots.

RESIRATORY SYSTEM:

The lungs weigh 555 grams and 552 grams, right and left respectively. There is a small amount of subpleural anthracotic pigment within the lobes. The pleural surfaces are free of exudates: right-sided pleural adhesions have been described above. The trachea and bonchi have smooth tan epithelium. The cut surfaces of the lungs are red-pin and have mild edema. The lung parenchyma is of the usual consistency and shows no evidence of neoplasm, consolidation, thromboemboli, fibrosis o calcification.

HEPATOBILIAY SYSTEM:

The liver weighs 2545 grams. The liver edge is somewhat blunted. The capsule is intact. The cut surfaces are red-brown and normal consistency. There are no focal lesions. The gallbladder contains 15 milliliters of dark green bile. There are no stones. The mucosa is unremarkable. The large bile ducts are patent and non-dilated.

HEMOLYMPHATIC SYSTEM:

The thymus is not identified. The spleen weighs 305 grams. The capsule is shiny, smooth and intact. The cut surfaces are firm and moderately congested. The lymphoid tissue in the spleen is within a normal range. The lymph nodes throughout the body are no enlarged.

Office of the Medical Examiner
Calusa County

Chris Alexander
00XX-2-767

GASTROINTESTINAL SYSTEM:

The tongue shows a small focus of sub mucosal hemorrhage near the tip. The esophagus is empty and the mucosa is unremarkable. The stomach contains an estimated 29 milliliters of thick sanguinous fluid. The gastric mucosa shows no evidence of ulceration. There is a mild flattening of the rugal pattern within the antrum with intense hyperemia. The duodenum contains bile-stained hick tan fluid. The jejunum, ileum, and the colon contain yellowish fluid with a thick, cloudy, particulate matter. There is no major alteration to internal and external inspection and palpitation except for a yellowish/white shiny discoloration of the mucosa. The vermiform appendix is identified. The pancreas is tan, lobulated and shows no neoplasia calcification or hemorrhage.

There are no intraluminal masses or pseudomenbrane.

UROGENITAL SYSTEM:

The kindeys are similar size and shape and weigh 159 grams and 176 grams, right and left, respectively. The capsules are intact and strip with ease. The cortical surfaces are purplish, congested and mildly granular. The cut surfaces reveal a well-defined corticomedullary unction. There are no structural abnormalities of the medullae, calyces or pelvis. The ureters are slender and patent. The urinary bladder has approximately 0.5 milliliters of cloudy yellow urine. The mucosa is unremarkable.

The penis and testes appear normal.

ENDOKRINE SYSTEM:

The adrenal glands have a normal configuration with the golden yellow cotices well demarcated from the underlying medullae and there is no evidence of hemorrhage. The thyroid gland is mildly fibrotic and has vocally pale gray parenchyma on sectioning. The pituitary gland is within normal limits.

MUSCULOSKELETAL SYTEM:

Postmortem radiographs of the body show no acute, healed or healing fractures of the head, neck appendicular skeleton or the axial skeleton. The muscles are normally formed.

CENTRAL NERVOUS SYSTEM:

The scalp has no hemorrhage or contusions. The calvarium is intact. There is no epidural, subdural or subarachnoid hemorrhage. The brain has a normal convolutional pattern and weighs 1270 grams. The meninges are clear. The cortical surfaces of the brain have mild to moderate flattening of the gyri with narrowing of the sulci.

EVIDENCE OF INJURIES:

There are six gunshot wounds. These are given Roman Numeral designations; however these designations are random and do not correspond to the degree of severity of injuries, nor to the sequence in which they have been inflicted.

I. Perforating gunshot wound of right upper chest:

State v. Alexander

Office of the Medical Examiner
Calusa County

Chris Alexander
00XX-2-767

An entrance gunshot wound is located on the decedent's right upper chest, 2 inches to the right of the right nipple. It is a 1/4 inch circular perforation with a symmetrical 1/8 inch dark margin of abrasion. No soot or stippling is seen in association with this wound.

After perforating the skin and soft tissues of the right chest, the bullet enters the right chest wall at the 5th intercostals space and subsequently fractures ribs #6-9, posterior-laterally and exits behind the right posterior chest wall through the 8th intercostal space. Powder residue is not visible in the wound track. There is moderate tissue disruption along the bullet track. There is no major or minor injury to any organ from this wound. No bullet is recovered.

This was an indeterminate/distant range perforating gunshot wound of the right chest which passes front to back, slightly left, and slightly downward.

II. Perforating gunshot wound of right lower chest:

An entrance gunshot wound is located in the decedent's right lower chest, 2 inches below and 1 inch to the right of the right nipple. It is a 1/4 inch round perforation with an asymmetric margin of abrasion which measures 1/4 inch at the superior aspect of the wound and 1/8 inch at the inferior aspect of the wound. No soot or stippling is seen in association with this wound.

After perforating the skin and soft tissues of the left lateral chest, the bullet enters the abdominal cavity via the 8th intercostals space, injures multiple loops of small bowel and penetrates the retroperitoneal soft tissues of the upper left pelvis. The bullet exits the left lower back. Powder residue is not visible in the wound track. There is slight tissue disruption along the bullet track. No bullet is recovered.

This was an indeterminate/distant range gunshot wound of the right chest which passes front to back and downward.

III. Perforating gunshot wounds of left groin:

There are two entrance gunshot wounds in the decedent's left pelvis area.

a. The first wound in the left groin area is located 1 inch to the left of the pubis. It is a 1/4 inch circular perforation with a symmetrical 1/8 inch dark margin of abrasion. No soot or stippling is seen in association with this wound. After perforating the skin, the wound extends through the muscles and soft tissues of the abdomen and punctures the prostate gland. The bullet perforates the psoas muscle and exits the body to the left of the sacrum.

b. The second wound in the left groin area is located 2 inches to the left of the pubis. It is a 1/4 inch circular perforation with a symmetrical 1/8 inch dark margin of abrasion. No soot or stippling is seen in association with this wound. After perforating the skin, the wound extends through the muscles and soft tissue of the abdomen and perforates the femoral artery. The bullet exits the body through the gluteus maximus to the left of the sacrum.

State v. Alexander

Office of the Medical Examiner
Calusa County

Chris Alexander
00XX-2-767

These are indeterminate/distant range gunshot wounds of the left groin which pass from front to back.

IV. Perforating gunshot wounds of right groin:

There are two gunshot wounds in the decedent's right pelvis area.

a. The first wound is in the right groin area located 1 and ¼ inches to the right of the pubis. It is a 1/4 inch circular perforation with a symmetrical 1/8 inch dark margin of abrasion. No soot or stippling is seen in association with this wound. After perforating the skin, the wound extends through the muscles and soft tissues of the abdomen and punctures the bladder. The bullet exits the body through the gluteus maximus to the right of the sacrum.

b. The second wound is in the right groin area located 3 inches to the right of the pubis. It is a 1/4 inch circular perforation with a symmetrical 1/8 inch dark margin of abrasion. No soot or stippling is seen in association with this wound. After perforating the skin, the wound extends through the muscles and soft tissues of the abdomen and punctures the right femoral artery. The bullet exits through the gluteus maximus to the left of the sacrum.

These are indeterminate/distant range gunshot wounds of the left groin which pass from front to back.

Enclosure 1 – Autopsy Diagram
Enclosure 2 – Blank Body Diagram

ST/GPS/lsr

Dictated: 06/08/00XX-2
Transcribed: 06/09/00XX-2
Finalized: 06/15/00XX-2

State v. Alexander

Office of the Medical Examiner
Calusa County

Chris Alexander
00XX-2-767

Enclosure 1

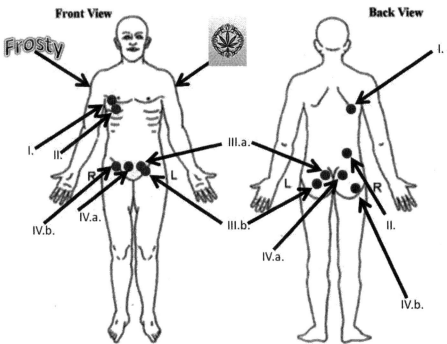

Autopsy Notes: Chris Alexander, conducted 06/09/20XX-2   *J.J. ME*

Office of the Medical Examiner
Calusa County

Chris Alexander
00XX-2-767

Enclosure 2

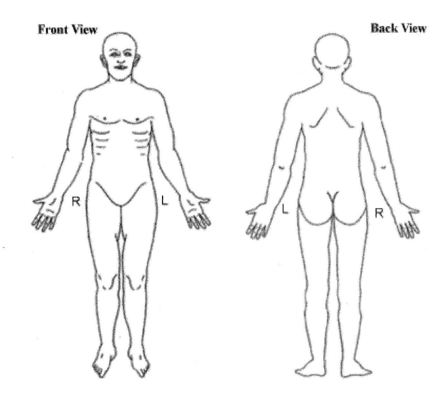

State v. Alexander   Tab D Page 133

EVIDENCE

Agency:	Pelican Bay Police Department		Calusa County
Collected By:	Officer Anece Baxter-White		
Item Number:		Case Number:	20XX(-2)1959
Date:	6-6-20XX-2	Time:	2345 hours

Description: Small Bag of white powder, field test positive for presence of cocaine, identified as exhibit 9 in the case file.

Remarks: Secured properly, carried to station and turned over to the evidence custodian.

CHAIN OF CUSTODY

Received From: Officer Anece Baxter-White *Anece Baxter-White*
Received By: Detective William Murphy *Bill Murphy*
Date: 6-7-20XX(-2)　　　Time: 0239 HOURS

Received From: Detective William Murphy – by Certified Mail
Received By: Doctor Steven Schwarz, Calusa County Forensic Laboratory *Felix Schwarz*
Date: 7-23-20XX(-2)　　　Time: 0932 Hours

Received From: Calusa County, Forensic Laboratory – by Certified Mail
Received By: Detective William Murphy *Bill Murphy*
Date: 10-10-20XX(-2)　　　Time: 1232 Hours

State v. Alexander

EVIDENCE

Agency:	Pelican Bay Police Department		Calusa County
Collected By:	Officer Scott Frost		
Item Number:		Case Number:	20XX(-2)1959
Date:	6-6-20XX-2	Time:	0232 hours

Description: Small Bag of green leafy substance, field test positive for presence of marijuana, identified as exhibit 10 in the case file.

Remarks: Secured properly, carried to station and turned over to the evidence custodian.

CHAIN OF CUSTODY

Received From: Officer Scott Frost *Scott Frost*
Received By: Detective William Murphy *Bill Murphy*
Date: 6-7-20XX(-2)   Time: 0339 HOURS

Received From: Detective William Murphy – by Certified Mail
Received By: Doctor Steven Schwarz, Calusa County Forensic Laboratory *Felix Schwarz*
Date: 7-23-20XX(-2)   Time: 0932 Hours

Received From: Calusa County, Forensic Laboratory – by Certified Mail
Received By: Detective William Murphy *Bill Murphy*
Date: 10-10-20XX(-2)   Time: 1232 Hours

State v. Alexander

CALUSA COUNTY FORENSIC LABORATORY
415 COUNTY ROAD 369
CALUSA COUNTY, FLORIDA 33459

August 4, 20XX-2

DRUG CHEMISTRY DIVISION REPORT

SUBJECT: Submitter Case Number: 20XX(-2)-9x-PBPD454
Laboratory Referral Number: 20XX(-2)-948
Subject: Chris Alexander

Exhibits:
1. 1 plastic bag containing white powder (Item 1)
2. 1 plastic bag containing green leafy substance (Item 2)

Findings:
Examination of white powder material in Exhibit 1 revealed the presence of cocaine. Amounts (grams):

Exhibit	Received	Used	Returned
1	45.0	0.5	44.5

Examination of green leafy substance material in Exhibit 2 revealed the presence of marijuana. Amounts (grams):

Exhibit	Received	Used	Returned
2	154.0	1.0	153.0

Stephen F. Schwarz, M.D.
Stephen F. Schwarz, Ph.D.
Forensic Chemist

CERTIFICATE

I certify that I am the custodian of records of the Calusa County Forensic Laboratory, and that the foregoing is a true copy of the record of this Laboratory.

James Holder, M.D.
JAMES HOLDER, M.D.
Director, Calusa County Forensic Laboratory

-Notes-

PDQ Alarm Systems, Inc.,
2914 49th Avenue South
Pelican Bay, XX 33606
727-555-9012

Mr. Christopher Alexander
6731 Lullaby Lane
Pelican Bay, XX 33707

Dear Sir/Ma'am:

In accordance with your *PDQ* Alarm system plan we are writing to inform you of the reported activity for your system during the time period May 15, 20XX-2 through June 15, 20XX-2. A review of the computer logs maintained on our system provides the following information:

Date:	Incident:	Action Taken:
20XX-2.05.16.2139	Alarm tripped – garage door	Called home IAW plan requirements. Homeowner Alexander answered phone call and indicated he had just come in through the garage and forgot to reset the system.
20XX-2.05.23.1649	Alarm tripped – front door	Called home IAW plan requirements. Homeowner's wife said children went out the door before the system was disarmed. Explained the fact that there is no lag time between opening of door and tripping of alarm.
20XX-2.06.06.2253	Alarm tripped – front door	Called home IAW plan requirements. Wife on the phone saying someone shot husband, send help. Very upset, almost incomprehensible. Called Police through 911 system and reported incident.

As always we appreciate your business and look forward to providing for all of your security related needs in the future.

Sincerely,

Russell Martin

Russell Martin
CEO, PDQ Alarm Systems

Individual Charges

www.sprintpcs.com

Customer	Account Number	Invoice Period	Page
Chris Alexander	0166000555-3	May 31 – Jun 30	5 of 16

Individual Charges for Chris Alexander (continued)
727-555-2260
cafrostie@sprintpcs.com

Voice Call Detail

Date	Time	Phone Number	Call Destination	Rate/Type	Minutes Used	Airtime Charges	LD/Additional Charges	Total Charges
5.31	1739	555-3624	Pelican Bay	📱	7	included	0.00	0.00
5.31	1943	555-3461	Incoming		2	included	0.00	0.00
6.1	1345	555-3327	Pelican Bay		12	included	0.00	0.00
6.1	1603	555-3463	Jacksonville		3	included	0.00	0.00
6.1	1954	555-3461	Incoming		2	included	0.00	0.00
6.2	1433	555-6633	Pelican Bay		15	included	0.00	0.00
6.2	1729	555-3624	Pelican Bay	📱	29	included	0.00	0.00
6.3	2012	555-3327	Pelican Bay		5	included	0.00	0.00
6.3	2213	555-1623	Incoming		2	included	0.00	0.00
6.5	2312	555-3463	Jacksonville		4	included	0.00	0.00
6.6	1501	01934-679	Juarez, Mx		2	included	0.00	0.00
6.6	1515	555-1623	Incoming		2	included	0.00	0.00
6.6	1621	555-3461	Incoming		2	included	0.00	0.00
6.6	1752	01934-679	Mexico City, Mx		2	included	0.00	0.00
6.6	2201	555-5172	Pelican Bay		4	included	0.00	0.00
6.6	2210	555-3624	Pelican Bay	📱	23	included	0.00	0.00

📱 - PCS Calling

EM Notes:
555-5172 - Alexander Home Number
555-3327 - Brandi Alexander Cell Phone
555-3624 - Nikki Long Cell Phone
555-6633 - Nikki's Hair Salon

Doctor Horrible

The Pelican Bay Star
November 3, 20XX-2
By Phillip Payne, State Court Correspondent

In January, the State Supreme Court took an unusual step. In the murder trial of 14-year-old Danny Wayne Morris, the court tossed out the testimony of the medical examiner who had conducted the autopsy of the body.

Why you may ask? The medical examiner in the case, Dr. Jeremiah Jones, had testified under oath that he could tell from the bullet wounds in the body that Morris and his brother simultaneously held the gun to fire the fatal shot. Unfortunately it is impossible to make such a determination from examining bullet wounds, a point the Supreme Court explained at length in their opinion.

Former Pelican Bay Police Chief B.J. Mills has been trying for years to draw attention to Dr. Jones. "There's no question in my mind that there are innocent people doing time due to the testimony of Dr. Jones," he says. "I reckon some may even be on death row."

Over the twenty years that Dr. Jones has been a medical examiner state Supreme Court justices, police officers, defense lawyers, crime lab experts and other state medical examiners have made public their concerns with his practice at one time or another.

Although Dr. Jones refused to speak talk with the paper, he did make the following observation on the witness stand during the Morris trial. He claimed under oath to perform anywhere from 1,500 to 1,800 autopsies a year. The National Association of Medical Examiners (NAME) says a medical examiner should perform no more than 250 autopsies per year. After 325, the organization refuses to certify an examiner's practice.

"That number cannot be done," says Antonio DeMarossa, author of The Complete Guide to Forensic Pathology, widely considered the guiding textbook. "After 250 autopsies, you start making small mistakes. At 300, you're going to get mental and physical strains on your body. Over 350, and you're talking about major fatigue and major mistakes."

For much of his career Dr. Jones, 71, has conducted autopsies as well as held two research and hospital positions and testified in court two to four times per week. After reviewing one Jones autopsy in a 2003 homicide case, Dr. James McDonald, who sits on NAME's ethics committee, sent a strongly-worded letter to the defendant's attorney describing Dr. Jones's conclusions as "near-total speculation," the quality of his report "pathetic." As a result of Dr. McDonald's letter, the prosecutor dropped the murder charge and the defendant pleaded guilty to the lesser charge of manslaughter.

Another medical examiner reviewed Dr. Jones's autopsy in a 1998 homicide and characterized his work as "near complete malpractice." In that case, Dr. Jones had determined that a woman had died of "natural causes." The diagnosis was later changed to homicide by blunt force to the head. According to the medical examiner that performed the second autopsy, Dr. Jones hadn't even emptied the woman's pockets, a standard autopsy procedure. No one has been prosecuted in the case. Dr. Jones declined repeated requests from me to comment.

Dr. Jones isn't a board-certified forensic pathologist, at least as the term is understood by his peers. The American Board of Pathology is considered the only reputable certifying organization for forensic pathology. Dr. Jones failed the board's exam in the 1980s. He still testifies in court that he's "board certified." But that's a reference to his membership in the American Academy of Forensic Examiners, which he has said publicly certified him without requiring him to take an exam.

State v. Alexander

Part of the problem is a lack of oversight. Elected county coroners and district attorneys shop out autopsies to private-practice medical examiners. The county pays doctors $550 for each autopsy, plus extra for other tests and services. Dr. Jones has dominated these referrals for years, a strong indication that coroners and district attorneys are happy with his work. And the state Supreme Court, although it tossed out his testimony in the Morris case, didn't stop him from testifying in other cases. Most experts agree that a medical examiner should be independent and find facts irrespective of their value to the prosecution.

Consider William Schifflett, convicted and sentenced to death in 2002 for the murder of his girlfriend's infant daughter. The indigent Schifflett asked the trial court for money to hire his own expert to review Dr. Jones's findings -- a crucial part of the state's case. He was denied. Schifflett's attorneys were able to get a former state medical examiner from a neighboring state to review Dr. Jones's autopsy for his appeal. Though the second autopsy raised real doubts about Schifflett's guilt, the state Supreme Court declined to even consider it, ruling that it was new evidence, and should have been introduced at trial.

That's not an uncommon ruling from an appellate court, but it illustrates just how important it is that state expert witnesses be reputable, credible, and accountable before ever stepping onto the witness stand.

Our state leaders should put an immediate end to Dr. Jones's autopsy operation. The state also needs to revisit every criminal case in which Dr. Jones has testified. Finally, we need to implement significant reforms as to how autopsies are conducted – we could start by requiring all contracted medical examiners to at least meet the profession's minimum standards. Until then, a cloud of suspicion hangs over every murder conviction that comes out of the state's courts.

DA Argues Infidelity, Money Motivated Killing

The Pelican Bay Star
December 7, 20XX-1
By Phillip Payne, State Court Correspondent

Pelican Bay -- Prosecutors are honing in on infidelity and money as reasons a former teacher might have killed her husband in 20XX-2.

Chris Alexander was shot six times in his living room, and his wife, Brandi, told police she believed he was killed after answering the front door.

Police recovered several .45 caliber shell casings in the foyer, outside the front door and in the flowerbed. But the only blood found in the house was under Chris Alexander in the living room.

Brandi Alexander also had traces of gunshot residue on her left hand. The defense plans to argue that it came from touching her husband's body.

The prosecution claims Brandi Alexander was angry about her husband's affair with another woman who spoke with him just minutes before he was killed.

That woman, Nikki Long, took the stand Wednesday afternoon and said she was on the phone with Chris Alexander for 30 minutes just moments before he was shot. Long said he had to hang up because his wife came in the room.

The district attorney told the jury that Brandi Alexander killed her husband for a $250,000 life insurance policy and because she found out he had at least two mistresses.

The former Public School teacher was arrested and charged in the slaying a week later.

State v. Alexander

Detective: Suspect Lied Night of Husband's Death

The Pelican Bay Star
December 9, 20XX-1
By Phillip Payne, State Court Correspondent

Pelican Bay -- Testimony in the second day of a former teacher's murder trial revealed that she lied to police on the night of her husband's slaying.

Officer Anece Baxter White told jurors Thursday that Brandi Alexander lied to her about a gun being in the couple's house. Only after she told her an empty gun holster was found under her bed did the Public School teacher say there was a .9-millimeter in the garage, Baxter White testified.

A friend of the victim, Chris Alexander, said in court that Alexander had owned a .45-caliber gun that is still missing -- the same type of gun used to kill Alexander.

An investigator testified he found no signs of forced entry or blood anywhere in the house except around the body of Chris Alexander. A neighbor who lives across the street also told the jury he heard gunshots the night of the killing, looked out and saw no one leave the Alexander house.

An aunt of Chris Alexander that went to the house the night of the crime testified that Brandi Alexander had gone into a bathroom to wash up. She later tested positive for gunshot residue on the back of her left hand.

Brandi Alexander was arrested and charged in the slaying a week after her husband's death.

Teacher's Attorney Blasts Investigation: Defense Claims Detective Left Details Out Of Report

The Pelican Bay Star
December 13, 20XX-2
By Phillip Payne, State Court Correspondent

Pelican Bay -- The defense for a former Public Schools teacher blasted police during her murder trial Monday, saying detectives did a sloppy and incomplete investigation.

Lead Detective Ed Morris spent most of the day on the stand telling jurors what Brandi Alexander told him about the night of her husband's death and defending his own report.

Defense attorney Ross Eastman ripped into Morris, claiming he'd left out details in his initial report that he included in his testimony -- facts such as inaccurate dates and who was at the crime scene the night of the slaying.

Morris told jurors he interviewed Brandi Alexander six days after the killing and that she had several inconsistencies in her story, mainly about the couple's security system. Alexander first said she heard the alarm go off while she was sleeping, then heard popping noises, Morris testified. But he said Alexander changed the story moments later, saying the popping sounds came first.

Brandi Alexander claims she found her husband shot on the living room floor and that someone else did it. She tested positive for gunshot residue, and there were no signs of forced entry or blood anywhere in the house except around the body.

Teacher's Murder Trial Resumes

The Pelican Bay Star
January 2, 20XX-1
By Phillip Payne, State Court Correspondent

Pelican Bay -- Testimony is expected to continue Thursday morning in the trial of a Public School teacher accused of killing her husband. Opening statements began Wednesday in the case.

The defense claims someone else shot Brandi Alexander' husband Chris as he answered their front door in June 20XX-2.

But the prosecution claims she killed her husband to collect a $250,000 life insurance policy. Prosecutors said Brandi Alexander was angry about her husband's affairs with two other women.

In court on Wednesday, one of those women claimed she spoke with Chris Alexander just minutes before he was killed.

Police recovered several .45 caliber shell casings in the house.

Brandi Alexander also had traces of gunshot residue on her left hand. The defense said that was because she touched her husband's body.

Juror Dismissed In Ex-Teacher's Murder Trial

The Pelican Bay Star

January 4, 20XX-1
By Phillip Payne, State Court Correspondent

Pelican Bay -- A juror was dismissed Friday in the murder trial of a former Public Schools teacher.

Brandi Alexander is accused of killing her husband, Chris Alexander, at their home.

Juror No. 5 was dismissed because she had been taking medication and was seen closing her eyes and not focusing on testimony Thursday.

The jury now has eight white members and four black members -- three of them women. Judge Jerry Parker noted a defense objection and moved forward.

Much of Friday's testimony focused on shell casings and bullet fragments in the house. Alexander was shot six times and died in his living room. Although the shell casings were found outside the front door, most of the bullet fragments were around and underneath the body.

The prosecution contended Brandi Alexander stood over her husband's body and shot him, sending bullets into the concrete underneath the living room carpet -- something a gun expert from the state crime lab said is possible.

Brandi Alexander claimed someone at their front door shot her husband while she was in the bedroom. She tested positive for traces of gunshot residue on the back of her left hand, investigators said.

The trial has ended for the weekend. Alexander could be sentenced to life in prison if she's found guilty.

Teacher Guilty!

The Pelican Bay Star
January 9, 20XX-1
By Phillip Payne, State Court Correspondent

It took a Calusa County Jury only two hours to reach a guilty verdict in Brandi Alexander's Alexander' murder trial.

"We the jury, find the defendant guilty as charged," read the court foreman.

Brandi Alexander showed no emotion Tuesday after she was found guilty of the 200XX-2 killing of her husband, Chris Alexander.

Chris Alexander' father said the verdict does little to numb his pain.

"I'm pleased with what the verdict was. I'm not happy, but pleased, because God confirmed what he showed me two and a half years ago," Chris Alexander Sr. said.

Chris Alexander was shot six times in the living room of the north Jackson home he shared with his wife in June 20XX-2. The gun has never been found.

During the trial, prosecutors alleged that Brandi Alexander killed her husband because he had two mistresses and also to cash in on a $250,000 life insurance policy.

Prosecutors also claimed gunshot residue found on her hand proved she fired the shots.

Defense attorneys called only one witness. The defense contended that Brandi Alexander was asleep in her bedroom when her husband was fatally shot and that she discovered his body after hearing popping noises.

"There's no direct evidence. There's not one piece of direct evidence you can seize or put your hands on and say 'I'm convinced beyond a reasonable doubt.' They build inference onto inference, and the law doesn't allow that," defense attorney Ross Eastman said.

After the verdict was read, Brandi Alexander' family members cried in the courtroom and did not want to speak as they left the courthouse.

Her attorneys said they will request a new trial.

Since the murder, Chris Alexander' family has continued a limited relationship with Brandi because of the couple's children.

Chris Alexander' father said he still questions why his son was murdered.

"When someone tells you point blank, 'I didn't have anything to do with your son's death,' and come to find out that person lied to you, that hurts. It really hurts." Mr. Alexander said.

Judge Jerry Parker sentenced Brandi Alexander to life in prison shortly after she was found guilty.

Retrial Set For Teacher Charged With Murder

The Pelican Bay Star
By Phillip Payne, State Court Correspondent

Pelican Bay -- A former public school teacher accused of killing her husband will be retried this week.

Brandi Alexander' retrial originally was scheduled for May, but attorneys for both sides said scheduling conflicts forced them to set a November date.

During her first trial, prosecutors claimed she killed Chris Alexander to cash in on a life insurance policy and because he had two mistresses.

Alexander was convicted in January and sentenced to life in prison, but that verdict was thrown out after Judge Jerry Parker ruled that prosecutors sought to keep blacks off the jury.

She was released on $150,000 bond.

The retrial starts Tuesday.

-Notes-

State of XXXXX
UNIFORM COMMITMENT TO CUSTODY
OF DEPARTMENT OF CORRECTIONS

THE CIRCUIT COURT OF CALUSA COUNTY, IN THE SPRING TERM of 20XX-8
IN THE CASE OF:

STATE OF XXXXXX

v.   CASE ID : 20XX(-8)1492   DIVISION: D

DEFENDANT   :   Chris   Alexander
AKA(S)   :   Frostie

IN THE NAME AND BY AUTHORITY OF THE STATE OF XXXXX, TO THE SHERRIFF OF SAID COUNTY AND THE DEPARTMENT OF CORRECTIONS OF SAID STATE, GREETING:

THE ABOVE NAMED DEFENDANT HAVING BEEN DULY CHARGED WITH THE OFFENSE SPECIFIED HEREIN IN THE ABOVE STYLED COURT, AND HAVING BEEN DULY CONVICTED AND ADJUDICATED GUILTY OF AND SENTENCE FOR SAID OFFENSE BY SAID COURT, AS APPEARS FROM THE ATTACHED CERTIFIED COPIES OF INFORMATION FILED JUDGMENT AND SENTENCE, AND FELONY DISPOSITION AND SENTENCE DATA FROM WHICH ARE HEREBY MADE PARTS HEREOF;

NOW THEREFORE, THIS TO COMMAND YOU, THE SAID SHERIFF, TO TAKE AND KEEP, AND, WITHIN A REASONABLE TIME AFTER RECEIVING THIS COMMITMENT, SAFELY DELIVER THE SAID DEFENDANT, TOGETHER WITH ANY PERTINENT INVESTIGATION REPORT PREPARED IN THIS CASE, INTO THE CUSTODY OF THE DEPARTMENT OF CORRECTIONS OF THE STATE OF XXXXX: AND THIS IS TO COMMAND YOU, THE SAID DEPARTMENT OF CORRECTIONS, BY AND THROUGH YOUR SECRETARY, REGIONAL DIRECTORS, SUPERINTENDANTS, AND OTHER OFFICIALS, TO KEEP AND SAFELY IMPRISON THE SAID DEFENDANT FRO THE TERM OF SAID SENTENCE IN THE INSTITUTION IN THE STATE CORRECTIONAL SYSTEM TO WHICH YOU, THE SAID DEPARTMENT OF CORRECTIONS, MAY CAUSE THE SAID DEFENDANT TO BE CONVEYED OR THEREAFTER TRANSFERRED. AND THESE PRESENTS SHALL BE YOUR AUTHORITY FOR THE SAME. HEREIN NOT FAIL.

WITNESS THE HONORABLE JEREMY PARKER
JUDGE OF THE SAID COURT, AS ALSO CONNIE EVANS
CLERK, AND THE SEAL THEREOF, THIS
24th DAY OF May 20XX-8

BY: *Margaret Mills*
DEPUTY CLERK

IN THE FIRST JUDICIAL CIRCUIT IN AND FOR
CALUSA COUNTY, STATE OF XXXXX

CIRCUIT CRIMINAL DIVISON

STATE OF XXXXX DIVISION: D
v.
CHRIS ALEXANDER CASE NUMBER: 20XX(-8)1492
DEFENDANT

CERTIFICATE OF SERVICE

    I, Connie Evans, Clerk of the Circuit Court of the County of Calusa, State of XXXXX, having by law the custody of the seal and all records, books, documents and papers of or appertaining to the Circuit Court, do hereby certify that a true and correct copy of the Judgment and Sentence has been hand delivered to the State Attorney and mailed to the Defense Attorney.

    IN WITNESS WHEREOF, I have hereunto set my hand and seal of said Circuit Court, this 24th day of May A.D. 20XX-8.

CONNIE EVANS
As Clerk of Circuit Court

Margaret Mills

As Deputy Clerk
Circuit Criminal Division

IN THE CIRCUIT COURT, 1ST JUDICIAL CIRCUIT
IN AND FOR CALUSA COUNTY, XXXXX
DIVISION : D
CASE NUMBER : 20XX(-8)1492

STATE OF XXXXX
v.
Chris Alexander
DEFENDANT

------JUDGMENT------

THE DEFENDANT, Chris Alexander, BEING PERSONALLY BEFORE
THIS COURT REPRESENTED WITH
PRIVATE ATTORNEY
Norm Pearson, Esquire
THE ATTORNEY OF RECORD AND THE STATE REPRESENTED BY ASSISTANT STATE ATTORNEY
George Peabody Smalley, AND HAVING

Been tried and found guilty by a jury of the following crime(s): 1

COUNT	CRIME	STATUTE	COURT ACTION	DATE
1	Possession of a Controlled Substance, to wit, MARIJUANA	80112	GUILTY	16 April 20XX-8
2	Sale of a Controlled Substance, to wit, Marijuana	80112a	GUILTY	16 April 20XX-8

And no cause being shown why the defendant should not be adjudicated guilty, it is ordered that the defendant is hereby adjudicated guilty of the above crime(s).

DEFENDANT Chris Alexander

                                                      Division   : D
                                                      Case Number : 20XX(-8)1492
                                                      OBTS Number : 98421119

-----------------SENTENCE-----------------

THE DEFENDANT, BEING PERSONALLY BEFORE THIS COURT, ACCOMPANIED BY THE DEFENDANT'S ATTORNEY OF RECORD, PRIVATE ATTORNEY Norm Pearson, Esquire AND HAVING BEEN ADJUDGED GUILTY HEREIN, AND THE COURT HAVING BEEN GIVEN THE DEFENDANT AN OPPORTUNITY TO BE HEARD AND TO OFFER MATTERS IN MITIGATION OF SENTENCE, AND TO SHOW CAUSE WHY THE DEFENDANT SHOULD NOT BE SENTENCED AS PROVIDED BY LAW AND NO CAUSE BEING SHOWN

IT IS THE SENTENCE OF THIS COURT THAT THE DEFENDANT:

Pay a fine of $2500.00, pursuant to appropriate XXXXX Statutes.

Is hereby committed to the custody of the Department of Corrections for a term of: 4 Years, sentence to be suspended pending successful completion of 4 years probation.

-----------------OTHER PROVISIONS-----------------

AS TO COUNT(S) : 1
THE FOLLOWING MANDATORY/MINIMUM PROVISIONS APPLY TO THE SENTENCE IMPOSED :

DEFENDANT Chris Alexander

                                                      Division   : D
                                                     Case Number : 20XX(-8)1492
                                                     OBTS Number : 98421119

-----------------OTHER PROVISIONS-----------------

Sentencing guidelines filed.

IN THE EVENT THE ABOVE SENTENCE IS TO THE DEPARTMENT OF CORRECTIONS, THE SHERIFF OF CALUSA COUNTY, XXXXX, IS HEREBY ORDERED AND DIRECTED TO DELIVER THE DEFENDANT TO THE DEPARTMENT OF CORRECTIONS AT THE FACILITY DESIGNATED BY THE DEPARTMENT TOGETHER WITH A COPY OF THIS JUDGMENT AND SENTENCE AND ANY OTHER DOCUMENTS SPECIFIED BY XXXXX STATUTE
THE DEFENDANT IN OPEN COURT WAS ADVISED OF THE RIGHT TO APPEAL FROM THIS SENTENCE BY FILING NOTICE OF APPEAL WITHIN 30 DAYS FROM THIS DATE WITH THE CLERK OF THIS COURT AND THE DEFENDANT'S RIGHT TO THE ASSISTANCE OF COUNSEL IN TAKING THE APPEAL AT THE EXPENSE OF THE STATE SHOWING OF INDIGENCY.

DONE AND ORDERED IN CALUSA COUNTY, XXXXX, THIS 24TH DAY OF May 20XX-8

State of XXXXX
UNIFORM COMMITMENT TO CUSTODY
OF DEPARTMENT OF CORRECTIONS

THE CIRCUIT COURT OF CALUSA COUNTY, IN THE SPRING TERM of 20XX-8
IN THE CASE OF:

STATE OF XXXXX   CASE ID : 20XX(-3)1898   DIVISION: D
v.
DEFENDANT   :   Nikki   Long
AKA(S)   :

IN THE NAME AND BY AUTHORITY OF THE STATE OF XXXXX, TO THE SHERIFF OF SAID COUNTY AND THE DEPARTMENT OF CORRECTIONS OF SAID STATE, GREETING:

    THE ABOVE NAMED DEFENDANT HAVING BEEN DULY CHARGED WITH THE OFFENSE SPECIFIED HEREIN IN THE ABOVE STYLED COURT, AND HAVING BEEN DULY CONVICTED AND ADJUDICATED GUILTY OF AND SENTENCE FOR SAID OFFENSE BY SAID COURT, AS APPEARS FROM THE ATTACHED CERTIFIED COPIES OF INFORMATION FILED JUDGMENT AND SENTENCE, AND FELONY DISPOSITION AND SENTENCE DATA FROM WHICH ARE HEREBY MADE PARTS HEREOF;

    NOW THEREFORE, THIS TO COMMAND YOU, THE SAID SHERIFF, TO TAKE AND KEEP, AND, WITHIN A REASONABLE TIME AFTER RECEIVING THIS COMMITMENT, SAFELY DELIVER THE SAID DEFENDANT, TOGETHER WITH ANY PERTINENT INVESTIGATION REPORT PREPARED IN THIS CASE, INTO THE CUSTODY OF THE DEPARTMENT OF CORRECTIONS OF THE STATE OF XXXXX: AND THIS IS TO COMMAND YOU, THE SAID DEPARTMENT OF CORRECTIONS, BY AND THROUGH YOUR SECRETARY, REGIONAL DIRECTORS, SUPERINTENDANTS, AND OTHER OFFICIALS, TO KEEP AND SAFELY IMPRISON THE SAID DEFENDANT FRO THE TERM OF SAID SENTENCE IN THE INSTITUTION IN THE STATE CORRECTIONAL SYSTEM TO WHICH YOU, THE SAID DEPARTMENT OF CORRECTIONS, MAY CAUSE THE SAID DEFENDANT TO BE CONVEYED OR THEREAFTER TRANSFERRED. AND THESE PRESENTS SHALL BE YOUR AUTHORITY FOR THE SAME. HEREIN NOT FAIL.

    WITNESS THE HONORABLE JEREMY PARKER
JUDGE OF THE SAID COURT, AS ALSO CONNIE EVANS
CLERK, AND THE SEAL THEREOF, THIS
21st DAY OF January 20XX-3

BY: *MARGARET MILLS*
DEPUTY CLERK

IN THE FIRST JUDICIAL CIRCUIT IN AND FOR
CALUSA COUNTY, STATE OF XXXXX

CIRCUIT CRIMINAL DIVISON

STATE OF XXXXX   DIVISION: D
V.
Nikki Long   CASE NUMBER: 20XX(-1)1898
DEFENDANT

CERTIFICATE OF SERVICE

    I, Connie Evans, Clerk of the Circuit Court of the County of Calusa, State of XXXXX, having by law the custody of the seal and all records, books, documents and papers of or appertaining to the Circuit Court, do hereby certify that a true and correct copy of the Judgment and Sentence has been hand delivered to the State Attorney and mailed to the Defense Attorney.

    IN WITNESS WHEREOF, I have hereunto set my hand and seal of said Circuit Court, this 21st day of January A.D. 20XX-3.

                                                      CONNIE EVANS
                                                      As Clerk of Circuit Court

MARGARET MILLS
As Deputy Clerk
Circuit Criminal Division

IN THE CIRCUIT COURT, 1ST JUDICIAL CIRCUIT
IN AND FOR CALUSA COUNTY, XXXXX
DIVISION : D
CASE NUMBER : 20XX(-3)1898

STATE OF XXXXX
VS
Nikki Long
DEFENDANT

--JUDGMENT--

THE DEFENDANT, Nikki Long, BEING PERSONALLY BEFORE
THIS COURT REPRESENTED WITH
PRIVATE ATTORNEY
Norm Pearson, Esquire
THE ATTORNEY OF RECORD AND THE STATE REPRESENTED BY ASSISTANT STATE ATTORNEY
George Peabody Smalley, AND HAVING

Been tried and found guilty by a jury of the following crime(s): 1

COUNT	CRIME	STATUTE	COURT ACTION	DATE
1	Filing a false police report	80107	GUILTY	14 Dec 20XX-4

And no cause being shown why the defendant should not be adjudicated guilty, it is ordered that the defendant is hereby adjudicated guilty of the above crime(s).

DEFENDANT Nikki Long

           Division : D
           Case Number : 20XX(-3)1898
           OBTS Number : 32323498

------------------------------SENTENCE------------------------------

THE DEFENDANT, BEING PERSONALLY BEFORE THIS COURT, ACCOMPANIED BY THE DEFENDANT'S ATTORNEY OF RECORD, PRIVATE ATTORNEY Norm Pearson, Esquire
AND HAVING BEEN ADJUDGED GUILTY HEREIN, AND THE COURT HAVING BEEN GIVEN THE DEFENDANT AN OPPORTUNITY TO BE HEARD AND TO OFFER MATTERS IN MITIGATION OF SENTENCE, AND TO SHOW CAUSE WHY THE DEFENDANT SHOULD NOT BE SENTENCED AS PROVIDED BY LAW AND NO CAUSE BEING SHOWN

IT IS THE SENTENCE OF THIS COURT THAT THE DEFENDANT:

Pay a fine of $750.00, pursuant to appropriate XXXXX Statutes. Is hereby committed to the custody of the Department of Corrections for a term of: 18 Months, sentence to be suspended pending successful completion of 2 years probation.

------------------------------OTHER PROVISIONS------------------------------

AS TO COUNT(S): 1
THE FOLLOWING MANDATORY/MINIMUM PROVISIONS APPLY TO THE SENTENCE IMPOSED:

None

DEFENDANT Nikki Long

           Division : D
           Case Number : 20XX(-3)1898
           OBTS Number : 32323498

------------------------------OTHER PROVISIONS------------------------------

Sentencing guidelines filed.

IN THE EVENT THE ABOVE SENTENCE IS TO THE DEPARTMENT OF CORRECTIONS, THE SHERIFF OF CALUSA COUNTY, XXXXX, IS HEREBY ORDERED AND DIRECTED TO DELIVER THE DEFENDANT TO THE DEPARTMENT OF CORRECTIONS AT THE FACILITY DESIGNATED BY THE DEPARTMENT TOGETHER WITH A COPY OF THIS JUDGMENT AND SENTENCE AND ANY OTHER DOCUMENTS SPECIFIED BY XXXXX STATUTE

THE DEFENDANT IN OPEN COURT WAS ADVISED OF THE RIGHT TO APPEAL FROM THIS SENTENCE BY FILING NOTICE OF APPEAL WITHIN 30 DAYS FROM THIS DATE WITH THE CLERK OF THIS COURT AND THE DEFENDANT'S RIGHT TO THE ASSISTANCE OF COUNSEL IN TAKING THE APPEAL AT THE EXPENSE OF THE STATE SHOWING OF INDIGENCY.

DONE AND ORDERED IN CALUSA COUNTY, XXXXX, THIS 21st DAY OF January 20XX-3

State of XXXXX
UNIFORM COMMITMENT TO CUSTODY
OF DEPARTMENT OF CORRECTIONS

THE CIRCUIT COURT OF CALUSA COUNTY, IN THE SPRING TERM of 20XX-8
IN THE CASE OF:

STATE OF XXXXX   CASE ID : 20XX(-6)1066   DIVISION: D
v.
DEFENDANT : Nikki   Long
AKA(S) :

IN THE NAME AND BY AUTHORITY OF THE STATE OF XXXXX, TO THE SHERRIFF OF SAID COUNTY AND THE DEPARTMENT OF CORRECTIONS OF SAID STATE, GREETING:

    THE ABOVE NAMED DEFENDANT HAVING BEEN DULY CHARGED WITH THE OFFENSE SPECIFIED HEREIN IN THE ABOVE STYLED COURT, AND HAVING BEEN DULY CONVICTED AND ADJUDICATED GUILTY OF AND SENTENCE FOR SAID OFFENSE BY SAID COURT, AS APPEARS FROM THE ATTACHED CERTIFIED COPIES OF INFORMATION FILED JUDGMENT AND SENTENCE, AND FELONY DISPOSITION AND SENTENCE DATA FROM WHICH ARE HEREBY MADE PARTS HEROF;

    NOW THEREFORE, THIS TO COMMAND YOU, THE SAID SHERIFF, TO TAKE AND KEEP, AND, WITHIN A REASONABLE TIME AFTER RECEIVING THIS COMMITMENT, SAFELY DELIVER THE SAID DEFENDANT, TOGETHER WITH ANY PERTINENT INVESTIGATION REPORT PREPARED IN THIS CASE, INTO THE CUSTODY OF THE DEPARTMENT OF CORRECTIONS OF THE STATE OF XXXXX: AND THIS IS TO COMMAND YOU, THE SAID DEPARTMENT OF CORRECTIONS, BY AND THROUGH YOUR SECRETARY, REGIONAL DIRECTORS, SUPERINTENDANTS, AND OTHER OFFICIALS, TO KEEP AND SAFELY IMPRISON THE SAID DEFENDANT FRO THE TERM OF SAID SENTENCE IN THE INSTITUTION IN THE STATE CORRECTIONAL SYSTEM TO WHICH YOU, THE SAID DEPARTMENT OF CORRECTIONS, MAY CAUSE THE SAID DEFENDANT TO BE CONVEYED OR THEREAFTER TRANSFERRED. AND THESE PRESENTS SHALL BE YOUR AUTHORITY FOR THE SAME. HEREIN NOT FAIL.

    WITNESS THE HONORABLE JEREMY PARKER
    JUDGE OF THE SAID COURT, AS ALSO CONNIE EVANS
    CLERK, AND THE SEAL THEREOF, THIS
    24th DAY OF February 20XX-6

BY: *MARGARET MILLS*
DEPUTY CLERK

IN THE FIRST JUDICIAL CIRCUIT IN AND FOR
CALUSA COUNTY, STATE OF XXXXX

CIRCUIT CRIMINAL DIVISON

STATE OF XXXXX DIVISION: D
v.
<u>Nikki Long</u> CASE NUMBER: 20XX(-6)1066
DEFENDANT

CERTIFICATE OF SERVICE

 I, Connie Evans, Clerk of the Circuit Court of the County of Calusa, State of XXXXX, having by law the custody of the seal and all records, books, documents and papers of or appertaining to the Circuit Court, do hereby certify that a true and correct copy of the Judgment and Sentence has been hand delivered to the State Attorney and mailed to the Defense Attorney.

 IN WITNESS WHEREOF, I have hereunto set my hand and seal of said Circuit Court, this 24th day of February A.D. 20XX-6.

CONNIE EVANS
As Clerk of Circuit Court

MARGARET MILLS
As Deputy Clerk
Circuit Criminal Division

IN THE CIRCUIT COURT, 1ST JUDICIAL CIRCUIT
IN AND FOR CALUSA COUNTY, XXXXX
DIVISION : D
CASE NUMBER : 20XX(-6)1066

STATE OF XXXXX
VS
Nikki Long
DEFENDANT

----------JUDGMENT----------

THE DEFENDANT, Nikki Long, BEING PERSONALLY BEFORE
THIS COURT REPRESENTED WITH
PRIVATE ATTORNEY
Norm Pearson, Esquire
THE ATTORNEY OF RECORD AND THE STATE REPRESENTED BY ASSISTANT STATE ATTORNEY
George Peabody Smalley, AND HAVING

Been tried and found guilty by a jury of the following crime(s): 1

COUNT	CRIME	STATUTE	COURT ACTION	DATE
1	Possession of a Controlled Substance, to wit, MARIJUANA	80112	GUILTY	9 January 20XX-6

And no cause being shown why the defendant should not be adjudicated guilty, it is ordered that the defendant is hereby adjudicated guilty of the above crime(s).

State v. Alexander

DEFENDANT Nikki Long

                                                    Division   :   D
                                                    Case Number :   20XX(-6)1066
                                                    OBTS Number :   32323498

---------------SENTENCE---------------

THE DEFENDANT, BEING PERSONALLY BEFORE THIS COURT, ACCOMPANIED BY THE DEFENDANT'S ATTORNEY OF RECORD, PRIVATE ATTORNEY Norm Pearson, Esquire AND HAVING BEEN ADJUDGED GUILTY HEREIN, AND THE COURT HAVING BEEN GIVEN THE DEFENDANT AN OPPORTUNITY TO BE HEARD AND TO OFFER MATTERS IN MITIGATION OF SENTENCE, AND TO SHOW CAUSE WHY THE DEFENDANT SHOULD NOT BE SENTENCED AS PROVIDED BY LAW AND NO CAUSE BEING SHOWN

IT IS THE SENTENCE OF THIS COURT THAT THE DEFENDANT:

Pay a fine of $500.00, pursuant to appropriate XXXXX Statutes. Is hereby committed to the custody of the Department of Corrections for a term of: 1 Year, sentence to be suspended pending successful completion of 2 years probation.

---------------OTHER PROVISIONS---------------

AS TO COUNT(S) : 1

THE FOLLOWING MANDATORY/MINIMUM PROVISIONS APPLY TO THE SENTENCE IMPOSED :

None

DEFENDANT Nikki Long

                                                    Division   :   D
                                                    Case Number :   20XX(-6)1066
                                                    OBTS Number :   32323498

---------------OTHER PROVISIONS---------------

Sentencing guidelines filed.

IN THE EVENT THE ABOVE SENTENCE IS TO THE DEPARTMENT OF CORRECTIONS, THE SHERIFF OF CALUSA COUNTY, XXXXX, IS HEREBY ORDERED AND DIRECTED TO DELIVER THE DEFENDANT TO THE DEPARTMENT OF CORRECTIONS AT THE FACILITY DESIGNATED BY THE DEPARTMENT TOGETHER WITH A COPY OF THIS JUDGMENT AND SENTENCE AND ANY OTHER DOCUMENTS SPECIFIED BY XXXXX STATUTE

THE DEFENDANT IN OPEN COURT WAS ADVISED OF THE RIGHT TO APPEAL FROM THIS SENTENCE BY FILING NOTICE OF APPEAL WITHIN 30 DAYS FROM THIS DATE WITH THE CLERK OF THIS COURT AND THE DEFENDANT'S RIGHT TO THE ASSISTANCE OF COUNSEL IN TAKING THE APPEAL AT THE EXPENSE OF THE STATE SHOWING OF INDIGENCY.

DONE AND ORDERED IN CALUSA COUNTY, XXXXX, THIS 24TH DAY OF February 20XX-6

Fundamental Trial Advocacy:
The Law, the Skill & the Art

Washington v. Hartwell
Cases and Materials

Charles H. Rose, III
Professor of Excellence in Trial Advocacy
Director, Center for Excellence in Advocacy
Stetson University College of Law

Notes

WASHINGTON V. HARTWELL

CHARLES H. ROSE III
Associate Professor of Law
Director, Center for Excellence in Advocacy
Stetson University College of Law

"We empower students to find within themselves their unique voices – to become the best possible advocates they can be."[1]

The following student at Stetson University College of Law gave of their time, expertise and creativity to assist in producing this case file. Without their help this project would still be an idea that was less than half way to completion. Each embodies the Stetson Spirit and I gratefully acknowledge their contributions. They are:

Center for Excellence in Advocacy Fellows-
Vilma Martinez
Allana Forté
Katherine Lambrose

Case File Project Volunteers-
Derrick Connell
Nadine David
Brian Dettman
Natasha Hines
Lindsay Moczynski

I wish to express my gratitude to the leadership at Stetson - Dean Darby Dickerson, Associate Dean Ellen Podgor, and Associate Dean Jamie Fox. They helped make this text possible through their unfailing support of creative scholarship.

The ideas behind using case files to teach are grounded in concepts of experiential learning. It is in doing that true education occurs.[2] These files are designed to create optimal "learning by doing" opportunities – the foundation upon which advocacy instruction, if not all learning, rests.

---

[1] Professor Charles H. Rose III, Director, Center for Excellence in Advocacy, www.law.stetson.edu/excellence/advocacy

[2] Myles Horton, the co-founder of the Highlander Folk School, referred to this with a phrase from a Spanish song that translated reads "We make the road by walking." One of the best captured thoughts about experiential learning I have ever read.

– Introduction –

These case files are scalable, adaptable, and relevant to the issues facing 21st century advocates. They are based on the lessons learned by Stetson's faculty, students and alumni, reflecting the same commitment to excellence embodied in our Law School's award winning advocacy teams and national reputation in Advocacy.

A commitment to the law, the skill and the art of advocacy creates persuasive advocacy. The foundation begins with the **process**: it's the way we train, the way we learn, and the way we practice. This is experiential learning. These case files focus the advocates on specific advocacy skills in a simulated real world environment, allowing participants to learn the skill and the law in the context of a moment in the trial. The exercises accompanying the case file develop advocacy **skills** through the rubric of the experiential learning process. This approach allows the advocate to develop **values** that contextually reflect the legal profession. These case files provide a structure for the **process**, **skills** and **values** involved in becoming a better advocate.

The goal of this effort is to design a well-crafted, challenging case file that promotes excellence in all facets of advocacy instruction. The way in which a case file is organized, presented and supported is a balancing act that either increases or decreases its effectiveness. The result of this balancing act is a unique, multi-media product that provides both academics and the practicing bar with modular course content producing varied levels of difficulty (novice, intermediate, and advanced), that is developed for, and measured by, quantifiable outcome assessments.

Washington v. Hartwell

CASE FILE CONTENTS

Tab A: Introduction..**166**

- Introduction to the Case
- Jury Instructions
- Verdict Form

Tab B: Court Filings..**178**

- Summons
- Complaint
- Answer and Affirmative Defenses
- Request for Documents
- Interrogatory

Tab C: Police Investigations..**200**

- Report of Incident – James Record
- Report of Investigation – Edwin Morris
    - 911 Call transcript
    - Photos of area
    - Diagrams of area
    - Photos of Oldest Decedent
    - Sun Up and Sun Down Report
    - Statement of Johnny Broadsides
    - Statement of Dimitri Merinov
    - Statement of Bill Hartwell
    - Statement of Marian Hartwell
    - Statement of Matt Bader
    - Video 1 of fleeing vehicle

- Video 2 of fleeing vehicle
- 9-1-1 call .mp3 file
- Affidavit of Lieutenant James Allen Record

Tab D: Newspaper Articles...236
- Calusa County Courier Article
- Pelican Bay Star - Letter to the Editor

Tab E: Statements of the Parties...238
- Statement of Charissa Washington
- Statement of Rebecca Hartwell

Tab F: Conviction Reports..243
- Dimitri Merinov Record of Conviction for Exhibition
- Matt Bader Record of Conviction for Cocaine Possession
- Rebecca Hartwell Record of Conviction for Reckless Driving
- Charissa Washington Record of Convictions for Filing a False Police Report and Possession of Marijuana

Washington v. Hartwell

INTRODUCTION

The children were black. The driver was white. The community was outraged. It was a media circus. Was it one vehicle, two or three? A van? A dark blue Honda? A Toyota? Or was it all three? The witnesses couldn't agree. The car sped away as a horrified crowd of about 200 emptied into the street and began shouting in outrage. Children's shoes and sandals were scattered on the pavement. Next to a puddle of blood was a pillow left behind by paramedics who had treated one of the victims. Were the non-working streetlights also to blame? Did someone hide the car? Was DNA removed from the evidence? What were the unsupervised children doing in a high-traffic area at night? Who would pay? After being sought for days, a high-profile criminal defense attorney, Steve Levine, finally announced that the driver would come forward.

On March 21, 20XX-2 at approximately 7:15 p.m., Ms. Rebecca Hartwell was driving her midnight blue Toyota Echo. She was travelling north on 39th Street. It is undisputed that at some point her car hit at least two of the four children crossing the street. She also fled the scene of the accident. The hit-and-run crash killed two brothers, aged 14 and 3, and seriously injured a 2-year-old boy and a 7-year-old girl. The 3 year old boy was caught underneath the grill of Ms. Hartwell's car and dragged approximately 150 feet before his body worked its way loose and came to final rest in the middle of 39th Street. The Toyota then fled the scene of the accident.

The criminal case has ended. Judge Jerry Parker oversaw the prosecution for negligent homicide that resulted in a hung jury on July 13, 20XX-1. The prosecution's office has indicated that they have no intention of retrying the case, citing evidentiary concerns and proof difficulties. Steve Levine contends that the nature of this trial caused the hung jury to have the effect of a dismissal with prejudice. The state's office has publically stated that they disagree with that assessment.

A civil case has been filed alleging both wrongful death and defamation. After filing answers and affirmative defenses to the Complaint, civil defense counsel moved for a change of venue. The Motion was denied.

LOCAL RULES: Calusa County follows the **Federal Rules of Civil Procedure** and has adopted the **Federal Rules of Evidence**. There are some local evidentiary and statutory distinctions litigants must consider. Those relevant Calusa County-specific rules and law have been provided in the law section of this case file.

PRELIMINARY JURY INSTRUCTIONS

You have now been sworn as the jury to try this case. This is a civil case involving a disputed claim or claims between the parties. Those claims and other matters will be explained to you later. By your verdict, you will decide the disputed issues of fact. I will decide the questions of law that arise during the trial, and before you retire to deliberate at the close of the trial, I will instruct you on the law that you are to follow and apply in reaching your verdict. It is your responsibility to determine the facts and to apply the law to those facts. Thus, the function of the jury and the function of the judge are well defined, and they do not overlap. This is one of the fundamental principles of our system of justice.

Before proceeding further, it will be helpful for you to understand how a trial is conducted. In a few moments, the attorneys for the parties will have an opportunity to make opening statements, in which they may explain to you the, issues in the case and summarize the facts that they expect the evidence will show. Following the opening statements, witnesses will be called to testify under oath. They will be examined and cross-examined by the attorneys. Documents and other exhibits also may be received as evidence.

After all the evidence has been received, the attorneys will again have the opportunity to address you and to make their final arguments. The statements that the attorneys now make and the arguments that they later make are not to be considered by you either as evidence in the case or as your instruction on the law. Nevertheless, these statements and arguments are intended to help you properly understand the issues, the evidence, and the applicable law, so you should give them your close attention. Following the final arguments by the attorneys, I will instruct you on the law.

You should give careful attention to the testimony and other evidence as it is received and presented for your consideration, but you should not form or express any opinion about the case until you have received all the evidence, the arguments of the attorneys, and the instructions on the law from me. In other words, you should not form or express any opinion about the case until you retire to the jury room to consider you verdict

The attorneys are trained in the rules of evidence and trial procedure, and it is their duty to make all objections they feel are proper. When a lawyer makes an objection, I will either overrule or sustain the objection. If I overrule an objection to a question, the witness will answer the question. If I sustain an objection, the witness will not answer, but you must not, speculate on what might have happened or what the witness might have said had I permitted the witness to answer the question. You should not draw any inference from the question itself.

During the trial, it may be necessary for me to confer with the attorneys out of your hearing, talking about matters of law and other matters that require consideration by me alone. It is impossible for me to predict when such a conference may be required or how long it will last. When such conferences occur, they will be conducted so as to consume as little of your time as necessary for a fair and orderly trial of the case.

At this time, the attorneys for the parties will have an opportunity to make their opening statements, in which they may explain to you the issues in this case and give you a summary of the facts they expect the evidence will show.

FINAL JURY INSTRUCTIONS

Members of the jury, I shall now instruct you on the law that you must follow in reaching your verdict. It is your duty as jurors to decide the issues, and only those issues, that I submit for determination by your verdict. In reaching your verdict, you should consider and weigh the evidence, decide the disputed issues of fact and apply the law on which I shall instruct you to the facts as you find them from the evidence.

The evidence in this case consists of the sworn testimony of the witnesses, all exhibits received into evidence, and all facts that may be admitted or agreed to by the parties. In determining the facts, you may draw reasonable inferences from the evidence. You may make deductions and reach conclusions which reason and common sense lead you to draw from the facts shown by the evidence in this case, but you should not speculate on any matters outside the evidence.

In determining the believability of any witness and the weight to be given the testimony of any witness, you may properly consider the demeanor of the witness while testifying; the frankness or lack of frankness of the witness; the intelligence of the witness; any interest the witness may have in the outcome of the case; the means and opportunity the, witness had to know the facts about which the witness testified; the ability of the witness to remember the matters about which the witness testified; and the reasonableness of the testimony of the witness, considered in the light of all the evidence in the case and in light of your own experience and common sense.

The issues for your determination on the wrongful death claim of Charissa Washington against Rebecca Hartwell is whether Rebecca Hartwell was negligent when she struck Ronald and Jordan Washington with the vehicle she operated on the evening of March 21, 20XX, and, if so, whether such negligence was a legal cause of the loss, injury, or damage suffered by Charissa Washington and/or the Estates Jordan and Ronald Washington.

"Negligence" is the failure to use reasonable care. Reasonable care is that degree of care which a reasonably careful person would use under like circumstances. Negligence may consist either of doing something that a reasonably careful person would not do under like circumstances or failing to do something that a reasonably careful person would do under like circumstances.

Negligence is a legal cause of loss, injury, or damage if it directly and in natural and continuous sequence produces or contributes substantially to producing such loss, injury, or damages that it can reasonably be said that but for the negligence the loss, injury, or damage would not have occurred.

If the greater weight of the evidence does not support the claim of Charissa Washington and/or the Estate, then your verdict should be for Rebecca Hartwell. "Greater weight of the evidence" means the more persuasive and convincing force and effect of the entire evidence in this case. However, if the greater weight of the evidence supports either Charissa Washington's individual claims or the Estate's claim, then you should consider the defenses raised by Rebecca Hartwell.

Rebecca Hartwell has raised a defense in this case which permits you, the jury, to determine whether persons who are not parties to this lawsuit may have also contributed to the injuries of the Washington's and/or the Estate. If you find that Rebecca Hartwell was negligent in her operation of her motor vehicle and that her negligence caused or contributed to the Washington's injury and/or the Estate's injury, you should determine what percentage of the total fault is chargeable to Rebecca Hartwell.

If you find that Ronald and Jordan Washington were negligent in their decision to cross the street and that their negligence caused or contributed to the injuries and/or the Estate's injury, you should determine what percentage of the total fault is chargeable to Ronald and Jordan Washington. In determining whether Ronald and Jordan Washington were negligent, you must consider whether they exercised reasonable care for their own safety. Reasonable care on the part of a child is that degree of care which a reasonably careful child of the same age, mental capacity, intelligence, training and experience would use under like circumstances.

At this point in the trial, you, as jurors, are deciding only if Rebecca Hartwell was negligent, and if Ronald and Jordan Washington were negligent. You will first return a verdict on that issue.

Additionally, the plaintiff, Charissa Washington, claims that the defendant, Rebecca Hartwell, defamed her when she made statements about the quality of Ms. Washington's parenting of the children on the day of the accident. These statements were allegedly made by Ms. Hartwell and published in the Pelican Daily Star.

In order to recover under her defamation claim(s), Charissa Washington must prove the following: that Rebecca Hartwell made the alleged statement(s); Rebecca Hartwell made the defamatory statement(s) with malice toward the Charissa Washington or with a reckless disregard for her interests; the defendant published the defamatory statement(s) to a person other than the defendant; the plaintiff was damaged; and the Plaintiff's damages were caused by the Rebecca Hartwell's defamatory statement(s).

A person acts with malice if she makes a false statement with knowledge of its falsity, or if she makes it for the specific purpose of injuring another person. A person acts with reckless disregard if she consciously disregards and is indifferent to the truth or falsity of the statement. It is not necessary for Charissa Washington to prove that Rebecca Hartwell deliberately intended to injure her. It is sufficient if Rebecca Hartwell acted with reckless disregard for the truth or falsity of her statements.

In determining whether Rebecca Hartwell acted with malice or reckless disregard, you may consider the following factors: a) did Rebecca Hartwell reasonably rely on the circumstances known to him when he made the statements; b) did the Rebecca Hartwell make the statement in good faith and believing it to be true; c) did the Defendant act with spite or ill will toward Charissa Washington; did she intend to injure her reputation, good name or feelings;

d) did Rebecca Hartwell attempt to minimize any harm to Charissa Washington by apologizing or retracting a statement within a reasonable time after determining a statement to be false?

Substantial truth is a defense to defamation. Substantially true means that the substance or gist of the statement is true. If the defendant proves that a statement was substantially true, then your verdict must be for the defendant with regard to that statement.

Qualified privilege is also a defense to a defamation claim. This jurisdiction recognizes a qualified privilege for statements made within certain business and social relationships. The privilege is qualified because it is not an absolute defense.

Burdens of Proof:

Charissa Washington has the burden of proving her claim of defamation, namely, that Rebecca Hartwell made a statement that defamed her; that it was communicated to another person; that she was injured by the defamatory statement; and that the Rebecca Hartwell made the statement with malice or reckless disregard. If you find that the Charissa Washington has proven each of these elements, then your verdict must be for the Charissa Washington, unless you find that the statement is true.

Rebecca Hartwell has the burden of proving the defense of truth. If you find that a statement was true, then your verdict must be for Rebecca Hartwell with regard to that statement.

Damages:

If you find for Charissa Washington on any of her claims for wrongful death/negligence and/or defamation, then you shall determine her damages in an amount that will justly and fairly compensate her for the harm caused by Rebecca Hartwell's defamatory statement or statements. In determining damages you may consider the injury to Charissa Washington's reputation and good name, any physical or mental suffering she may have sustained, and any loss of earnings or harm to business and employment relations. You may also, in your discretion, assess punitive damages against Rebecca Hartwell as punishment and as a deterrent to others. If you find that punitive damages should be assessed against Rebecca Hartwell, you may consider the financial resources of Rebecca Hartwell in fixing the amount. Punitive damages are awarded to punish the Defendant, not to compensate the Plaintiff.

Your verdict must be based on the evidence that has been received and the law on which I have instructed you. In reaching your verdict, you are not to be swayed from the performance of your duty by prejudice, sympathy, or any other sentiment for or against any party.

When you retire to the jury room, you should select one of your members to act as foreperson, to preside over your deliberations, and to sign your verdict. Your verdict must be unanimous; that is, your verdict must be agreed to by each of you. You will be given a verdict form, which I shall now read and explain to you.

(READ VERDICT FORM)

When you have agreed on your verdict, the foreperson, acting for the jury, should date and sign the verdict form and return it to the courtroom. You may now retire to consider your verdict.

IN THE CIRCUIT COURT OF FIRST JUDICIAL DISTICT
CALUSA COUNTY, XXXXX
CIVIL DIVISION

CHARISSA WASHINGTON,
   Plaintiff,

v.

REBECCA HARTWELL,
   Defendant.

CASE NO.: 20XX-1439

DIVISION: A

JURY VERDICT

The jury must answer the following interrogatories. The foreperson is to answer the interrogatories for the jury and sign the verdict.

Interrogatory No. 1: Did Rebecca Hartwell fail to exercise reasonable care during the March 21, 20XX-2 incident?

   YES _____
   NO _____

Interrogatory No. 2: If the answer to No. 1 is *YES*, was Rebecca Hartwell's negligence the direct cause of damage to Charissa Washington?

   YES _____
   NO _____

Interrogatory No. 3: If the answer to No. 1 is *YES*, did Charissa Washington contribute in any way to the cause of her damage?

   YES _____
   NO _____

Interrogatory No. 4: Please determine the amount of damages necessary to justly and fairly compensate the Plaintiff:

   Amount $ _____

Interrogatory No. 5: Did Defendant make a defamatory statement about the Plaintiff?

   YES _____
   NO _____

Interrogatory No. 6: Did Defendant make the defamatory statement with malice toward the Plaintiff, or with a reckless disregard for her interests?

    YES _____
    NO   _____

Interrogatory No. 7: Did Defendant publish the defamatory statement to a person other than the Plaintiff?

    YES _____
    NO   _____

Interrogatory No. 8: Was the defamatory statement true?

    YES _____
    NO   _____

Interrogatory No. 9: Was the defamatory statement made on a subject in which the Defendant had an important interest or duty--either legal, moral, business, or social--and made to another person having a like interest or duty?

    YES _____
    NO   _____

Interrogatory No. 10: If the answer to No. 5 is *YES*, then did the defamatory statement injure the Plaintiff?

    YES _____
    NO   _____

Interrogatory No. 11: If the answer to Numbers 1 and 7 is *YES*, then you may assess punitive damages against Defendant. Please indicate the amount of punitive damages, if any, you assess against Defendant:

    Amount $ _____

The members of the jury have unanimously answered the Interrogatories in the manner I have indicated.

_____

Foreperson

IN THE FIRST JUDICIAL CIRCUIT
IN AND FOR CALUSA COUNTY, XXXXX
CIRCUIT CIVIL DIVISION

CHARISSA WASHINGTON, Individually and
as Personal Representative of the Estate of
JORDAN AND RONALD WASHINGTON,
Deceased, f/b/o any Survivors,

    Plaintiff,

v.   Case No. 20XX-1439

REBECCA HARTWELL,

    Defendant.
_____/

SUMMONS

THE STATE OF XXXXX:
TO EACH SHERIFF OF THE STATE:

YOU ARE COMMANDED to serve this summons and a copy of the complaint or petition in this action on defendant:

    Rebecca Hartwell
    1929 15th Avenue North
    Pelican Bay, XXXXX 33707

Each defendant is required to serve written defenses to the complaint or petition on:

    Scott Frost, Esq.
    Frost, Dunkelheit & Associates, P.L.
    412 Central Avenue
    Pelican Bay, XXXXX 33707
    Plaintiff's Attorney

within 20 days after service of this summons on that defendant, exclusive of the day of service, and to file the original of the defenses with the clerk of this court either before service on plaintiff's attorney or immediately thereafter. If Defendant fails to do so, a default will be entered against that Defendant for the relief demanded in the complaint or petition.

    DATED on this 14th day of August 20XX.

                                                Connie Evans
                                                As Clerk of the Court
                                                By <u>Beth Mills</u>
                                                As Deputy Clerk

SUMMONS

IMPORTANT

A lawsuit has been filed against you. You have 20 calendar days after this summons is served on you to file a written response to the attached complaint with the clerk of this court. A phone call will not protect you. Your written response, including the case number given above and the names of the parties, must be filed if you want the court to hear your side of the case. If you do not file your response on time, you may lose the case, and your wages, money, and property may thereafter be taken without further warning from the court. There are other legal requirements. You may want to call an attorney right away. If you do not know an attorney, you may call an attorney referral service or a legal aid office (listed in the phone book).

If you choose to file a written response yourself, at the same time you file your written response to the court you must also mail or take a copy of your written response to the APlaintiff=s Attorney@ named below.

IMPORTANTE

Usted ha sido demando legalmente. Tiene 20 dias, contados a partir del recibo de esta notificacion, para contestar la demanda adjunta, por escrito, y presentarla ante este tribunal. Una llamada telefonica ca no lo protegera. Si usted desea que el tribunal considere su defensa, debe presentar su respuesta por escrito, incluyendo el numero del caso y los nombres de las partes interesadas. Si usted no contesta la demanda a tiempo, puiese perder el caso y podria ser despojado de sus ingresos y propiedades, o privado de sus derechos, sin previo aviso del tribunal. Existen otros requisitos legales. Si lo desea, puede usted consultar a un abogado inmediatamente. Si no conoce a un abogado, puede llamar a una de las oficinas de asistencia legal que aparecen en la guia telefonica.

Si desea responder a la demanda por su cuenta, al mismo tiempo en que presenta su respuesta ante el tribunal, debera usted enviar por correo o entregar una copia de su respuesta a la persona denominada abajo como APlaintiff=s Attorney@ (Demandante o Abogado del Demandante).

IMPORTANTE

De poursuites judiciares ont ete entreprises contre vous. Vous avez 20 jours consecutifs a partir de la date de l=assignation de cette citation pour deposer une reponse ecrite a la plainte ci-jointe aupres de ce tribunal. Un simple coup de telephone est insuffisant pour vous preteger. Vous etes obliges de deposer votre reponse ecrite, avec mention du numero de dossier ci-dessus et du nom des parties nommees ici, si vous souhaitez que le tribunal entende votre cause. Si vous ne desposez pas votre reponse ecrite dans le relai requis, vous risquez de predre la cause ainsi que votre salaire, votre argent, et vos biens peuvent etre saisis par la suite, sans aucun preavis ulterieur du tribunal. Il y a d=autres obligations juridiques et vous pouvez requerir les services immediats d=un avocat. Si vous ne connaissez pas d=avocat, vous pourriez telephoner a un service de reference d=avocats ou a un bureau d=assistance juridique (figurant a l=annuaire de telephones).

Si vous choisissez de deposer vous-meme une reponse ecrite, il vous faudra egalement, en mem temps que cette formalite, faire parvenir ou expedier une copie de votre reponse ecrite au APlaintiff=s Attorney@ (Plaignant ou a son avocat) nomme cidessous.

Washington v. Hartwell

IN THE FIRST JUDICIAL CIRCUIT
IN AND FOR CALUSA COUNTY, XXXXX
CIRCUIT CIVIL DIVISION

CHARISSA WASHINGTON, Individually and
as Personal Representative of the Estate of
JORDAN AND RONALD WASHINGTON,
Deceased, f/b/o any Survivors,

    Plaintiff,

v.   Case No. 20XX-1439

REBECCA HARTWELL,

    Defendant.
_____/

COMPLAINT AND DEMAND FOR JURY TRIAL

    COMES NOW the Plaintiff, CHARISSA WASHINGTON, Individually, and as Parent and Personal Representative of the Estates of JORDAN WASHINGTON, a minor, and RONALD WASHINGTON, a minor, by and through the undersigned counsel, as and for their Complaint for damages against Defendant, REBECCA HARTWELL, states as follows:

JURISDICTION, PARTIES, AND VENUE

1. This is an action for damages in excess of fifteen thousand dollars ($15,000.00).

2. All conditions precedent to the bringing of this action have occurred or have been performed.

3. At all times material hereto, Plaintiff, CHARISSA WASHINGTON, was and is a resident of Calusa County, XXXXX. Plaintiff, CHARISSA WASHINGTON, was the mother of JORDAN WASHINGTON, deceased and RONALD WASHINGTON, deceased.

4. At all times material hereto, CHARISSA WASHINGTON, was duly appointed as Personal Representative of the Estates of JORDAN WASHINGTON and RONALD WASHINGTON,

5. At all times material hereto, the decedent, JORDAN WASHINGTON, a minor, upon his death left CHARISSA WASHINGTON, his mother, as survivor as defined by XXXXX Stat. § 718.18.

6. At all times material hereto, the decedent, RONALD WASHINGTON, a minor, upon his death left CHARISSA WASHINGTON, his mother, as survivor as defined by XXXXX Stat. § 718.18.

7. At all times material hereto, the Defendant, REBECCA HARTWELL, was and is a resident of Calusa County, XXXXX.

8. On or around March 21, 2008, the Defendant, REBECCA HARTWELL, was operating a Toyota Echo, VIN A610W909O4656B, on 39th Street at or near the University Community Center in Calusa County, XXXXX.

9. At said time, JORDAN WASHINGTON and RONALD WASHINGTON were walking on 39th Street at or near the University Community Center in Pelican Bay, Calusa County, XXXXX.

10. At said time, the Defendant, REBECCA HARTWELL, negligently operated her vehicle, colliding with JORDAN WASHINGTON and RONALD WASHINGTON. JORDAN WASHINGTON and RONALD WASHINGTON were killed as a result of the Defendant's car striking them. Defendant, REBECCA HARTWELL, fled the scene.

11. In no way were JORDAN WASHINGTON and RONALD WASHINGTON responsible for their injuries.

12. Since the death of JORDAN WASHINGTON and RONALD WASHINGTON the Defendant, REBECCA HARTWELL, has continued to make disparaging, public remarks concerning the Plaintiffs.

13. Venue is proper in this action as the subject accident took place in Calusa County, XXXXX.

COUNT I

THE ESTATE'S WRONGFUL DEATH CLAIM OF JORDAN WASHINGTON

14. Plaintiff realleges and reavers paragraphs #1–13 as fully set forth herein and would further state:

15. At all times material hereto, the Defendant, REBECCA HARTWELL, was the owner of the vehicle that struck victim, JORDAN WASHINGTON. As a driver on public roads the Defendant, REBECCA HARTWELL, had a duty to operate her vehicle as a reasonably prudent driver. Defendant, REBECCA HARTWELL, had a duty to exercise reasonable care and to safeguard the public, and in particular the victim, JORDAN WASHINGTON, and refrain from striking him with her motor vehicle.

16. At all times material hereto, the Defendant, REBECCA HARTWELL, breached the aforesaid duty by failing to drive as a reasonably prudent driver and striking the Plaintiff, JORDAN WASHINGTON.

17. As a direct, proximate, and foreseeable result of the negligence of the Defendant, REBECCA HARTWELL, the Plaintiff, JORDAN WASHINGTON, was fatally injured.

18. As a direct, proximate, and foreseeable result of the negligence of the Defendant, REBECCA HARTWELL, the Plaintiff, CHARISSA WASHINGTON, as Personal Representative of the ESTATE OF JORDAN WASHINGTON, deceased, sustained the following losses as set forth in XXXXX Stat. § 768.21:

    A.   <u>AS TO THE ESTATE OF JORDAN WASHINGTON, DECEASED:</u>

1) Medical and/or funeral expenses due to the decedent's injury/death that would have become a charge against the Estate or that were paid for on behalf of the decedent; and

B. <u>AS TO THE SURVIVING PARENT, CHARISSA WASHINGTON:</u>

1) Value of future lost support and services from the date of the decedent's death with interest;

2) Value of loss of son's companionship;

3) Mental pain and suffering from the date of the injury/death into the future; and

4) Medical and/or funeral expenses due to the decedent's death.

WHEREFORE, Plaintiff, CHARISSA WASHINGTON, as Personal Representative of the ESTATE OF JORDAN WASHINGTON, demands judgment for damages against the Defendant, REBECCA HARTWELL, according to law, together with post-judgment interest and costs, and demands trial by jury of all issues triable as of right by jury.

COUNT II

WRONGFUL DEATH CLAIM OF RONALD WASHINGTON

19. Plaintiff re-alleges and readopts paragraphs #1–13 as fully set forth herein and would further state:

20. At all times material hereto, the Defendant, REBECCA HARTWELL, was the owner of the vehicle that struck Plaintiff, RONALD WASHINGTON. As a driver on public roads the Defendant, REBECCA HARTWELL, had a duty to operate her vehicle as a reasonably prudent driver. Defendant, REBECCA HARTWELL, had a duty to exercise reasonable care and to safeguard the public, and in particular the Plaintiff, RONALD WASHINGTON, and refrain from striking him with her motor vehicle.

21. At all times material hereto, the Defendant, REBECCA HARTWELL, breached the aforesaid duty by failing to drive as a reasonably prudent driver and striking the Plaintiff, RONALD WASHINGTON.

22. As a direct, proximate, and foreseeable result of the negligence of the Defendant, REBECCA HARTWELL, the Plaintiff, RONALD WASHINGTON, was fatally injured.

23. As a direct, proximate, and foreseeable result of the negligence of the Defendant, REBECCA HARTWELL, the Plaintiff, CHARISSA WASHINGTON, as Personal Representative of the ESTATE OF RONALD WASHINGTON, deceased, sustained the following losses as set forth in XXXXX Stat. § 768.21:

A. AS TO THE ESTATE OF RONALD WASHINGTON, DECEASED:

1) Medical and/or funeral expenses due to the decedent's injury/death that would have become a charge against the Estate or that were paid for on behalf of the decedent; and

B. AS TO THE SURVIVING PARENT, CHARISSA WASHINGTON:

1) Value of future lost support and services from the date of the decedent's death with interest;

2) Value of loss of son's companionship;

3) Mental pain and suffering from the date of the injury/death into the future; and

4) Medical and/or funeral expenses due to the decedent's death.

WHEREFORE, Plaintiff, CHARISSA WASHINGTON, as Personal Representative of the ESTATE OF RONALD WASHINGTON, demands judgment for damages against the Defendant, REBECCA HARTWELL, according to law, together with post-judgment interest and costs, and demands trial by jury of all issues triable as of right by jury.

COUNT III

DEFAMATION OF CHARISSA WASHINGTON BY REBECCA HARTWELL

24. Plaintiff realleges and reavers paragraphs #1–11 as fully set forth herein and would further state:

25. Defendant, REBECCA HARTWELL, knowingly made false and defamatory statements to third parties alleging that the Plaintiff, CHARISSA WASHINGTON, was an inferior mother and could not look over her children.

26. These statements were made without reasonable care as to the truth or falsity of the statements. In failing to verify the accuracy of her statements, the Defendant, REBECCA

HARTWELL, acted negligently and/or intentionally knew her statement was not substantially true.

27. The statement exposed the Plaintiff, CHARISSA WASHINGTON, to hatred, ridicule, contempt, embarrassment, humiliation, disgrace, and/or public ridicule within the greater Calusa County Area and throughout the United States.

28. The Defendant's defamatory statements resulted in actual damages and would cause a reasonable person to believe the Plaintiff, CHARISSA WASHINGTON, was and is an incompetent mother.

29. As a direct and proximate result of the defamatory statements made by the Defendant, REBECCA HARTWELL, the Plaintiff, CHARISSA WASHINGTON, has suffered damages resulting from, but not limited to: being shunned in social circles, being unable to function in the public arena, being laughed at and emotionally destroyed by her peers.

WHEREFORE, the Plaintiff, CHARISSA WASHINGTON, demands judgment for damages against the Defendant, REBECCA HARTWELL, together with costs and demands a trial by jury of all issues triable as of right by jury.

Scott Frost
Scott Frost, Esq.
Frost, Dunkelheit & Associates, P.L.
412 Central Avenue
Pelican Bay, XXXXX 33707
(727) 555-3548
XXXXX Bar No. 4521XX
Counsel for Plaintiff

IN THE FIRST JUDICIAL CIRCUIT
IN AND FOR CALUSA COUNTY, XXXXX
CIRCUIT CIVIL DIVISION

CHARISSA WASHINGTON, Individually and
as Personal Representative of the Estate of
JORDAN AND RONALD WASHINGTON,
Deceased, f/b/o any Survivors,

    Plaintiff,

v.   Case No. 20XX-1439

REBECCA HARTWELL,

    Defendant.
_____/

ANSWER AND AFFIRMATIVE DEFENSES

COMES NOW, the Defendant, REBECCA HARTWELL, by and through the undersigned attorney, and files this Answer to the Plaintiff's Complaint, and as grounds therefore and would state:

1. Denied. Defendant finds the current action unfounded.

2. This paragraph stated legal conclusions to which no response is necessary. To the extent a response is necessary, same are denied.

3. Admitted upon information and belief.

4. Admitted upon information and belief

5. Admitted upon information and belief.

6. Admitted upon information and belief.

7. Admitted for jurisdictional purposes only.

8. Admitted that Defendant, Hartwell, has a Toyota Echo and was driving it on the aforesaid street.

9. Admitted upon information and belief.

10. Denied. After reasonable investigation Defendant is without sufficient knowledge or information to form a belief as to the truth or falsity of the averments contained in this paragraph, therefore same are denied and strict proof to the contrary is demanded at time of trial.

11. Denied. Plaintiffs and their mother are wholly responsible for the unfortunate accident.

12. Denied. After reasonable investigation Defendant is without sufficient knowledge or information to form a belief as to the truth or falsity of the averments contained in this paragraph, therefore same are denied and strict proof to the contrary is demanded at time of trial.

13. Admitted.

COUNT I

NEGLIGENCE OF REBECCA HARTWELL TO JORDAN WASHINGTON

14. Admit in Part. Defendant was the owner and driver of vehicle. Deny in Part. Defendant did not breach said duty.

15. Denied. After reasonable investigation Defendant is without sufficient knowledge or information to form a belief as to the truth or falsity of the averment contained in this paragraph therefore same are denied and strict proof to the contract is demanded at time of trial.

16. Denied. After reasonable investigation Defendant is without sufficient knowledge or information to form a belief as to the truth or falsity of the averments contained in this paragraph, therefore same are denied and strict proof to the contrary is demanded at time of trial.

17. Denied. After reasonable investigation Defendant is without sufficient knowledge or information to form a belief as to the truth or falsity of the averments contained in this paragraph, therefore same are denied and strict proof to the contrary is demanded at time of trial.

COUNT II

NEGLIGENCE OF REBECCA HARTWELL TO RONALD WASHINGTON

18. Denied. After reasonable investigation Defendant is without sufficient knowledge or information to form a belief as to the truth or falsity of the averments contained in this paragraph, therefore same are denied and strict proof to the contrary is demanded at time of trial.

19. Admitted.

20. Denied. After reasonable investigation Defendant is without sufficient knowledge or information to form a belief as to the truth or falsity of the averments contained in this paragraph, therefore same are denied and strict proof to the contrary is demanded at time of trial.

21. Denied. After reasonable investigation Defendant is without sufficient knowledge or information to form a belief as to the truth or falsity of the averments contained in this paragraph, therefore same are denied and strict proof to the contrary is demanded at time of trial.

22. Denied. After reasonable investigation Defendant is without sufficient knowledge or information to form a belief as to the truth or falsity of the averments contained in this paragraph, therefore same are denied and strict proof to the contrary is demanded at time of trial.

23. Defendant is without knowledge and therefore Denied. After reasonable investigation Defendant is without sufficient knowledge or information to form a belief as to the truth or falsity of the averments contained in this paragraph, therefore same are denied and strict proof to the contrary is demanded at time of trial.

24. Defendant is without knowledge and therefore Denied. After reasonable investigation Defendant is without sufficient knowledge or information to form a belief as to the truth or falsity of the averments contained in this paragraph, therefore same are denied and strict proof to the contrary is demanded at time of trial.

COUNT III

DEFAMATION OF CHARISSA WASHINGTON BY REBECCA HARTWELL

25. After reasonable investigation Defendant is without sufficient knowledge or information to form a belief as to the truth or falsity of the averments contained in this paragraph, therefore same are denied and strict proof to the contrary is demanded at time of trial.

26. After reasonable investigation Defendant is without sufficient knowledge or information to form a belief as to the truth or falsity of the averments contained in this paragraph, therefore same are denied and strict proof to the contrary is demanded at time of trial.

27. After reasonable investigation Defendant is without sufficient knowledge or information to form a belief as to the truth or falsity of the averments contained in this paragraph, therefore same are denied and strict proof to the contrary is demanded at time of trial.

28. After reasonable investigation Defendant is without sufficient knowledge or information to form a belief as to the truth or falsity of the averments contained in this paragraph, therefore same are denied and strict proof to the contrary is demanded at time of trial.

29. After reasonable investigation Defendant is without sufficient knowledge or information to form a belief as to the truth or falsity of the averments contained in this paragraph, therefore same are denied and strict proof to the contrary is demanded at time of trial.

30. 28. After reasonable investigation Defendant is without sufficient knowledge or information to form a belief as to the truth or falsity of the averments contained in this paragraph, therefore same are denied and strict proof to the contrary is demanded at time of trial.

FIRST AFFIRMATIVE DEFENSE

The actions of the two deceased children were superseding, intervening causes in whole or in part, to the accident which occurred and damages sustained that absolve the Defendant of liability. In the alternative, Plaintiff was without time to react to the children playing in the street with no lights on. Therefore, Defendant did not breach any duty and is not liable for this accident.

SECOND AFFIRMATIVE DEFENSE

Plaintiff Complaint should be dismissed pursuant to Fed. R. Civ. P. 12(b)(6) for failure to state a claim upon which relief can be granted.

THIRD AFFIRMATIVE DEFENSE

This Defendant is entitled to an apportionment of damages in accordance with Section 768.81 of the XXXXX Statutes. Any judgment entered against this Defendant must be based on the fault, if any, of this Defendant, and not on the basis of the doctrine of joint and several liability. Additionally, the Plaintiffs' recovery must be reduced based upon the percentage of fault attributed to any co-Defendant or any non-party who is found to be at fault for the incident alleged by the Plaintiffs, including but not limited to the Calusa County and Progress Energy. Future discovery will determine what additional parties, if any, were at fault and will be named in accordance with the Fabre and Nash decisions.

FOURTH AFFIRMATIVE DEFENSE

The Plaintiffs have failed to join indispensable parties to this litigation.

FIFTH AFFIRMATIVE DEFENSE

The negligence of the Plaintiff, CHARISSA WASHINGTON, proximately contributed to causing the accident complained of and any resultant damages sustained by Plaintiff, CHARISSA WASHINGTON, because she failed to conduct herself in a reasonable manner and ordinary due care as a parent in supervising her. Thus Plaintiff is barred from recovery herein to the extent that such negligence proximately contributed to causing the complained of accident and/or any resultant damages sustained by the Plaintiff.

Washington v. Hartwell

Plaintiff's defamation count is barred by the truth defense.

WHEREFORE, REBECCA HARTWELL, having answered the allegations asserted in the Plaintiff's Complaint, Defendants demand strict proof of all allegations not expressly admitted herein. Further Defendant, REBECCA HARTWELL, demands dismissal of the claims against her and judgment in her favor together with all costs of defense, including attorney's fees, as may be recoverable by law.

Steve Levine, Esquire
Steve Levine & Associates LLP
415 Central Avenue
Pelican Bay, XXXXX 33707
XXXXX Bar No. 453XX
(727)555-7317
Attorney for Defendant

IN THE FIRST JUDICIAL CIRCUIT
IN AND FOR CALUSA COUNTY, XXXXX
CIRCUIT CIVIL DIVISION

CHARISSA WASHINGTON, Individually and
as Personal Representative of the Estate of
JORDAN AND RONALD WASHINGTON,
Deceased, f/b/o any Survivors,

    Plaintiff,

v.   Case No. 20XX-1439

REBECCA HARTWELL,

    Defendant.
_____/

PLAINTIFF=S FIRST REQUEST FOR PRODUCTION OF DOCUMENTS
TO DEFENDANT, REBECCA HARTWELL

    Pursuant to XXXXX Rule of Civil Procedure 1.350(a), Plaintiff, CHARISSA WASHINGTON., requests that Defendant, REBECCA HARTWELL, respond to the following requests for documents within forty-five (45) days after service of process. Plaintiff further requests that said documents be produced for inspection and photocopying at the office of Frost, Dunkelheit & Associates, P.L., 412 Central Avenue, Pelican Bay, XXXXX 33707 forty-five days from the date of service of this request. If the date and time of inspection are inconvenient, please promptly contact the undersigned attorney to reschedule. Alternatively, photocopies of the requested documents may be mailed by said date to the aforesaid address in lieu of the inspection.

DEFINITIONS

1.   As used herein, the terms "you" and "your" shall mean Defendant, REBECCA HARTWELL.

2.   As used herein, the phrase "accident" shall mean the collision of defendant's 20XX-5 Toyota Echo and the Five Children of Ms. Charissa Washington that occurred on March 21, 20XX-2, as alleged in the Complaint and Demand for Jury Trial.

3.   As used herein, the term "document(s)" is defined as follows. One, the term refers to all writings of any kind, including originals and all non-identical copies, whether different from the original by reason of any notation made on such copies or otherwise. Two, the term "document(s)" includes the following without limitation: correspondence, memoranda, notes, diaries, statistics, letters, materials, invoices, orders, directives, interviews, telegrams, minutes, reports, studies, statements, transcripts, summaries, pamphlets, books, intraoffice and interoffice communications, notations of conversation, telephone call records, bulletins, printed forms,

teletype, telefax, worksheets, electronic mail, e-mail, and regularly-kept records. Three, the term "document(s)" also includes the following without limitation: photographs, digital images, charts, graphs, microfiche, microfilm, videotape, audiotape, motion pictures, computer data, and information contained on a fixed or floppy computer disc.

REQUESTS

Please produce the following:

1. All photographs and/or digital images of decedents taken after the auto accident.

2. All photographs and/or digital images of your vehicle taken after the auto accident.

3. All photographs and/or digital images of the accident scene taken after the auto accident.

4. All repair estimates for damage to your vehicle arising from the auto accident.

5. All documents showing who owned the vehicle which you drove in the auto accident.

6. All documents showing whether you were acting within the course and scope of your employment at the time of the auto accident.

7. All documents which you contend would support your affirmative defenses.

8. All of your insurance coverage documents for all auto policies, umbrella policies, or excess policies which may provide coverage for the auto accident.

9. All recorded statements taken by you related to the auto accident.

10. All witness statements received by you related to the auto accident.

11. Paperwork establishing ownership of defendant's dance studio.

12. Copies of all newspaper clippings kept by defendant, defendant's family, or by others at the request of the defendant concerning the accident and death of Jordan and Ronald Washington.

Scott Frost, Esquire
Scott Frost, Esq.
Frost, Dunkelheit & Associates, P.L.
412 Central Avenue
Pelican Bay, XXXXX 33707
(727) 555-3548
XXXXX Bar No. 4521XX
Counsel for Plaintiff

IN IN THE FIRST JUDICIAL CIRCUIT
IN AND FOR CALUSA COUNTY, XXXXX
CIRCUIT CIVIL DIVISION

CHARISSA WASHINGTON, Individually and
as Personal Representative of the Estate of
JORDAN AND RONALD WASHINGTON,
Deceased, f/b/o any Survivors,

    Plaintiff,

v.   Case No. 20XX-1439

REBECCA HARTWELL,

    Defendant.
_____/

PLAINTIFF'S FIRST SET OF INTERROGATORIES

Pursuant to XXXXX Rule of Civil Procedure 1.340(a), Plaintiff, CHARISSA WASHINGTON, hereby requests that Defendant, REBECCA HARTWELL, answer the following Interrogatory Numbers 1-10 under oath within forty-five (45) days after service of process.

DEFINITIONS

1.   As used herein, the terms "you" and "your" shall mean Defendant, REBECCA HARTWELL.

2.   As used herein, the phrase "auto accident" shall mean the striking of children on 39th street on March 21, 20XX-2 as alleged in the Complaint and Demand for Jury Trial.

Scott Frost

Scott Frost, Esq.
Frost, Dunkelheit & Associates, P.L.
412 Central Avenue
Pelican Bay, XXXXX 33707
(727) 555-3548
XXXXX Bar No. 4521XX
Counsel for Plaintiff

INTERROGATORIES TO DEFENDANT, REBECCA HARTWELL

1. Please state the full legal name(s) and physical address(es) of each and every person who owned the vehicle which you were operating at the time of the auto accident.

   Rebecca Hartwell
   1929 15th Avenue North
   Pelican Bay, XXXXX 33707

2. Were you acting within the course and scope of your employment at the time of the auto accident? If and only if your answer is yes, please state the complete legal name of your employer, your employer's physical business address, your job title, and your dates of employment for that employer.

   No

3. Describe any and all policies of insurance which you contend cover or may cover you for the allegations set forth in Plaintiff's Complaint, detailing as to such policies the name of the insurer, the policy number, the effective dates of the policy, the available limits of liability, and the name and address of the custodian of the policy.

   GEICO – liability limit is 300,000 dollars.
   Policy Number - 5673901-12
   Effective Dates – December 2, 20xx-3 through June 2, 20xx-2
   GEICO of XXXXX
   1820 Bayshore Hills
   Pelican Bay, XXXXX 33453

4. Were you married at the time of the auto accident? If and only if your answer is yes, please state the full legal name of your husband, his last known residential address, the date of your marriage to him, and the state of your marriage.

   No – never married.

5. State the facts upon which you rely for each affirmative defense in your Answer.

   Upon the advice of counsel I direct you to review their written response as my agent to this interrogatory.

6. Do you contend any person or entity other than you is, or may be, liable in whole or part for the claims asserted against you in this lawsuit? If so, state the full name and address of each such person or entity, the legal basis for your contention, the facts or evidence upon which your contention is based, and whether or not you have notified each such person or entity of your contention.

   Upon the advice of counsel I direct you to review their written response as my agent to this interrogatory.

7. Do you contend that any individual or entity not named as a party to this action was at fault, in whole or in part, in causing or contributing to cause the subject incident or subject injuries? If so, state the full name and address of each such person or entity, the legal basis for your contention, the facts or evidence upon which your contention is based, and whether or not you have notified each such person or entity of your contention.

   Upon the advice of counsel I direct you to review their written response as my agent to this interrogatory.

8. List the names and addresses of all persons who are believed or known by you, your agents or attorneys to have any knowledge concerning any of the issues in this lawsuit; and specify the subject matter about which the witness has knowledge.

> *Upon the advice of counsel I direct you to review their written response as my agent to this interrogatory.*

9. Describe in detail each act or omission on the part of any party to this lawsuit that you contend constituted negligence that was a contributing legal cause of the incident in question.

> *Upon the advice of counsel I direct you to review their written response as my agent to this interrogatory.*

10. To the best of your recollection, please set forth the following:

    a. the date of the auto accident. *March 21, 20XX-2.*
    b. the time of the auto accident. *7:15 p.m.*
    c. the weather conditions at the time of the auto accident. *Sun had just gone down, it was hot, dry.*
    d. what you saw happen to the five children immediately after the collision. *I never saw the children until they struck my windshield and car door.*

OATH OF DEFENDANT, REBECCA HARTWELL

STATE OF *XXXXX*

COUNTY OF *Calusa*

I, REBECCA HARTWELL, am the Defendant in this lawsuit and hereby swear by my notarized signature below that the Answers to Plaintiff's Interrogatory Numbers 1-10 are both true and correct to the best of my personal knowledge.

DEFENDANT:

Rebecca Hartwell
SIGNATURE OF REBECCA HARTWELL

REBECCA HARTWELL, who is either personally known to the undersigned Notary Public or has produced XXXXX Driver's License Number as identification, appeared and signed these Interrogatory Answers under oath on the 5th day of May 20XX.

Vilma Rodriguez
Vilma Rodriguez
NOTARY PUBLIC
STATE OF XXXXX
My Commission Expires: October XX, 20XX +2

Washington v. Hartwell

	Offense Incident Report # 20XX(-2)10101
	Pelican Bay Police Department
	Investigator: James Record
	Subject: Accident Scene on 39th Street Near the University Center, called in by a 9-1-1 call.

Address: 39th Street – between 15th and 15th Avenue South, Pelican Bay

Felony: Vehicular Homicide	**Victim(s):** Ronald Washington, Jordan Washington, Laquinta Washington, August Washington, Charles Washington

Narrative

Page 1 of 3.

Responded to a radio dispatch- investigate a hit and run involving three children on 15th Avenue South and 39th Street. Area is dangerous part of town – drug dealers, bad living areas, homeless folks, very violent area of town. Upon arrival I saw what appeared to be two different large gangs of people milling around, screaming, throwing beer bottles and shouting for revenge. There was one other person already there in uniform but I did not get their badge number or precinct. I arrived within three minutes of the call, but crowds had already gathered. It was an ugly crowd scene. Spent at least 45 minutes getting people out of the accident area. They kept coming back, walking around, moving pieces of the debris. I had to arrest one person for picking up what they described as "evidence" of the crime. There were plastic, glass, and metal car parts scattered in the road. I saw both sneakers and sandals that had been knocked loose from feet. They appeared to be in the southbound lane.

The first victim I approached was an adolescent boy lying on the pavement near the center stripe. He wasn't moving and his head and mouth were bleeding. The second victim, a little girl, was a few feet away from the boy, to the west. She was laying in the southbound lane. She was badly hurt with a broken leg, but was talking. She kept saying "the big white van hit me." I could not be sure how many bodies there were. Farther up the street, people were yelling, "there's two more up here!" The people had moved the third victim; it was little boy no more than 3 years old. He wasn't moving. He was on the center line of 39th Street.

	PELICAN BAY POLICE DEPARTMENT CALUSA COUNTY, FLORIDA	ARREST NUMBER: n/a
		COMPLAINT NUMBER: 20XX(-2)10101

NARRATIVE (cont'd):

Page 2 of 3.

It looked like the boy was dragged about 150 feet by the vehicle going northbound. There was a fourth child but we couldn't tell how badly hurt he was because the street lights were not working. Three ambulances and a rescue chopper rushed the children to a local hospital.

We only secured the scene after the rescue efforts were completed. The crowds were angry and it took a great deal of time to control them. We marked plastic car parts, metal car parts, sneakers, and sandals. We didn't really know what we were looking for or what would be important, there was so much debris. I found Toyota parts and parts from a Honda Accord. Some of them were on the road and some were laying on the side of the road by the Royal Garden Apartments.

There was debris everywhere. I watched as several groups of folks moved pieces of the accident debris around. I stopped them but was not able to get everything back into its original location.

I took witness statements from Johnny Broadsides, Dimitri Merinov and Matt Bader. Another boy whose name I did not get said that he remembered sitting on the bench when he saw a white van speeding, then he heard a loud boom. A 13-year-old remembered the children standing on the grass between the sidewalk and the road. They were holding hands, as if they were about to cross the street.

PELICAN BAY POLICE DEPARTMENT
CALUSA COUNTY, FLORIDA

ARREST NUMBER: n/a

COMPLAINT NUMBER: 20XX(-2)10101

NARRATIVE (cont'd):

Page 3 of 3.

A few seconds later the teen saw the children tumbling over a white van like dominoes. He did not see any other vehicle strike the children.

Several witnesses said two vehicles were involved and a few said that three were involved. Stories varied. One said that a Honda dragged a child down the street before flipping off its lights and speeding away. People did not agree on the models or their makes, which direction they were traveling, which ones had actually struck the children. No one got a license plate number. I received different descriptions and it appears at this time that at least two, if not three, vehicles were involved.

One witness saw a dark Toyota strike the youngest child, drag him around 150 feet, stop, turn off their lights, turn on their lights and then leave.

Investigation will continue by accident reconstruction technicians.
Attached files: 1. Sketch of the Accident Scene, Photos, statements of Broadsides and Merinov

REPORTING OFFICER	James Record	DATE REPORTED	22 Mar 20XX-2
REPORTING OFFICER	James Record (SIGNATURE)	BR549 (OFFICER BADGE)	22 Mar 20XX-2 (DATE)
REVIEWING SUPERVISOR	Robert Burrell (SIGNATURE)	BR9240 (OFFICER BADGE)	22 Mar 20XX-2 (DATE)

CALUSA POLICE DEPARTMENT
CALUSA COUNTY

INVESTIGATION REPORT
PAGE 1 OF 2

Report No	Date:	Complaining Witness:
20XX-203230355	3/23/20XX-02	Charissa Washington
Investigating Officer:		**Suspect:**
Detective Edwin Morris		Rebecca Hartwell
Division:		**Address:**
Homicide		Royal Garden Apartments
Victim(s):	**Age(s):**	**General Description:**
Ronald Washington, Jordan Washington	14, 3	Two African American males, ages 14 and 3

Investigator's Notes:

March 23, 20XX-2:

Case assigned to Homicide division. Opened case file, began investigation.

On March 21, 20XX:-2 Officer James Record responded to an accident scene. They were called in to deal with a hit and run that resulted in the death of two children. Chief Hightower assigned case to my division on March 23, 20XX-2. No accident scene reconstruction was conducted the day of the accident, and the video of the scene was destroyed by Officer Record when he inadvertently incorrectly attempted to download the materials to his department laptop. Investigation plan includes developing diagrams, interviewing witnesses and securing evidence if available. Inserted transcript of 911 call (exhibit 1) and photos of oldest child into case file (exhibits 2, 3, and 4).
Investigation continues.

March 28, 20XX-2.
Developed diagrams of the relevant areas (exhibit 5, 6 and 7 of this report)
Secured overhead shots of accident area from Google Maps (exhibits 8 and 9)
Secured street shot of accident area by basketball court from Google Maps (exhibit 10)
Inserted Sun Up and Sun Down Report into the case file (exhibit 11)
Interviewed Bill Hartwell.
Interviewed Marian Hartwell.
Investigation continues.

April 7, 20XX-2.
Received statements from Johnny Broadsides (exhibit 12) and Dimitri Merinov (exhibit 13) from Officer Record. Reviewed and inserted into the case file.

May 12, 20XX-2.
Statements given by Mr. Hartwell (exhibit 14) and Mrs. Hartwell (exhibit 15) on 28 March returned by their attorney Steve Levine. Placed in the file once received.

CALUSA POLICE DEPARTMENT
CALUSA COUNTY

INVESTIGATION REPORT
PAGE 2 OF 2

July 7, 20XX-2.
Located Mr. Bader, brought him in for questioning. He provided a statement (exhibit 16). He also provided two video files from his cell phone that night (exhibits 17 and 18). Procured MP3 of the 911 call (exhibit 19) Requested an additional statement from Officer Record.

July 13, 20XX-2. Officer Record provides affidavit (exhibit 20).

Subsequent investigation revealed that probable cause exists to believe that Rebecca Hartwell drove the vehicle that struck both Ronald and Jordan Washington on the night of 21 March 20XX-2.
Investigation continues.

July 13, 20XX-1. Hung jury in the case of State v. Hartwell. Case file closed.

/--Nothing Follows--------------------------------------/

Sworn and subscribed in my presence, July 13, 20XX-1.

Signature: *Edwin Morris*

Supervisor: Robert Burrell

Supervisor's Signature *Robert Burrell*

Case Status: Closed   Date: 072320XX-1

I swear and affirm that the report above and the attached files are true and correct to the best of my Belief and Knowledge.

Signature: *Edwin Morris*

Transcript of 911 Call
21 March 20XX-2
7:17 p.m.

1. **OPERATOR**: This is 911, what is your emergency?

2. **CALLER**: I'm at the University Community Center on 39th Street and I just saw an accident. You guys need to get out here right now, man.

3. **OPERATOR**: Sir, please describe what happened.

4. **CALLER**: I was playing basketball down here and just a second ago I just heard an accident. There's...aww man...there's like three kids just got hit by a car. And, and, I think there might be another that got hit too. Hurry up and get down here! I think these kids are dying!

5. **OPERATOR**: Sir, how many vehicles were involved?

6. **CALLER**: I don't know, there was one stopped here like it was involved in it or something and another stopped further down the road. It started its engine and sped off. I think that one was involved.

7. **OPERATOR**: So, both vehicles have left?

8. **CALLER**: Yeah! They both just took off!

9. **OPERATOR**: Can you please describe those vehicles sir?

10. **CALLER**: I dunno. I'm pretty sure the one stopped here closer to the Center was a Ford Econoline Van, white I think. The other one looked like a small Toyota or Honda, some dark color or something.

11. **OPERATOR**: Sir, the police and paramedics should be arriving very soon, they may need your assistance when they arrive so please remain calm and stay where you are, OK?

12. **CALLER**: OK Just hurry up!

I hereby certify that the above transcript is a true and accurate copy of the tape maintained on file in the office of the emergency response center, Calusa County Sherriff's Department, Pelican Bay, Florida.

Charlotte Jones
Administrative Clerk
Calusa County Sherriff's Department
May 6, 20XX-2

Exhibit 1

Washington v. Hartwell

Exhibit 2

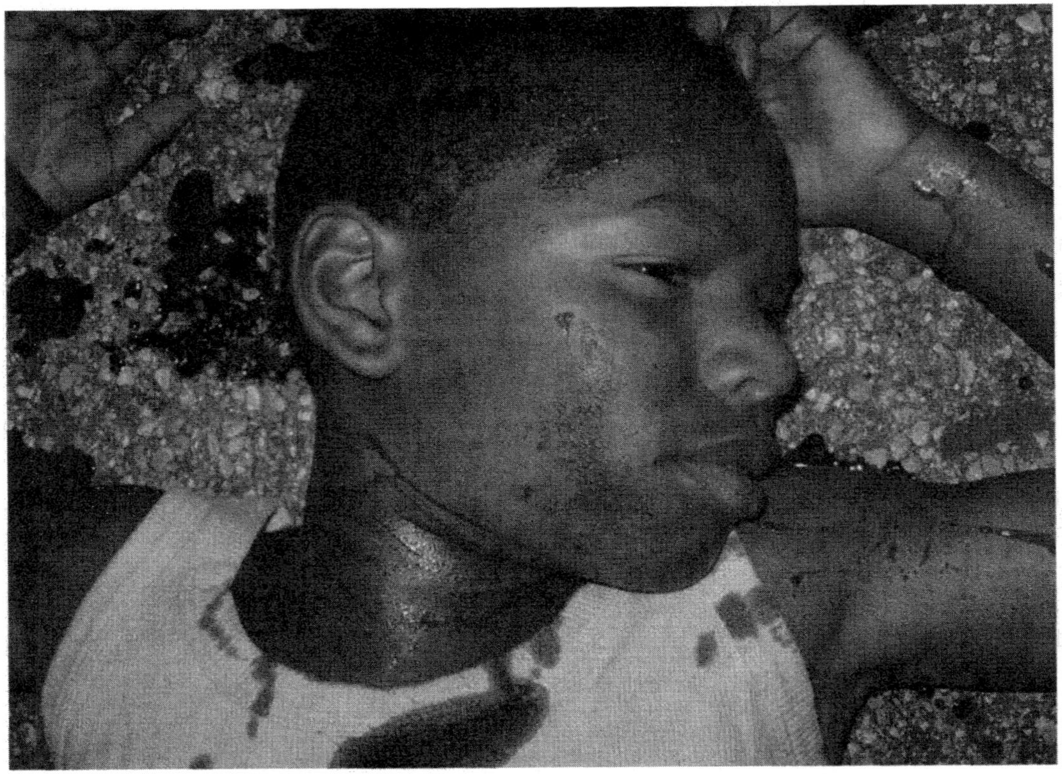

Exhibit 3

Tab C Page 206

Washington v. Hartwell

Exhibit 4

Tab C Page 207

Washington v. Hartwell

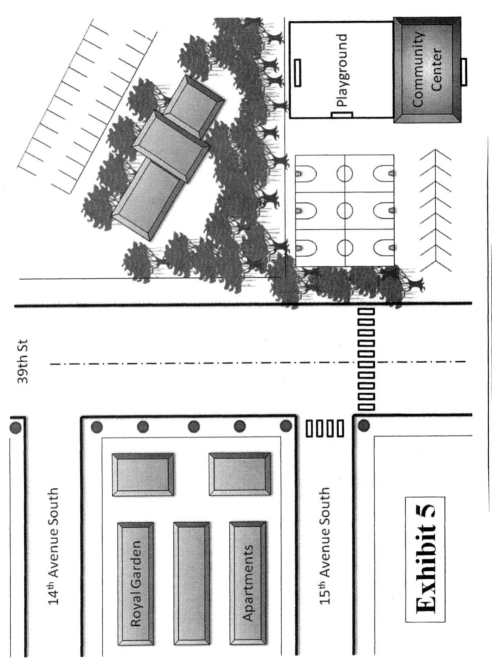

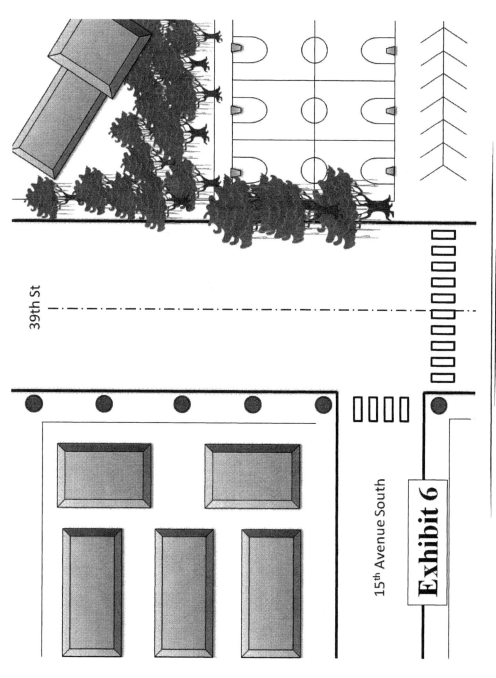

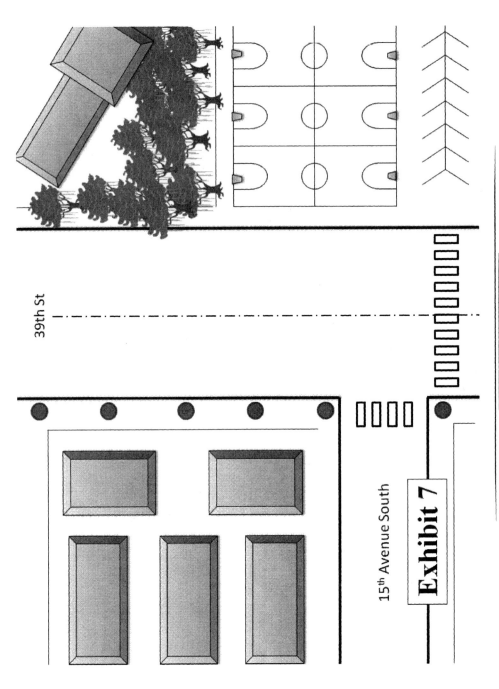

Exhibit 8

Washington v. Hartwell

Tab C Page 211

Exhibit 9

Tab C Page 212

Washington v. Hartwell

Exhibit 10

Tab C Page 213

Washington v. Hartwell

SUNRISE AND SUNSET FOR U.S.A. – PELICAN BAY – MARCH 20XX-2

Pelican Bay, XXXXX, United States

Rising and setting times for the Sun

Date	Sunrise	Sunset	Length of day This day	Difference	Solar noon Time	Altitude	Distance (10⁶ km)
Mar 1, 20XX-2	6:55 AM	6:31 PM	11h 35m 18s	+ 1m 38s	12:43 PM	54.5°	148.223
Mar 2, 20XX-2	6:54 AM	6:31 PM	11h 36m 56s	+ 1m 38s	12:43 PM	54.9°	148.259
Mar 3, 20XX-2	6:53 AM	6:32 PM	11h 38m 34s	+ 1m 38s	12:42 PM	55.3°	148.296
Mar 4, 20XX-2	6:52 AM	6:33 PM	11h 40m 13s	+ 1m 38s	12:42 PM	55.7°	148.333
Mar 5, 20XX-2	6:51 AM	6:33 PM	11h 41m 52s	+ 1m 38s	12:42 PM	56.0°	148.371
Mar 6, 20XX-2	6:50 AM	6:34 PM	11h 43m 31s	+ 1m 39s	12:42 PM	56.4°	148.410
Mar 7, 20XX-2	6:49 AM	6:34 PM	11h 45m 11s	+ 1m 39s	12:42 PM	56.8°	148.448
Mar 8, 20XX-2	6:48 AM	6:35 PM	11h 46m 50s	+ 1m 39s	12:41 PM	57.2°	148.488
Mar 9, 20XX-2	6:47 AM	6:36 PM	11h 48m 30s	+ 1m 39s	12:41 PM	57.6°	148.528
Mar 10, 20XX-2	6:46 AM	6:36 PM	11h 50m 10s	+ 1m 39s	12:41 PM	58.0°	148.568
Mar 11, 20XX-2	6:45 AM	6:37 PM	11h 51m 50s	+ 1m 40s	1:41 PM	58.4°	148.609
Mar 12, 20XX-2	6:44 AM	6:37 PM	11h 53m 30s	+ 1m 40s	1:40 PM	58.8°	148.649
Mar 13, 20XX-2	6:43 AM	6:38 PM	11h 55m 11s	+ 1m 40s	1:40 PM	59.2°	148.690
Mar 14, 20XX-2	6:42 AM	6:38 PM	11h 56m 51s	+ 1m 40s	1:40 PM	59.6°	148.732
Mar 15, 20XX-2	7:40 AM	7:39 PM	11h 58m 32s	+ 1m 40s	1:39 PM	60.0°	148.773

Mar 16, 20XX-2	6:39 AM	6:40 PM	12h 00m 12s	+ 1m 40s	1:39 PM	60.4°	148.814
Mar 17, 20XX-2	6:38 AM	6:40 PM	12h 01m 53s	+ 1m 40s	1:39 PM	60.7°	148.856
Mar 18, 20XX-2	6:37 AM	6:41 PM	12h 03m 34s	+ 1m 40s	1:39 PM	61.1°	148.897
Mar 19, 20XX-2	6:36 AM	6:41 PM	12h 05m 14s	+ 1m 40s	1:38 PM	61.5°	148.939
Mar 20, 20XX-2	6:35 AM	6:42 PM	12h 06m 55s	+ 1m 40s	1:38 PM	61.9°	148.980
Mar 21, 20XX-2	7:34 AM	6:42 PM	12h 08m 36s	+ 1m 40s	1:38 PM	62.3°	149.021
Mar 22, 20XX-2	7:33 AM	7:43 PM	12h 10m 16s	+ 1m 40s	1:37 PM	62.7°	149.063
Mar 23, 20XX-2	7:31 AM	7:43 PM	12h 11m 57s	+ 1m 40s	1:37 PM	63.1°	149.104
Mar 24, 20XX-2	7:30 AM	7:44 PM	12h 13m 37s	+ 1m 40s	1:37 PM	63.5°	149.146
Mar 25, 20XX-2	7:29 AM	7:44 PM	12h 15m 18s	+ 1m 40s	1:37 PM	63.9°	149.187
Mar 26, 20XX-2	7:28 AM	7:45 PM	12h 16m 58s	+ 1m 40s	1:36 PM	64.3°	149.229
Mar 27, 20XX-2	7:27 AM	7:45 PM	12h 18m 38s	+ 1m 40s	1:36 PM	64.7°	149.270
Mar 28, 20XX-2	7:26 AM	7:46 PM	12h 20m 18s	+ 1m 40s	1:36 PM	65.1°	149.312
Mar 29, 20XX-2	7:25 AM	7:47 PM	12h 21m 58s	+ 1m 39s	1:35 PM	65.5°	149.354
Mar 30, 20XX-2	7:23 AM	7:47 PM	12h 23m 38s	+ 1m 39s	1:35 PM	65.9°	149.396
Mar 31, 20XX-2	7:22 AM	7:48 PM	12h 25m 18s	+ 1m 39s	1:35 PM	66.2°	149.439

All times are in local time for Pelican Bay

Note that Daylight Saving Time started on March 22, 20XX-2 at 2:00 AM and this is accounted for above.
March Equinox (Vernal Equinox) is on Tuesday, March 20, 20XX-2 at 7:07 PM in Pelican Bay.

© Timeanddate.com

- Time and Date uses the tables of times for sunrise and sunset provided by the National Weather Service.

Exhibit 11

Exhibit 12

Officer Initials: JR

PELICAN BAY POLICE DEPARTMENT
CALUSA COUNTY, FLORIDA

VOLUNTARY STATEMENT
(NOT UNDER ARREST)
PAGE 216 OF 2

My name is **Johnny Broadsides**. I am **17** years old.

At the time of this statement, I am not under arrest nor am I being investigated for the commission of any crime or offense. I have given this statement voluntarily and I offer this information for whatever purpose it may serve.

1. On March 21, 20XX-2 I saw and heard some of what happened in the accident outside
2. the University Community Center. I worked the night before, so I didn't get up on the
3. 21st till around 3 in the afternoon. I hung out with my boys on the street corner most
4. of the afternoon and then we went over to the community center courts to play some
5. b-ball. We'd been playing for around two hours when we all heard this horrible thud and
6. kids screaming. We ran up the street looking for what happened. I say a white van
7. stopped in the road pretty close to the b-ball courts and up the road around 100 feet
8. or so were two cars, a Toyota and some kind of Honda. Kids were lying in the street,
9. looking like something you would see on the tv screen from Baghdad. Blood was
10. everywhere. I'm pretty fast so I ran up to the Honda and began beating on the
11. window telling them to get out. The person inside, I think it was a woman, freaked out
12. and took off. She almost ran my foot over! I then ran up about another 10 feet to

1 the Toyota. There was this baby lying in the road and it looked so bad.... I

2 started screaming and hollering at the Toyota. It peeled out of there before I got

3 a chance to see who was driving it, but I remember seeing blood and other stuff

4 smeared all over the left side of that car. It was awful. I have never been in

5 trouble with the law and I don't know none of them kids. Best that way I suppose

6 cause it might be too hard to take if I could put a name to the baby's face. Still

7 keeps me up at night. Some folks should not be in our neighborhood when they don't

8 belong. It just ain't right — they better watch out cause sometimes things happen to

9 folks who don't belong here. You know how things are down here.

I certify that the facts given in this statement consist of __2__ pages and are correct to the best of my knowledge. I have reviewed this statement and signed my name below.

Johnny Broadsides
Signature of person giving statement   Witness

March 23, 20XX-2
Date   Witness

Official Use Only

Lt. James Record   *James Record*
Officer   Officer Signature   Date
(Printed Name)

Page 2 of 2

JB

Washington v. Hartwell   Tab C Page 217

Exhibit 13

Officer Initials: JR

PELICAN BAY POLICE DEPARTMENT
CALUSA COUNTY, FLORIDA

VOLUNTARY STATEMENT
(NOT UNDER ARREST)
PAGE 218 OF 2

My name is __Dimitri Merinov__. I am __24__ years old.

At the time of this statement, I am not under arrest nor am I being investigated for the commission of any crime or offense. I have given this statement voluntarily and I offer this information for whatever purpose it may serve.

1 On March 21, 20XX-2 I saw and heard some of what happened in the accident outside
2 the University Community Center. I got off of work at the United Express sorting
3 facility at about 12:00p that afternoon. I worked an early shift from 4:00a to
4 12:00p. I was going to play in a 3-on-3 basketball tournament that night at the
5 Community Center, so when I came home from work I wanted to sleep for a few hours.
6 I woke up and got ready a little before 5:30. My game started at 6:00 and I got
7 there about 10 minutes before that. When I was playing I noticed the four kids who
8 were involved in the accident at the park watching the games. I recognized them
9 because they live next to me in my building. I played my game and finished at 6:50. A
10 little after 7:00 I was cooling off and talking with a few people when I heard like a
11 muffled "boom, boom" come from the street in front of the Community Center. I grabbed
12   Page _1_ of _3_   D.M.

my camera phone from my bag and ran out there. I could see that two vehicles were stopped in the road both going the same direction I guess. One was a white panel van and the other was a dark colored Toyota and they were pretty far apart. The van was a little closer to me and when I got there it was driving slowly and then sped off. The Toyota was about 150 feet down the road and it had stopped. I know it was a manual transmission because it looked like it stalled out because it stared again I heard the gears grinding before it finally lurched and sped off. I got video of it with my camera phone. I walked into the street and saw the three of the neighbor kids I recognized hurt badly in the road, but the fourth wasn't with them. It looked like they got hit. I heard bystanders say that they saw the van and the Toyota hit them. Someone screamed from where the Toyota was stopped and said that there was another of the kids down there about 150 feet away. Some other people said that the Toyota dragged the kid all the way down the street to where it stopped. I'm really upset because I know these kids and their mother. Monique Washington is my neighbor and a good friend of mine. I heard her crying and upset all day the next day when she came home. I stopped by her house to check on her and she told me two of her kids died. She said she thought it was "all her fault." I guess I should tell you

1 that I have a criminal record. About five years ago I was convicted of petit theft

2 here in Pelican Bay. About four years ago I was convicted of trespassing. I'm working

3 hard now at my job and trying I'm trying get past all that.

I certify that the facts given in this statement consist of __3__ pages and are correct to the best of my knowledge. I have reviewed this statement and signed my name below.

Dimitri Merinov
Signature of person giving statement   Witness

March 23, 20XX-2
Date   Witness

Official Use Only

Lt. James Record	*James Record*	
Officer (Printed Name)	Officer Signature	Date

Sworn Statement of Bill Hartwell March 28, 20XX-2

BH Page 1 of 3

Exhibit 14

1 My name is Bill Hartwell. I've worked as a postal worker since 1979. I'm married
2 to my wonderful wife, Marian, and we live in Pelican Bay in Calusa County, FL. We have
3 two daughters, Rebecca, 28, and Gina, 23. My wife moved here from Cuba as a little
4 girl. But both of my daughters grew up here in Calusa County. We are a tight-knit
5 family, and my girls are wonderful children. And smart, too. As babies they only spoke
6 Spanish. It wasn't until Rebecca went to pre-school that she learned English. But she
7 was a great student all the way from her time at St. Mary's Elementary School through
8 high school. She always made 'A's and 'B's at Incarnation High.

9 As kids Rebecca and Gina were constantly dancing. Probably since Rebecca was
10 8, she was doing ballet. The girls absolutely loved it. They took it serious, and I could
11 tell they were serious about it. I even converted our garage into a dance studio. Wooden
12 slab floor, a wall of mirrors, it even had the ballet bar. I did it all in a single weekend.
13 The kids loved it. I used to watch them practice, and I'd give them pointers. I would tell
14 them if they forgot to point their toes when they jumped. I had a pretty good eye for
15 those sorts of things.

16 And it must have helped, too. Rebecca is a dance teacher at Northside Elementary
17 Magnet School. She also has her own studio. She is the owner/director of the Dance,
18 Dance, Dance Studio. Her studio is located Pelican Bay, about 5 miles from the
19 University Community Center. Pelican Bay Her students loved her. They really looked
20 up to her and admired her. She touched the hearts of all of her students through her
21 dancing.

22 That night of March 21 changed our lives, though. Not only Rebecca's life, but
23 also our whole family's. I will never forget when I first learned about this. My wife told
24 me. I was working the night shift at the post office when Marian called me. Rebecca
25 called her mom first. Then Marian called me and told me what happened. I couldn't
26 speak. It was tragic. I knew that this would affect my family for the rest of their lives.

27 I immediately went home. Nobody was there. Jamie – that's Gina's boyfriend –
28 and Marian went down to meet Rebecca and get her car. I was at the house when
29 Marian and Jamie got back. Rebecca was with them. She looked awful. Tear-streaked
30 face. I tried to hold her. She was limp. She felt so frail.

31 We were all sitting in the house, and that's when Rebecca and I found out that
32 two children had died. When Jamie told Rebecca she broke down. She balled up in a
33 fetal position and cried. She was afraid and said that she should have been the one to
34 die. She wanted to go back to the scene of the accident. I told her not to go back. She
35 tried to get up and leave the house but I grabbed her and stopped her. She was crazy out
36 of her head with grief and I didn't think she could even drive. When I first found out
37 about the accident, I wanted Rebecca to go back and turn herself in, I really did, but it
38 was too late now and I didn't know what to do. I just knew I wanted to keep Rebecca
39 safe and do the right thing for those kids and I couldn't see how I could do both. I

Washington v. Hartwell

1 wanted to protect my baby and I thought that more than anything else we needed to talk
2 with a lawyer before we did anything else. We needed to think through this and

Sworn Statement of Bill Hartwell March 28, 20XX-2

1 figure out what to do. It was late, I think sometime after midnight. If we could all just
2 get through the night, then I would figure out who to call to make things better. I
3 planned to do it in the morning.

4 Rebecca's car was still in the driveway, her 20XX-5 Toyota Echo. I guess my wife
5 drove it to the house. I went to look at the car.

6 The hood and bumper on the driver's side were damaged—part of the bumper was torn
7 off. The windshield was cracked. The driver's side airbag had deployed. The front end
8 had blood... and...other stuff...I don't know...blood...lots of it... all over the front end of
9 the car. Horrible. I almost passed out from seeing it. I decided we needed to move it
10 into the garage, we just couldn't leave it out in the driveway.

11 The garage hadn't been used as a dance studio for years; it was mainly just
12 storage. It hdl the the car fine. After Jamie drove the car into the garage, I used the
13 hose, Lysol and paper towels to clean the blood and other stuff off the car. I also wiped
14 away blood from the driver-side windshield and door. There was a handprint on the left
15 rear window, like someone had been beating on it. I threw everything out—even the
16 Lysol can—in a black garbage bag. I wasn't sure what to do with it so I placed it in the
17 garbage cans in the garage, then took the cans to the curb. Initially, no one except Steve
18 really ever asked me about the location of the stuff I used to clean the car. Not even the
19 police. I actually kind of forgot about it—with all that was going on—I guess the garbage
20 collectors picked it up. They pick up on Fridays. By the time I was asked about it at
21 deposition, well, it was gone. I don't know if they ever found it. It never came up at
22 trial.

23 Man, that was a rough night. Rebecca was suicidal. I was really concerned. But
24 we made it through the night, and the next morning, I told the family to stick to their
25 normal schedule until I found a lawyer. I don't know if that was the right thing to do,
26 but I didn't know what else to do. We needed to talk to a lawyer. We needed to figure
27 out what we should do.

28 It was hard to know what to do. It was hard to know what happened. I don't
29 think Rebecca even knew what happened. Rebecca never told me she hit any kids; she
30 told me a body flew into her windshield. Because this was not her usual route home, I
31 asked her if she saw anyone in the street, crossing the street. "Suitcase City"—that's the
32 area she was in—is not a great neighborhood. What I mean to say is-- I mean, well, she
33 just usually takes the interstate home. I don't feel comfortable with her driving in that
34 part of town.

35 Rebecca said the first time she saw the body is when it flew into her windshield. The
36 body could have been thrown into the windshield, I don't really know. It's not like we
37 were trying to hide the truth. We weren't trying to hide anything from anyone. We just
38 didn't know exactly what happened. And I don't think Rebecca is responsible for the
39 death of those two boys. I will go to my grave saying that. I don't want to speak ill of

Washington v. Hartwell

1 anyone, but those children should not have been out on a street like that by themselves
2 - it just isn't right.

3   The family did go about their business, though. They stuck to their normal
4 schedules. I told them we should. Rebecca even taught school that Thursday.
5 Somehow we all made it through the day after the accident. I think it was that night,
6 Thursday night, we went to Marian's

Sworn Statement of Bill Hartwell   March 28, 20XX-2

1 parents' house in Pelican Bay. Everyone went, including the dogs. We moved in
2 temporarily and tried to figure out what to do next.

3   I called Steve Levine on Friday. I'm so glad that I did. He really seemed to
4 understand our pain, our fears. He didn't have to help us, you know. He didn't have to
5 help my daughter. He didn't have to take this case. But he did. He really helped us
6 figure out what we needed to do to straighten out this mess.

7   Levine knew what to do. Both he and Rebecca knew that she had to tell the police
8 what happened. Levine knew we needed to try to visit the family. On Saturday Levine
9 drove us to Mrs. Washington's home so that we could tell her how deeply sorry we were
10 about this terrible tragedy. It wasn't the right time though. Mrs. Washington still
11 needed time.

12   We stayed at Marian's parents until the news conference on Monday morning at
13 10 a.m. in Levine's office. We were finally able to come forward. Finally, Rebecca could
14 tell Mrs. Washington and everyone how truly sorry she was for Mrs. Washington loss.
15 Finally, Mrs. Washington could know that her family is in our thoughts and prayers.

BH Page 3 of 3.

Signed: *Bill Hartwell*
March 28, 20XX-2

Witnessed by: Detective Edwin Morris

Signed, *Edwin Morris*

March 28, 20XX-2

Sworn Statement of Marian Hartwell　　　　　　　　　　　　　　March 28, 20XX-2

MH Page 1 of 3　　　　　　　　　　　　　　　　　　　　　　　　**Exhibit 15**

My name is Marian C. Hartwell. I am a teacher's aid at Lake Cypress Elementary School in Pelican Bay. I'm married to Bill Hartwell, and we live in Pelican Bay, Calusa County, FL. We have two daughters, Rebecca, 28, and Gina, 23.

My family moved to Florida from Cuba when I was just a little girl. I met Bill here and we have raised both of our daughters here in Calusa County. We are a very close family. Both of my daughters are wonderful people and very smart. We taught them to speak Spanish and that was their only language until they began school. Rebecca learned to speak English very well after she began pre-school. She was an excellent student. She attended Most Holy Redeemer Elementary School and then Riverridge High School where she always made 'A's and 'B's.

Both of my daughters were constantly dancing as children. They both loved to dance and took their dance classes very seriously. Rebecca began ballet around age 8. Bill converted the garage into a dance studio so that the girls could practice at home. Rebecca received a bachelor's degree in dance education from the University of South Florida. She is now a dance teacher at Northside Elementary School and she owns her own dance studio, The Dance, Dance, Dance Studio of Pelican Bay. All of her students really look up to her and admire her. Rebecca touches people through her love of dance.

March 21st was a horrible night that changed the lives of everyone in this family. Rebecca called me after the accident. She was sobbing and tried to explain to me what happened. Rebecca told me that a body had hit her windshield and that it was about to crack open. I told Rebecca to continue on towards the dance studio and to stay there. The studio was closer to Rebecca than our house and I didn't think that Rebecca should be driving because she was so upset. Bill was working the night shift at the post office. I had to call him to break the news. Bill wanted Rebecca to turn around and turn herself in. But when Rebecca called back she told me that she could not do that. I think she was just too upset. She was crying so hard, I could barely understand her. She wasn't making any sense. I think she was just too scared to go back, scared of what she would see.

After I spoke with my husband, I went with Gina's boyfriend Jamie to meet Rebecca and get her car. We drove by the scene of the accident first. We saw the ambulances and the sheriff's cruisers. I noticed a man standing in the street and I asked him what happened. He told me that a man had hit four children and that two of them were dead. I just started to cry. I couldn't believe that two children were gone. I felt some relief that this man was telling me a man had hit the children.

Sworn Statement of Marian Hartwell   March 28, 20XX-2

1   Rebecca kept calling me. She had arrived at the dance studio and was panicked.
2 She told me that she was going to go to Publix and take all the pills she could. I told
3 Jamie to get there as fast he could. We found the car that Rebecca was driving in the
4 back of the studio. I went inside and found Rebecca alone, trembling. She was in shock.
5 I put my jacket around her, helped her to the car that Jamie was driving, and I drove her
6 car home.

7   When we got back to the house, Bill was home. We all sat in the house and just
8 waited. Jamie broke the news to Rebecca that two of the children that had been hit had
9 died. Rebecca just fell apart when she heard the news, curling up in a ball and just
10 sobbing. She was so scared and said that she should have been the one to die. She kept
11 saying, "I want to die." I want to die."

12   Later, Rebecca said that she wanted to go back to the scene of the accident, but
13 Bill told her not to. She stopped talking. She wouldn't eat. We were so worried. Bill and
14 I decided that the only way we could help and protect Rebecca at this point was to hire a
15 lawyer. It was after midnight, so we decided that we would wait until morning and then
16 make some calls. It was a long night for the whole family. Rebecca was suicidal and we
17 needed to stay with her to keep her safe. The next morning, Bill told me and the girls
18 that we were to follow our normal routine. We all followed Bill' order. I went to work.
19 Rebecca even taught school that day. She called me once that day and told me that she
20 couldn't take it and that she wanted to turn herself in.

21   I knew how Bill felt about this, so I told her to finish her day at work. Thursday
22 night, the whole family stayed with my parents at their home in Tampa. We even took
23 the dogs with us. We decided to stay there temporarily. It was comforting to be around
24 family while we decided what to do next. On Friday, Bill called Steve Levine. He is the
25 best lawyer in town. Steve was able to take the case and assud us that he could help
26 Rebecca. I knew Steve was going to help us straighten everything out.

27   Steve decided that he and Rebecca would tell the police what happened. He also
28 thought that Rebecca should visit the family of the children that had been hit. That
29 Saturday, Steve drove us to the home of Mrs. Washington. The car ride was silent. We
30 were all so nervous. We were going to explain to her how terribly sorry Rebecca was, we
31 all were. We were met at the door by a friend of the family who explained that this was
32 simply not the right time.

33   The whole family stayed with my parents until the news conference was held on
34 Monday morning. It was at 10am at Steve's office. It was then that Rebecca was able to
35 come forward and explain how sorry she was to everyone. Steve explained Rebecca's
36 side of the story and let Rebecca apologize to Mrs. Washington.

1   Rebecca never tried to explain to us what happened. But she never said that she
2 hit

Sworn Statement of Marian Hartwell　　　　　　　　　　　　　　March 28, 20XX-2

1 anyone, either. She did say that a body flew into her windshield. Bill asked her if she
2 had seen anyone trying to cross the street and Rebecca said that the first time she saw
3 anyone was when the body hit her windshield. She kept saying, "No. No. No. I don't
4 know. No." She was never a perfect driver, but I believe Rebecca. I believe that she did
5 not hit those children.

6   I don't want to say anything bad about anybody else, but really, how could you let
7 your babies walk around like that in the dark? It just can't be believed that something
8 like that could happen this way. It just breaks my heart for those little ones. Nobody
9 deserves to lose their babies, even folks that don't work to pay for them. I don't want to
10 lose my baby to jail either. What good would that do for anyone?

MH Page 3 of 3.

Signed: *Marian Hartwell*
      March 28, 20XX-2

Witnessed by: Detective Edwin Morris

Signed, *Edwin Morris*
      March 28, 20XX-2

Sworn Statement of Matt Bader July 7, 20XX-2

MB Page 1 of 2

Exhibit 16

My name is Matt Bader. I am 25 years old. I live at 715 Bower Avenue in Pelican Bay, Florida. On Wednesday, March 21st, 20XX-2 I was at a neighborhood cookout in the park between 15th Avenue South and 14th Avenue South; off 39th Street. After dinner and a few beers I played basketball with a bunch of other guys from the neighborhood. There was a pretty good size crowd watching us with a lot of kids and adults. When I went to get another drink, I looked at my watch. I noticed that it was about 10 minutes after 7:00 pm. The sun had set about 15 minutes before that, but it was still light enough to play basketball. As I was finishing my drink, I saw a few of the kids leaving the park headed to their home.

I recognized the kids as living on the other side of 39th Street. There was an older kid; I can't remember his name, carrying a younger kid. There were also two other smaller kids walking next to him. I think that they were his brothers and sisters. I remember that they were all holding hands as they walked back to their house. When they began to cross 39th Street, between 15th Avenue South and 14th Avenue South, I noticed that a few of the streetlights were not working. I believe that about six of them were out. While I was standing there, I wondered when those lights were ever going to get fixed.

I happened to look south when the kids began to cross the street. As soon as the kids stepped off the curb into 39th Street, I saw a dark car speeding towards them. It was painted a dark color and looked like a Honda Civic or a Toyota from the early 1990's or the late 1980's. I know the speed limit there was 30 miles per hour but that car was going much faster, like 45 miles per hour or so. I tried to yell but the kids couldn't hear me. I began to run to where the kids were, but there was nothing I could do; it happened so fast. I wish I could change what happened.

The dark car plowed into the kids. First the car hit the older boy carrying his younger brother or sister with a loud slapping or smacking sound. The little kid went flying off into the air. The older boy hit the front of the car's grill and seemed to roll up onto its hood and then smash into the car's front windshield before ending up in the intersection. Those kids were all holding hands! After the car hit the older boy carrying his younger brother or sister, the car also hit the two other kids. It was sick! One of them was knocked out of the way but the other. It was terrible, the other kid seemed to get caught under the car and dragged about half a block before tumbling out from under the car around 14th Avenue South. It happened so fast. The slapping or smacking sound was so loud that everyone in the park heard it and came running.

The car's driver must have known what happened because the dark car that hit the kids stopped for a few seconds. Then the driver turned the cars outside headlights lights off. There were no lights inside the car. I saw a dark shape but could not make out any details. The car's window's also looked like they were tinted. The car must have had a manual transmission because when the car's lights went out, I heard some

Washington v. Hartwell

1 grinding sounds; like shifting gears. The driver rapidly shifted gears and gunned the
2 engine. Then the car took off, faster than it had been going

Sworn Statement of Matt Bader　　　　　　　　　　　　　　　　　　July 7, 20XX-2

1 before it hit the kids. That driver must have known that something bad happened
2 because it hit at least three of the kids directly. Afterwards, the car stopped for a few
3 seconds before I heard the gears grinding as the driver made a quick getaway. I
4 remember seeing lots of kid's shoes in the street and a puddle of blood. It happened so
5 fast I didn't even think to look at the license plate.

6 　　　　Almost immediately after the car going northbound on 39th Street hit those kids,
7 a van, coming southbound hit the two kids that were walking together that were
8 knocked into the van's way by the car. I got a good look at the outside of the van. The
9 van was white and looked like a Ford Econoline Van. There was a ladder on top. I
10 noticed that the van did not seem to be going that fast. It appeared to be going the
11 speed limit and was not going nearly as fast as the car was. I couldn't really see the
12 driver clearly, but it did not look like the Van's driver could even see the kids. After
13 hitting one of the kids the van stopped briefly and then left. What the car's driver did
14 was sick. I don't' understand why the car's driver didn't stop. I hope they catch that
15 driver. I also hope that someone learns something from this tragedy and fixes the
16 streetlights and puts in some speed bumps! I brought in my cell phone. It has two
17 videos taken that night. Both were emailed to me by someone else who must have been
18 there that night. I don't know who took them but they sure look accurate to me.

19 　　　　I affirm that the foregoing statement was provided of my free will and that I was
20 under no duress. This statement reflects my complete and total recollection of the
21 events that occurred on 21 March 20XX-2.

MH Page 2 of 2.

Signed: *Matthew Bader*

July 7, 20XX-2

Witnessed by: Detective Edwin Morris

Signed, *Edwin Morris*

　　July 7, 20XX-2

Exhibit 17

Washington v. Hartwell

Tab C Page 229

Exhibit 18

MP3 File of 911 Call

- Please download and listen to the MP3 file for the 911 call.

- Compare this file to the official transcript provided previously

Exhibit 19

Washington v. Hartwell

Affidavit - Lieutenant James Record   July 13, 20XX-2

JAR - Page 1 of 2.

Exhibit 16

My name is James Allen Record. I hereby swear under penalty of perjury that the following is a true and accurate recounting of all relevant events related to my involvement in this case. I have prepared this affidavit at the request of the prosecuting attorney in the case of *State v. Hartwell*. I am a Lieutenant at the Pelican Bay Police Department, where I have worked for 12 years. I am 34 years of age.

I am currently assigned to the patrol division. On March 21, 20XX-2, probably around 7:15 p.m., I received a radio dispatch to investigate a hit and run involving three children on 15th Avenue South and 39th Street. That area is a stretch of Pelican Bay that is notorious for its drug dealers, cramped living spaces, and abandoned buildings. It is not a good place and our department has a lot of trouble down there, particularly with gangs and drugs. I was the first responding officer to the scene. It took me less than three minutes to get there, but there were already crowds of people swarming 39th street. It was an ugly crowd scene and I spent at least 15 minutes getting people out of the accident area. They kept coming back.

When I got there I immediately saw plastic and metal car parts scattered in the road, and sneakers and sandals that had been knocked loose from feet. The first victim I found was an adolescent boy who was lying on the pavement near the center stripe. He wasn't moving and his head and mouth were bleeding. The second victim, a little girl, was a few feet way from the boy. She was badly hurt with a broken leg, but she was talking.

Nobody could be sure how many bodies there were. Farther up the street, people were yelling, "there's another one up here!" I made my way through the crowd to the third victim; it was little boy, he couldn't have been more than 3 years old, and he wasn't moving. It appeared as though the boy was dragged about 150 feet by the vehicle that had hit him.

A tall man in the crowd found the fourth and smallest child. He was conscious, but it was impossible to tell how badly he was hurt because some of the streetlights were not working along that section of the road.

Three ambulances and a rescue chopper rushed the children to a local hospital and after they cleared the scene, a few other deputies and I started taping off the scene. We had to push back the crowd several times in an effort to preserve and mark the scattered evidence. We marked plastic car parts, metal car parts, sneakers, and sandals. We didn't really know what we were looking for or what would be important, there was so much debris. The most promising piece of evidence was a piece of black fender molding. On the inside, it said: T O Y O T A. I also found what appeared to be a hubcap from a Honda Accord. I could not tell how long the hubcap had been there but it was laying by the side of the road across the street from where the children were hit, near the Royal Garden Apartments.

1   As the crime scene technicians collected the marked evidence, I took several witnesses
2   aside to give statements. A boy, about 16 years old, said that he remembered sitting on
3   the bench when he saw a white van speeding, then he heard a loud boom. A 13-year-old
4   remembered the children

Affidavit - Lieutenant James Record　　　　　　　　　　　　　　July 13, 20XX-2

1   standing on the grass between the sidewalk and the road. They were holding hands, as if
2   they were about to cross the street. Then a few seconds later, the teen saw the children
3   tumbling over a white van like dominoes.

4   Unfortunately, most of the statements were full of inconsistencies. Several witnesses
5   said two vehicles were involved and a few said that three were involved. According to
6   one person, a Honda had dragged a child down the street before flipping off its lights
7   and speeding away. We had a difficult time getting a solid description of the vehicles.
8   People did not agree on the models or their makes, which direction they were traveling,
9   which ones had actually struck the children. No one got a license plate number.

10 As best I could tell, a car driving north on 39th Street - described as a late 1980s or early
11 1990s Honda Civic or a Toyota with tinted windows - was the first to strike the children.
12 Then a second vehicle, traveling south - described as a white Ford Econoline van with a
13 work ladder on top - hit them. JAR - Page 2 of 2.

James Allen Record
James Allen Record
July 13, 20XX-2

-Notes-

Calusa County Courier

Calusa County, Florida   Tuesday, March 27, 20XX-2

Children Killed, School Teacher Comes Forward

Teacher casts blame on mother

By Suzie Slander

Yesterday a driver finally came forward in the tragic fatal accident that killed two children, ages 14 and 3, last Wednesday night at the intersection of 15th Avenue and 39th Street. The driver, Rebecca Hartwell, is a 28 year-old school teacher at Northside Elementary. She is also the owner-operator of the Dance, Dance, Dance Studio of Pelican Bay. Hartwell admitted that she was one of the drivers at the scene, but denied fault. Hartwell, surrounded by family and her lawyer, read a prepared statement yesterday at a press conference. Afterwards, in response to questions, Hartwell claimed that the children were "thrown into [her] car after being hit by another vehicle." Some witnesses claim Hartwell hit the children and then, with the 3 year old wedged under her car, drove another 150 feet, turned off her lights, and then sped away. Hartwell attempted to explain why she left the scene with the following: "It was dark; I was scared; I knew I had not caused the accident." Hartwell also appeared to blame the mother of the children for the accident, alluding that the mother was unfit, either an alcoholic or drug abuser, and placed the children in danger by allowing them to cross such a busy street at night. Speculation continues to swirl surrounding the case. Some witnesses state that a van hit the children and others claim there was a third car involved. Police continue to investigate the tragic accident.

After her prepared statement and unexpected remarks, Rebecca Hartwell and her family left the press conference together, hand-in-hand. Further attempts to ask the Hartwell's questions were met by their attorney stating that they did not have any further comment at this time.

The accident scene where the Washington children died looks much different in the light of day.

Jimmy Jones, CCC Photographer

Have you seen this van, or a van like it on 39th street the evening of March 21, 200XX-2? If so please call Crime Stoppers at 1-866-555-1234.

Pelican Bay Star Editorials
"Where People Talk"

Dear Ms. Washington and Citizens of Calusa County,

It is with my deepest sympathy that I come to you today. My heart goes out to Ms. Washington. My heart goes out to her children. And my heart goes out to our community.

To Ms. Washington, I can only say this--I cannot even begin to imagine the pain of losing a child, let alone two children. No one should have to go through that level of sorrow. I pray to God that you find peace during this difficult time.

To her surviving children, I pray that you are able to find comfort, as well as a safe environment to grow and live. To Jordan and Ronald, I pray your souls rest in peace.

To the community of Pelican Bay and Calusa Couty: I grieve with you. It was horrific, tragic, and senseless. I too cannot understand, for the life of me, why those four young children were left alone in such a neighborhood, at night, to cross a busy poorly lit street. The children were left to fend for themselves, and no children deserve that type of treatment; no children should be forced into that type of danger. I do not know if drugs or alcohol were involved, but those children should not have been left alone. That type of irresponsible conduct saddens and infuriates me. If an adult had been with those children, this would not have happened.

I did not hit those children. They were thrown into my car after being hit by another vehicle. It was dark; I was scared; I knew I had not caused the accident. I left because I did not know what to do. I regret not reacting with more calm and clarity after the accident. But my concern for Ms. Washington, her children, and the community is what has brought me before you today. I plead to the driver of the vehicle that hit these children—please come forward. Please. Thank you.

Sincerely,

Rebecca Hartwell
Rebecca Hartwell

Note: The opinions and statements expressed by Ms. Hartwell in the above letter to the editor, which we have printed in its entirety, in no way reflects the positions or opinions of the Pelican Bay Star* – the editors.

*The Pelican Bay Star is a Media Services Division Company ©PBS, All rights reserved.

Sworn Statement of Charissa Washington May 3, 20XX-1

CW page 1 of 3.

My name is Charissa Washington and I am 29 years old. I go by the name Rissa. I was born in Georgia, but I moved to Florida when I was a baby. I have never been married but I am a good woman and great mother. I had my first child, Jordan, when I was 15. I always wanted to be a teacher, but when Jordan was born I was unable to stay in school. My father helped me raise Jordan, and I took odd jobs to make a living. After Jordan, I had another son, who is now 10 and is living with his father. Then, I had four more children, August, Ronald, Charles, and my baby Laquinta.

I was pregnant with my seventh child that horrible spring. I love my children very much, and I try to give them the best life I can. I always worried about them because we did not live in a good neighborhood. We didn't have much – we are always moving from place to place, but we always had each other and were a good family. I did have trouble with the Department of Children and Family Services, DCF, but that was all a misunderstanding about a bad boyfriend. As God is my witness I did not know that he beat his own children. The minute I found out he was gone. He never hurt my babies though, the only person that did that was Ms. Hartwell. I don't know what rumors you may have heard about me and drug use, but I am here to tell you right now that I have never, ever taken any kind of illegal drug – I don't even drink.

Wednesday, March 21st was the worst day of my life. The kids had just gotten home from school, and they wanted to go play at the park. I told them that it was getting cold and that I didn't want them to go, but Jordan really wanted to go. He told me to stop treating him like a baby. He is very good with the babies, and I knew that he would watch them, so I told said they could go because I thought it would be safe. I walked the kids to the park because I am always nervous about the traffic and cars on the street by my apartment. The park is over there by the basketball courts and the community center. I told them to stay there until I would be back to pick them up before dark. I went back home, never knowing that was the last time I would see two of my boys alive. I saw that it was getting dark, so I went get the kids from the park. That was when a neighbor ran up yelling, so I started to run towards my babies.

I ran, even though I was pregnant, up to where my children were lying on the ground. People around told me to step back, and that I should not look. I saw Jordan lying there on the ground, bleeding from his head and mouth. Then I heard August scream. It was the worst feeling that a mother could have. I felt helpless, watching my babies there on the street, but there was nothing to do until help arrived. I knelt on the roadside until the ambulance came.

When I got to the hospital, there was nothing to do but wait. When I saw the chaplain come up to me, I knew that it was bad. He told me that Ronald was dead. I do not remember what happened after that, I felt like I was sleep walking in a dream. I remember falling down onto the floor screaming for my babies and they were nowhere for me to find them. Somebody picked me up off the floor and gave me a pill to calm me down. I remember that my family got to the hospital a bit later. I didn't know how I would make it without my kids, and when my family came to the hospital I started crying, "What am I going to do without my babies?" They had not caught the person who hit my children, so I went on the news and pled for whoever did this to turn themselves in. I said that I had no hate in my heart, but that I had a hole that needed to be filled. I needed to know who did this.

Luckily, a man named Mitchell Ritchie heard about what happened and wanted to help, so he called me up and told me that he would bury my babies in caskets. I picked one out for Jordan, and Mr. Ritchie ordered one specially made for Ronald. I was so grateful for Mr. Ritchie's kindness. At the funeral, when I saw my babies lying in their caskets, I screamed. It did not look like Ronald's face lying there, and I will always be haunted by that image. I fell before the caskets and I cried, and then I kissed each of my babies on the cheek to say goodbye. I said, "Mama be home to see you after awhile."

That weekend after the accident, a lawyer drove Mr. and Mrs. Hartwell over to my house. They were the parents of the girl who hit my children. I couldn't believe that they would come over so soon, I was such a mess, I told them that I was in no condition to see them that night.

Later, on the news, Jennifer Hartwell, the girl who hit my babies, expressed her apology to me by reading it off a piece of paper. It did not seem sincere or heartfelt. She did not explain what happened, and she came off looking like a victim when I was the one who lost my babies. I didn't know what to do, and when I talked to my friends about it, they told me that Jennifer Hartwell's lawyer was some important powerful lawyer who knew judges, and that Jennifer would probably not have to go to jail. It just made me so angry that someone could do something like this and not have to go to jail. I figured since she had a lawyer I better get me one too, just in case justice wasn't done you know, no other reason.

Everyone was talking about how she would not have to go to jail because she was white. Some people just see me as just a black girl who lived in the 'hood with a whole bunch of kids and no daddy. That important lawyer vowed to protect Jennifer Hartwell, but who was there to protect my kids? My lawyer told me that she would not be charged with murder, and I didn't understand how this was possible – she killed my babies. I vowed to Jesus that if she didn't go to jail I was still going to make her pay, under the law if nothing else.

Later that summer, I had my baby, Heaven. I had been so upset and unable to eat that my baby only weighed 5 pounds when she was born. My lawyer tried to get me to get a tubal ligation, but I had a dream where Jordan told me not to do it, so I knew it wasn't the right time. My lawyer was not happy about that.

Washington v. Hartwell

Sworn Statement of Charissa Washington May 3, 20XX-1

1 They told me that I was not guilty of child neglect, but I knew that already, I would never neglect
2 my babies. But, I still felt guilty for that day. I was even losing my hair and I was so upset about
3 it. I still wish every day that I had not let them go to the park that day.
4 In the spring of 20XX-1, I was able to move my family to a new house with money from a
5 settlement with Pelican Bay Electric Co. A Jacksonville law firm helped me with that case. They
6 are different lawyers from the one I have now for this suit. We are very happy in our new house,
7 and we feel safe here. It has helped me move on, although I still hear my dead babies
8 whispering to me, asking me to forgive. I just hope they can forgive me.

CW Page 3 of 3.

Signed: *Charissa Washington*
April 29, 200XX-2

Witnessed by: Private Investigator Dana Stubbs
Signed, *Dana Stubbs*
May 3, 20XX-1

Sworn Statement of Rebecca Hartwell May 4, 20XX-1

RH page 3 of 3.

1 My name is Rebecca Hartwell and I am 28 years old. I live with my parents, Marian and
2 Bill, and my sister Gina, 23, in Pelican Bay, Florida. I would say that I grew up in a close-knit,
3 Catholic, family. My mother is a Cuban immigrant and both my sister and I grew up speaking
4 Spanish until we started pre-school. I went to St. Mary's Elementary School and then
5 Incarnation High School. I always loved school and generally did pretty well, usually getting A's
6 and B's. I went on to get my bachelor's in dance education from the University of South Florida.

7 Even though I loved school, my true love was dancing, and this has been my passion
8 since childhood. My father was even kind enough to convert our old garage into a mini dance
9 studio for me. I was constantly dancing, and I think at times I took dancing even more seriously
10 than anything else in my life.

11 Even though I do not have children of my own, I am around them and work with them every
12 day. I work at Northside Elementary school, teaching dance to children in the community. And I
13 love them. My kids make me want to get up early and go to work every day. I love to bring the
14 joy of dance into the lives of children.

15 In addition to teaching dance at Muller Elementary, I also own and operate my own dance
16 studio, The Dance, Dance, Dance Studio of Pelican Bay. My parents helped me get started and
17 provided financial backing. Dancing has been such a positive outlet for me that I want to give all
18 the children I teach the opportunity to discover dance and allow it to affect their lives. My
19 dance studio is only about 5 miles from the University Community Center, if only I hadn't take
20 that road that night.

21 The night of March 21st was a nightmare come to life. I left Northside late that night,
22 around 7pm, because I was helping the art teacher with a project for the school dedication
23 ceremony coming up later that week. It was already dark when I drove out of the school parking
24 lot in my Toyota Echo and headed for home.

25 I didn't take my usual route home. I turned right down north onto 39th street near the
26 University. Usually the traffic lights are in my favor at that time of night—I can get home a little
27 faster that way. All of the lights ahead looked good. I remember that I could see the traffic
28 lights really well because several of the street lights were out. It was that time of day when the
29 sun finally goes down completely and it really gets dark.

30 Not long after making the turn onto 39th, I was startled by something crashing hard into my
31 windshield. It was so loud. I hadn't seen anything. My first thought was what was that?
32 Followed pretty quickly by a Hail Mary.

33 It seemed like a body, but I couldn't be sure. There was no chance for me to even slam
34 on my brakes because the object crashed into my car and then flew off my windshield so quickly.
35 it seemed that something had dropped from the sky onto my windshield. I can't remember
36 much

Sworn Statement of Rebecca Hartwell May 4, 20XX-1

else immediately after that, except for someone screaming! I guess my adrenaline kicked in to "fight or flight"—the only thing my body would let me do was to keep driving down the road.

Something jarred me—I heard what sounded like cracking ice. This sent me back into reality. I couldn't stop shaking and I couldn't catch my breath. I stopped the car.

My windshield was literally shattering in front of my eyes. I called my mother. I tried to tell her that something had stuck my windshield and that it was badly cracked. I'm not sure if she really understood what I was saying because I was crying so hard. She told me that I should drive over to the dance studio because it was closer to where I was than our house.

When I got to the dance studio, my mother was there and so was my sister's boyfriend Jamie. I had parked my car behind the studio in its usual spot. I was still crying and shaking. My mom told me that I insisted that I wanted to immediately go back to the area where the accident happened. I know I couldn't have driven my car back to the site—it was too unsafe to drive again with the windshield in that condition. Mom says I told them that I couldn't believe this was happening and that I wanted them to take me to Publix so I could buy sleeping pills. All I wanted to do was to take all the sleeping pills I could. put me into Jamie's car and drove me to our house.

When we got back home my father was there waiting for us. He hugged me. I was numb. I wanted to die.

At some point, my parents and Jamie sat me down and told me that on their way to the studio they had driven past the scene of the accident on 39th St. My mother told me she spoke with a bystander who told her that a car had stuck several children in the street and that two of them had died. I completely fell apart. All I could think about was whether these were my kids from Northside. I rolled onto the floor into the fetal position and just cried uncontrollably. If I could have traded my life to have one of those children back, I would have.

I kept asking my parents to take me to the scene of the accident in their car. I needed to go back there and explain what happened. They were only looking out for my safety. They kept telling me that it wasn't a good idea in the state I was in to go back there. That it was dangerous. That I needed to rest.

I couldn't eat, sleep or even talk. My parents told me they were going to get a lawyer first thing in the morning. My mother sat up with me the entire night. The next morning, my father insisted that we continue our normal routine to get our minds off things. I went to work the next day. The whole day I could barely speak. I didn't tell anyone what had happened. All I kept thinking about was how much I wanted to go back to the scene. I even called my mother and told her how much I wanted to go back there and tell the police what had happened. Because my parents were going to hire an attorney, they told me I should wait until I got professional advice before doing anything.

That night, my entire family went to stay with my grandparents in Pelican Bay. I wasn't sleeping and frankly, I think I may have taken those sleeping pills if it wasn't for my entire family

Washington v. Hartwell

Sworn Statement of Rebecca Hartwell May 4, 20XX-1

1 keeping watch over me. My parents even refused to answer investigators' questions and risked
2 being held in contempt and sent to jail for me.

3   On Friday, my dad got in contact with Steve Levine, a criminal defense attorney. He told
4 my family that he would be able to help me to get everything straightened out. Just as I hoped,
5 as soon as I got in touch with Steve, I was able to go to the police and tell them everything that
6 had happened. I also told Steve that I wanted to visit Ms. Washington, the mother of the
7 children who had been hit. I wanted to tell her how very truly sorry I was for her loss and that
8 her children were in my prayers.

9 Unfortunately, when we arrived at the door we were met by a friend of the family who told us
10 that Ms. Washington wasn't ready to speak with me at that time.

11   I went to confession on Sunday. I felt so horrible. I told Father Michaels everything. He
12 was kind. Understanding. He did not judge me and did not give me extraordinary penance. He
13 told me to be gentle with myself—that I needed to be still in order to hear God's counsel. That
14 God would guide me and Mr. Levine. That He would forgive me.

15   That Monday, Mr. Steve Levine and I held a press conference. I had written a letter
16 explaining how and why I was coming forward and how very sorry I was for Ms. Washington'
17 loss. I was able to read this letter with the hope that Ms. Washington would hear it and
18 understand what had happened. I wanted her to know that I wasn't a heartless, thoughtless
19 person. I love children. I work with them every day and I love inspiring and teaching them. I
20 got scared and let her fear get the best of me. I wish I could have been more level-headed and
21 calm when the accident happened. The night of March 21st was a nightmare, one I've been
22 reliving every day since then.

RH page 3 of 3.

Signed: *Rebecca Hartwell*

April 29, 20XX-2

Witnessed by: Private Investigator

Signed, *Dana Stubbs*

May 4, 20XX-1

State of XXXXX
UNIFORM COMMITMENT TO CUSTODY
OF DEPARTMENT OF CORRECTIONS

THE CIRCUIT COURT OF CALUSA COUNTY, IN THE SPRING TERM of 20XX-4
IN THE CASE OF:

STATE OF XXXXX   CASE ID : 00XX(-4)1308   DIVISION: D
VS
DEFENDANT   :   Merinov   Dimitri
AKA(S)   :   Ivan

IN THE NAME AND BY AUTHORITY OF THE STATE OF XXXXX, TO THE SHERRIFF OF SAID COUNTY AND THE DEPARTMENT OF CORRECTIONS OF SAID STATE, GREETING:

    THE ABOVE NAMED DEFENDANT HAVING BEEN DULY CHARGED WITH THE OFFENSE SPECIFIED HEREIN IN THE ABOVE STYLED COURT, AND HAVING BEEN DULY CONVICTED AND ADJUDICATED GUILTY OF AND SENTENCE FOR SAID OFFENSE BY SAID COURT, AS APPEARS FROM THE ATTACHED CERTIFIED COPIES OF INFORMATION FILED JUDGMENT AND SENTENCE, AND FELONY DISPOSITION AND SENTENCE DATA FROM WHICH ARE HEREBY MADE PARTS HEROF;

    NOW THEREFORE, THIS TO COMMAND YOU, THE SAID SHERIFF, TO TAKE AND KEEP, AND, WITHIN A REASONABLE TIME AFTER RECEIVING THIS COMMITMENT, SAFELY DELIVER THE SAID DEFENDANT, TOGETHER WITH ANY PERTINENT INVESTIGATION REPORT PREPARED IN THIS CASE, INTO THE CUSTODY OF THE DEPARTMENT OF CORRECTIONS OF THE STATE OF XXXXX: AND THIS IS TO COMMAND YOU, THE SAID DEPARTMENT OF CORRECTIONS, BY AND THROUGH YOUR SECRETARY, REGIONAL DIRECTORS, SUPERINTENDANTS, AND OTHER OFFICIALS, TO KEEP AND SAFELY IMPRISON THE SAID DEFENDANT FRO THE TERM OF SAID SENTENCE IN THE INSTITUTION IN THE STATE CORRECTIONAL SYSTEM TO WHICH YOU, THE SAID DEPARTMENT OF CORRECTIONS, MAY CAUSE THE SAID DEFENDANT TO BE CONVEYED OR THEREAFTER TRANSFERRED. AND THESE PRESENTS SHALL BE YOUR AUTHORITY FOR THE SAME. HEREIN NOT FAIL.

                         WITNESS THE HONORABLE JEREMY PARKER
                         JUDGE OF THE SAID COURT, AS ALSO CONNIE EVANS
                         CLERK, AND THE SEAL THEREOF, THIS
                         14th DAY OF February 20XX-4

               BY: *Margaret Mills*
                         DEPUTY CLERK

IN THE FIRST JUDICIAL CIRCUIT IN AND FOR
CALUSA COUNTY, STATE OF XXXXX

CIRCUIT CRIMINAL DIVISON

STATE OF XXXXX   DIVISION: D
v.
<u>DIMITRI MERINOV</u>   CASE NUMBER: 00XX(-4)1308
DEFENDANT

CERTIFICATE OF SERVICE

I, Connie Evans, Clerk of the Circuit Court of the County of Calusa, State of XXXXX, having by law the custody of the seal and all records, books, documents and papers of or appertaining to the Circuit Court, do hereby certify that a true and correct copy of the Judgment and Sentence has been hand delivered to the State Attorney and mailed to the Defense Attorney.

IN WITNESS WHEREOF, I have hereunto set my hand and seal of said Circuit Court, this 14th day of February A.D. 20XX-4.

                                                      CONNIE EVANS
                                                      As Clerk of Circuit Court

                                                      Margaret Mills
                                                      As Deputy Clerk
                                                      Circuit Criminal Division

IN THE CIRCUIT COURT, 1ST JUDICIAL CIRCUIT
IN AND FOR CALUSA COUNTY, XXXXX
DIVISION   : D
CASE NUMBER : 00XX(-4)1308

STATE OF XXXXX
VS
Dimitri Merinov
DEFENDANT

--JUDGMENT--

THE DEFENDANT, Dimitri Merinov,   BEING PERSONALLY BEFORE
THIS COURT REPRESENTED WITH
PRIVATE ATTORNEY
John Saunders, Esquire
THE ATTORNEY OF RECORD AND THE STATE REPRESENTED BY ASSISTANT STATE ATTORNEY
NICHOLAS COX, AND HAVING

Been tried and found guilty by a jury of the following crime(s): 3

COUNT	CRIME	STATUTE	COURT ACTION	DATE
1	~~LEWD OR LASCIVIOUS MOLESTATION~~	~~80004~~	NOT GUILTY	6 January 20XX-4
2	~~SEXUAL BATTERY~~	~~794011~~	NOT GUILTY	6 January 20XX-4
3	LEWD OR LASCIVIOUS EXHIBITION	800047	ADJG GUILTY	6 January 20XX-4

And no cause being shown why the defendant should not be adjudicated guilty, it is ordered that the defendant is hereby adjudicated guilty of the above crime(s).

AND PURSUANT TO SECTION 943.325, XXXXX STATUTES, HAVING BEEN CONFICTED OF ATTEMPTS OR OFFENSES RELATING TO SEXUAL BATTERY (CH. 794) OR LEWD AND LASCIVIOUS CONDUCT (CH. 800) THE DEFENDANT SHALL BE REQUIRED TO SUBMIT BLOOD SPECIMENS

Washington v. Hartwell   Tab F Page 245

DEFENDANT Dimitri Merinov
                                                Division : D
                                                Case Number : 00XX(-4)1308
                                                OBTS Number : 12394872

-------------------------SENTENCE-------------------------

THE DEFENDANT, BEING PERSONALLY BEFORE THIS COURT, ACCOMPANIED BY THE DEFENDANT'S ATTORNEY OF RECORD, PRIVATE ATTORNEY John Saunders, Esquire
AND HAVING BEEN ADJUDGED GUILTY HEREIN, AND THE COURT HAVING BEEN GIVEN THE DEFENDANT AN OPPORTUNITY TO BE HEARD AND TO OFFER MATTERS IN MITIGATION OF SENTENCE, AND TO SHOW CAUSE WHY THE DEFENDANT SHOULD NOT BE SENTENCED AS PROVIDED BY LAW AND NO CAUSE BEING SHOWN

IT IS THE SENTENCE OF THIS COURT THAT THE DEFENDANT:

Pay a fine of $3000.00, pursuant to appropriate XXXXX Statutes.
Is hereby committed to the custody of the Department of Corrections for a term of: 3 Years

-------------------------OTHER PROVISIONS-------------------------

AS TO COUNT(S) : 3
THE FOLLOWING MANDATORY/MINIMUM PROVISIONS APPLY TO THE SENTENCE IMPOSED :

JAIL CREDIT: It is further ordered that the defendant shall be allowed a total of 223 DAYS as credit for time incarcerated before imposition of this sentence.

DEFENDANT Dimitri Merinov
                                          Division   : D
                                          Case Number : 00XX(-4)1308
                                          OBTS Number : 12394872

-------------------------OTHER PROVISIONS-------------------------

Sentencing guidelines filed.

IN THE EVEN THE ABOVE SENTENCE IS TO THE DEPARTMENT OF CORRECTIONS, THE SHERIFF OF CALUSA COUNTY, XXXXX, IS HEREBY ORDERED AND DIRECTED TO DELIVER THE DEFENDANT TO THE DEPARTMENT OF CORRECTIONS AT THE FACILITY DESIGNATED BY THE DEPARTMENT TOGETHER WITH A COPY OF THIS JUDGMENT AND SENTENCE AND ANY OTHER DOCUMENTS SPECIFIED BY XXXXX STATUTE
THE DEFENDANT IN OPEN COURT WAS ADVISED OF THE RIGHT TO APPEAL FROM THIS SENTENCE BY FILING NOTICE OF APPEAL WITHIN 30 DAYS FROM THIS DATE WITH THE CLERK OF THIS COURT AND THE DEFENDANT'S RIGHT TO THE ASSISTANCE OF COUNSEL IN TAKING THE APPEAL AT THE EXPENSE OF THE STATE SHOWIN OF INDIGENCY.
DONE AND ORDERED IN CALUSA COUNTY, XXXXX, THIS 14TH DAY OF February 20XX-4

State of XXXXX
UNIFORM COMMITMENT TO CUSTODY
OF DEPARTMENT OF CORRECTIONS

THE CIRCUIT COURT OF CALUSA COUNTY, IN THE SPRING TERM of 20XX-4
IN THE CASE OF:

STATE OF XXXXX   CASE ID : 20XX(-3)1978   DIVISION: D
VS
DEFENDANT :   Bader   Matthew
AKA(S)   :   Nick

IN THE NAME AND BY AUTHORITY OF THE STATE OF XXXXX, TO THE SHERRIFF OF SAID COUNTY AND THE DEPARTMENT OF CORRECTIONS OF SAID STATE, GREETING:

THE ABOVE NAMED DEFENDANT HAVING BEEN DULY CHARGED WITH THE OFFENSE SPECIFIED HEREIN IN THE ABOVE STYLED COURT, AND HAVING BEEN DULY CONVICTED AND ADJUDICATED GUILTY OF AND SENTENCE FOR SAID OFFENSE BY SAID COURT, AS APPEARS FROM THE ATTACHED CERTIFIED COPIES OF INFORMATION FILED JUDGMENT AND SENTENCE, AND FELONY DISPOSITION AND SENTENCE DATA FROM WHICH ARE HEREBY MADE PARTS HEROF;

NOW THEREFORE, THIS TO COMMAND YOU, THE SAID SHERIFF, TO TAKE AND KEEP, AND, WITHIN A REASONABLE TIME AFTER RECEIVING THIS COMMITMENT, SAFELY DELIVER THE SAID DEFENDANT, TOGETHER WITH ANY PERTINENT INVESTIGATION REPORT PREPARED IN THIS CASE, INTO THE CUSTODY OF THE DEPARTMENT OF CORRECTIONS OF THE STATE OF XXXXX: AND THIS IS TO COMMAND YOU, THE SAID DEPARTMENT OF CORRECTIONS, BY AND THROUGH YOUR SECRETARY, REGIONAL DIRECTORS, SUPERINTENDANTS, AND OTHER OFFICIALS, TO KEEP AND SAFELY IMPRISON THE SAID DEFENDANT FRO THE TERM OF SAID SENTENCE IN THE INSTITUTION IN THE STATE CORRECTIONAL SYSTEM TO WHICH YOU, THE SAID DEPARTMENT OF CORRECTIONS, MAY CAUSE THE SAID DEFENDANT TO BE CONVEYED OR THEREAFTER TRANSFERRED. AND THESE PRESENTS SHALL BE YOUR AUTHORITY FOR THE SAME. HEREIN NOT FAIL.

         WITNESS THE HONORABLE JEREMY PARKER
         JUDGE OF THE SAID COURT, AS ALSO CONNIE EVANS
         CLERK, AND THE SEAL THEREOF, THIS
         24th DAY OF JUNE 20XX-3

BY: *Margaret Mills*
DEPUTY CLERK

IN THE FIRST JUDICIAL CIRCUIT IN AND FOR
CALUSA COUNTY, STATE OF XXXXX

CIRCUIT CRIMINAL DIVISON

STATE OF XXXXX   DIVISION: D
v.
MATTHEW BADER   CASE NUMBER: 20XX(-3)1978
DEFENDANT

CERTIFICATE OF SERVICE

I, Connie Evans, Clerk of the Circuit Court of the County of Calusa, State of XXXXX, having by law the custody of the seal and all records, books, documents and papers of or appertaining to the Circuit Court, do hereby certify that a true and correct copy of the Judgment and Sentence has been hand delivered to the State Attorney and mailed to the Defense Attorney.

IN WITNESS WHEREOF, I have hereunto set my hand and seal of said Circuit Court, this 24th day of June A.D. 20XX-3.

                                                   CONNIE EVANS
                                                   As Clerk of Circuit Court

                                                   Margaret Mills
                                                   As Deputy Clerk
                                                   Circuit Criminal Division

IN THE CIRCUIT COURT, 1ST JUDICIAL CIRCUIT
IN AND FOR CALUSA COUNTY, XXXXX
DIVISION : D
CASE NUMBER : 20XX(-3)1978

STATE OF XXXXX
VS
Matthew Bader
DEFENDANT

--JUDGMENT--

THE DEFENDANT, Matthew Bader, BEING PERSONALLY BEFORE
THIS COURT REPRESENTED WITH
PRIVATE ATTORNEY
Raymond Tillery, Esquire
THE ATTORNEY OF RECORD AND THE STATE REPRESENTED BY ASSISTANT STATE ATTORNEY
Lee Heller-Pearlman, AND HAVING

Been tried and found guilty by a jury of the following crime(s): 1

COUNT	CRIME	STATUTE	COURT ACTION	DATE
1	Possession of a Controlled Substance, to wit, COCAINE	80112	GUILTY	16 May 20XX-3

And no cause being shown why the defendant should not be adjudicated guilty, it is ordered that the defendant is hereby adjudicated guilty of the above crime(s).

Washington v. Hartwell

DEFENDANT Matthew Bader

Division : D
Case Number : 20XX(-3)1978
OBTS Number : 23488721

-----SENTENCE-----

THE DEFENDANT, BEING PERSONALLY BEFORE THIS COURT, ACCOMPANIED BY THE DEFENDANT'S ATTORNEY OF RECORD, PRIVATE ATTORNEY Raymond Tillery, Esquire
AND HAVING BEEN ADJUDGED GUILTY HEREIN, AND THE COURT HAVING BEEN GIVEN THE DEFENDANT AN OPPORTUNITY TO BE HEARD AND TO OFFER MATTERS IN MITIGATION OF SENTENCE, AND TO SHOW CAUSE WHY THE DEFENDANT SHOULD NOT BE SENTENCED AS PROVIDED BY LAW AND NO CAUSE BEING SHOWN

IT IS THE SENTENCE OF THIS COURT THAT THE DEFENDANT:

Pay a fine of $500.00, pursuant to appropriate XXXXX Statutes.
Is hereby committed to the custody of the Department of Corrections for a term of: 1 Year, 6 Months

-----OTHER PROVISIONS-----

AS TO COUNT(S) : 1
THE FOLLOWING MANDATORY/MINIMUM PROVISIONS APPLY TO THE SENTENCE IMPOSED :

JAIL CREDIT: It is further ordered that the defendant shall be allowed a total of 275 DAYS as credit for time incarcerated before imposition of this sentence.

DEFENDANT Matthew Bader

Division : D
Case Number : 20XX(-3)1978
OBTS Number : 23488721

-----OTHER PROVISIONS-----

Sentencing guidelines filed.

IN THE EVENT THE ABOVE SENTENCE IS TO THE DEPARTMENT OF CORRECTIONS, THE SHERIFF OF CALUSA COUNTY, XXXXX, IS HEREBY ORDERED AND DIRECTED TO DELIVER THE DEFENDANT TO THE DEPARTMENT OF CORRECTIONS AT THE FACILITY DESIGNATED BY THE DEPARTMENT TOGETHER WITH A COPY OF THIS JUDGMENT AND SENTENCE AND ANY OTHER DOCUMENTS SPECIFIED BY XXXXX STATUTE THE DEFENDANT IN OPEN COURT WAS ADVISED OF THE RIGHT TO APPEAL FROM THIS SENTENCE BY FILING NOTICE OF APPEAL WITHIN 30 DAYS FROM THIS DATE WITH THE CLERK OF THIS COURT AND THE DEFENDANT'S RIGHT TO THE ASSISTANCE OF COUNSEL IN TAKING THE APPEAL AT THE EXPENSE OF THE STATE SHOWING OF INDIGENCY.
DONE AND ORDERED IN CALUSA COUNTY, XXXXX, THIS 24TH DAY OF June 20XX-3

State of XXXXX
UNIFORM COMMITMENT TO CUSTODY
OF DEPARTMENT OF CORRECTIONS

THE CIRCUIT COURT OF CALUSA COUNTY, IN THE SPRING TERM of 20XX-10
IN THE CASE OF:

STATE OF XXXXX   CASE ID : 20XX(-11)1898   DIVISION: D
VS
DEFENDANT :   Rebecca   Hartwell
AKA(S)   :

IN THE NAME AND BY AUTHORITY OF THE STATE OF XXXXX, TO THE SHERIFF OF SAID COUNTY AND THE DEPARTMENT OF CORRECTIONS OF SAID STATE, GREETING:

THE ABOVE NAMED DEFENDANT HAVING BEEN DULY CHARGED WITH THE OFFENSE SPECIFIED HEREIN IN THE ABOVE STYLED COURT, AND HAVING BEEN DULY CONVICTED AND ADJUDICATED GUILTY OF AND SENTENCE FOR SAID OFFENSE BY SAID COURT, AS APPEARS FROM THE ATTACHED CERTIFIED COPIES OF INFORMATION FILED JUDGMENT AND SENTENCE, AND FELONY DISPOSITION AND SENTENCE DATA FROM WHICH ARE HEREBY MADE PARTS HEROF;

NOW THEREFORE, THIS TO COMMAND YOU, THE SAID SHERIFF, TO TAKE AND KEEP, AND, WITHIN A REASONABLE TIME AFTER RECEIVING THIS COMMITMENT, SAFELY DELIVER THE SAID DEFENDANT, TOGETHER WITH ANY PERTINENT INVESTIGATION REPORT PREPARED IN THIS CASE, INTO THE CUSTODY OF THE DEPARTMENT OF CORRECTIONS OF THE STATE OF XXXXX: AND THIS IS TO COMMAND YOU, THE SAID DEPARTMENT OF CORRECTIONS, BY AND THROUGH YOUR SECRETARY, REGIONAL DIRECTORS, SUPERINTENDANTS, AND OTHER OFFICIALS, TO KEEP AND SAFELY IMPRISON THE SAID DEFENDANT FRO THE TERM OF SAID SENTENCE IN THE INSTITUTION IN THE STATE CORRECTIONAL SYSTEM TO WHICH YOU, THE SAID DEPARTMENT OF CORRECTIONS, MAY CAUSE THE SAID DEFENDANT TO BE CONVEYED OR THEREAFTER TRANSFERRED. AND THESE PRESENTS SHALL BE YOUR AUTHORITY FOR THE SAME. HEREIN NOT FAIL.

           WITNESS THE HONORABLE JEREMY PARKER
           JUDGE OF THE SAID COURT, AS ALSO CONNIE EVANS
           CLERK, AND THE SEAL THEREOF, THIS
           21st DAY OF January 20XX-10

BY: *Margaret Mills*
DEPUTY CLERK

IN THE FIRST JUDICIAL CIRCUIT IN AND FOR
CALUSA COUNTY, STATE OF XXXXX

CIRCUIT CRIMINAL DIVISON

STATE OF XXXXX   DIVISION: D
v.
<u>Rebecca Hartwell</u>   CASE NUMBER: 20XX(-11)1898
DEFENDANT

CERTIFICATE OF SERVICE

    I, Connie Evans, Clerk of the Circuit Court of the County of Calusa, State of XXXXX, having by law the custody of the seal and all records, books, documents and papers of or appertaining to the Circuit Court, do hereby certify that a true and correct copy of the Judgment and Sentence has been hand delivered to the State Attorney and mailed to the Defense Attorney.

    IN WITNESS WHEREOF, I have hereunto set my hand and seal of said Circuit Court, this 21st day of January A.D. 20XX-10.

CONNIE EVANS
As Clerk of Circuit Court

Margaret Mills

As Deputy Clerk
Circuit Criminal Division

IN THE CIRCUIT COURT, 1ST JUDICIAL CIRCUIT
IN AND FOR CALUSA COUNTY, XXXXX
DIVISION : D
CASE NUMBER : 20XX(-11)1898

STATE OF XXXXX
VS
Rebecca Hartwell
DEFENDANT

------JUDGMENT------

THE DEFENDANT, Rebecca Hartwell, BEING PERSONALLY BEFORE THIS COURT REPRESENTED WITH PRIVATE ATTORNEY
John Head, Esquire
THE ATTORNEY OF RECORD AND THE STATE REPRESENTED BY ASSISTANT STATE ATTORNEY
George Peabody Smalley, AND HAVING

Been tried and found guilty by a jury of the following crime(s): 1

COUNT	CRIME	STATUTE	COURT ACTION	DATE
1	Reckless Driving	80120	GUILTY	13 Dec 20XX-11

And no cause being shown why the defendant should not be adjudicated guilty, it is ordered that the defendant is hereby adjudicated guilty of the above crime(s).

DEFENDANT Rebecca Hartwell

Division : D
Case Number : 20XX(-11)1898
OBTS Number : 32323496

---SENTENCE---

THE DEFENDANT, BEING PERSONALLY BEFORE THIS COURT, ACCOMPANIED BY THE DEFENDANT'S ATTORNEY OF RECORD, PRIVATE ATTORNEY John Head, Esquire
AND HAVING BEEN ADJUDGED GUILTY HEREIN, AND THE COURT HAVING BEEN GIVEN THE DEFENDANT AN OPPORTUNITY TO BE HEARD AND TO OFFER MATTERS IN MITIGATION OF SENTENCE, AND TO SHOW CAUSE WHY THE DEFENDANT SHOULD NOT BE SENTENCED AS PROVIDED BY LAW AND NO CAUSE BEING SHOWN

IT IS THE SENTENCE OF THIS COURT THAT THE DEFENDANT:

Pay a fine of $1500.00, pursuant to appropriate XXXXX Statutes.
Is hereby committed to the custody of the Department of Corrections for a term of: 24 Months, 18 months of said sentence to be suspended pending successful completion of 4 years probation.

---OTHER PROVISIONS---

AS TO COUNT(S) : 1
THE FOLLOWING MANDATORY/MINIMUM PROVISIONS APPLY TO THE SENTENCE IMPOSED :

None

DEFENDANT Rebecca Hartwell

Division : D
Case Number : 20XX(-11)1898
OBTS Number : 32323497

---OTHER PROVISIONS---

Sentencing guidelines filed.

IN THE EVENT THE ABOVE SENTENCE IS TO THE DEPARTMENT OF CORRECTIONS, THE SHERIFF OF CALUSA COUNTY, XXXXX, IS HEREBY ORDERED AND DIRECTED TO DELIVER THE DEFENDANT TO THE DEPARTMENT OF CORRECTIONS AT THE FACILITY DESIGNATED BY THE DEPARTMENT TOGETHER WITH A COPY OF THIS JUDGMENT AND SENTENCE AND ANY OTHER DOCUMENTS SPECIFIED BY XXXXX STATUTE
THE DEFENDANT IN OPEN COURT WAS ADVISED OF THE RIGHT TO APPEAL FROM THIS SENTENCE BY FILING NOTICE OF APPEAL WITHIN 30 DAYS FROM THIS DATE WITH THE CLERK OF THIS COURT AND THE DEFENDANT'S RIGHT TO THE ASSISTANCE OF COUNSEL IN TAKING THE APPEAL AT THE EXPENSE OF THE STATE SHOWIN OF INDIGENCY.
DONE AND ORDERED IN CALUSA COUNTY, XXXXX, THIS 21st DAY OF January 20XX-10

State of XXXXX
UNIFORM COMMITMENT TO CUSTODY
OF DEPARTMENT OF CORRECTIONS

THE CIRCUIT COURT OF CALUSA COUNTY, IN THE SPRING TERM of 20XX-4
IN THE CASE OF:

STATE OF XXXXX   CASE ID : 20XX(-5)1918   DIVISION: D
v.
DEFENDANT :   Charissa   Washington
AKA(S)   :   Rissa

IN THE NAME AND BY AUTHORITY OF THE STATE OF XXXXX, TO THE SHERRIFF OF SAID COUNTY AND THE DEPARTMENT OF CORRECTIONS OF SAID STATE, GREETING:

THE ABOVE NAMED DEFENDANT HAVING BEEN DULY CHARGED WITH THE OFFENSE SPECIFIED HEREIN IN THE ABOVE STYLED COURT, AND HAVING BEEN DULY CONVICTED AND ADJUDICATED GUILTY OF AND SENTENCE FOR SAID OFFENSE BY SAID COURT, AS APPEARS FROM THE ATTACHED CERTIFIED COPIES OF INFORMATION FILED JUDGMENT AND SENTENCE, AND FELONY DISPOSITION AND SENTENCE DATA FROM WHICH ARE HEREBY MADE PARTS HEROF;

NOW THEREFORE, THIS TO COMMAND YOU, THE SAID SHERIFF, TO TAKE AND KEEP, AND, WITHIN A REASONABLE TIME AFTER RECEIVING THIS COMMITMENT, SAFELY DELIVER THE SAID DEFENDANT, TOGETHER WITH ANY PERTINENT INVESTIGATION REPORT PREPARED IN THIS CASE, INTO THE CUSTODY OF THE DEPARTMENT OF CORRECTIONS OF THE STATE OF XXXXX: AND THIS IS TO COMMAND YOU, THE SAID DEPARTMENT OF CORRECTIONS, BY AND THROUGH YOUR SECRETARY, REGIONAL DIRECTORS, SUPERINTENDANTS, AND OTHER OFFICIALS, TO KEEP AND SAFELY IMPRISON THE SAID DEFENDANT FRO THE TERM OF SAID SENTENCE IN THE INSTITUTION IN THE STATE CORRECTIONAL SYSTEM TO WHICH YOU, THE SAID DEPARTMENT OF CORRECTIONS, MAY CAUSE THE SAID DEFENDANT TO BE CONVEYED OR THEREAFTER TRANSFERRED. AND THESE PRESENTS SHALL BE YOUR AUTHORITY FOR THE SAME. HEREIN NOT FAIL.

          WITNESS THE HONORABLE JEREMY PARKER
          JUDGE OF THE SAID COURT, AS ALSO CONNIE EVANS
          CLERK, AND THE SEAL THEREOF, THIS
          21st DAY OF April 20XX-4

          BY: *Margaret Mills*
          DEPUTY CLERK

IN THE FIRST JUDICIAL CIRCUIT IN AND FOR
CALUSA COUNTY, STATE OF XXXXX

CIRCUIT CRIMINAL DIVISON

STATE OF XXXXX   DIVISION: D
v.
<u>Charissa Washington</u>   CASE NUMBER: 20XX(-5)1918
DEFENDANT

CERTIFICATE OF SERVICE

    I, Connie Evans, Clerk of the Circuit Court of the County of Calusa, State of XXXXX, having by law the custody of the seal and all records, books, documents and papers of or appertaining to the Circuit Court, do hereby certify that a true and correct copy of the Judgment and Sentence has been hand delivered to the State Attorney and mailed to the Defense Attorney.

    IN WITNESS WHEREOF, I have hereunto set my hand and seal of said Circuit Court, this 21st day of April A.D. 20XX-4.

                                    CONNIE EVANS
                                    As Clerk of Circuit Court

                                    <u>*Margaret Mills*</u>
                                    As Deputy Clerk
                                    Circuit Criminal Division

IN THE CIRCUIT COURT, 1ST JUDICIAL CIRCUIT
IN AND FOR CALUSA COUNTY, XXXXX
DIVISION   : D
CASE NUMBER : 20XX(-5)1918

STATE OF XXXXX
v.
Charissa Washington
DEFENDANT

--JUDGMENT---

THE DEFENDANT, Charissa Washington   BEING PERSONALLY BEFORE
THIS COURT REPRESENTED WITH
PRIVATE ATTORNEY
Norm Pearson, Esquire
THE ATTORNEY OF RECORD AND THE STATE REPRESENTED BY ASSISTANT STATE ATTORNEY
George Peabody Smalley, AND HAVING

Been tried and found guilty by a jury of the following crime(s): 1

COUNT	CRIME	STATUTE	COURT ACTION	DATE
1	Filing a false police report	80107	GUILTY	21 April 20XX-4

And no cause being shown why the defendant should not be adjudicated guilty, it is ordered that the defendant is hereby adjudicated guilty of the above crime(s).

Washington v. Hartwell

DEFENDANT Charissa Washington

             Division : D
             Case Number : 20XX(-5)1918
             OBTS Number : 37624344

---SENTENCE---

THE DEFENDANT, BEING PERSONALLY BEFORE THIS COURT, ACCOMPANIED BY THE DEFENDANT'S ATTORNEY OF RECORD, PRIVATE ATTORNEY Norm Pearson, Esquire
AND HAVING BEEN ADJUDGED GUILTY HEREIN, AND THE COURT HAVING BEEN GIVEN THE DEFENDANT AN OPPORTUNITY TO BE HEARD AND TO OFFER MATTERS IN MITIGATION OF SENTENCE, AND TO SHOW CAUSE WHY THE DEFENDANT SHOULD NOT BE SENTENCED AS PROVIDED BY LAW AND NO CAUSE BEING SHOWN

IT IS THE SENTENCE OF THIS COURT THAT THE DEFENDANT:

Pay a fine of $1500.00, pursuant to appropriate XXXXX Statutes.
Is hereby committed to the custody of the Department of Corrections for a term of: 12 Months, sentence to be suspended pending successful completion of 4 years probation.

---OTHER PROVISIONS---

AS TO COUNT(S) : 1
THE FOLLOWING MANDATORY/MINIMUM PROVISIONS APPLY TO THE SENTENCE IMPOSED :

None

DEFENDANT Charissa Washington

             Division : D
             Case Number : 20XX(-5)1918
             OBTS Number : 37624344

---OTHER PROVISIONS---

Sentencing guidelines filed.

IN THE EVENT THE ABOVE SENTENCE IS TO THE DEPARTMENT OF CORRECTIONS, THE SHERIFF OF CALUSA COUNTY, XXXXX, IS HEREBY ORDERED AND DIRECTED TO DELIVER THE DEFENDANT TO THE DEPARTMENT OF CORRECTIONS AT THE FACILITY DESIGNATED BY THE DEPARTMENT TOGETHER WITH A COPY OF THIS JUDGMENT AND SENTENCE AND ANY OTHER DOCUMENTS SPECIFIED BY XXXXX STATUTE
THE DEFENDANT IN OPEN COURT WAS ADVISED OF THE RIGHT TO APPEAL FROM THIS SENTENCE BY FILING NOTICE OF APPEAL WITHIN 30 DAYS FROM THIS DATE WITH THE CLERK OF THIS COURT AND THE DEFENDANT'S RIGHT TO THE ASSISTANCE OF COUNSEL IN TAKING THE APPEAL AT THE EXPENSE OF THE STATE SHOWIN OF INDIGENCY.
DONE AND ORDERED IN CALUSA COUNTY, XXXXX, THIS 21st DAY OF April 20XX-4

State of XXXXX
UNIFORM COMMITMENT TO CUSTODY
OF DEPARTMENT OF CORRECTIONS

THE CIRCUIT COURT OF CALUSA COUNTY, IN THE SPRING TERM of 20XX-8
IN THE CASE OF:

STATE OF XXXXX   CASE ID : 20XX(-6)2132   DIVISION: D
VS
DEFENDANT : Charissa Washington
AKA(S) : Rissa

IN THE NAME AND BY AUTHORITY OF THE STATE OF XXXXX, TO THE SHERRIFF OF SAID COUNTY AND THE DEPARTMENT OF CORRECTIONS OF SAID STATE, GREETING:

THE ABOVE NAMED DEFENDANT HAVING BEEN DULY CHARGED WITH THE OFFENSE SPECIFIED HEREIN IN THE ABOVE STYLED COURT, AND HAVING BEEN DULY CONVICTED AND ADJUDICATED GUILTY OF AND SENTENCE FOR SAID OFFENSE BY SAID COURT, AS APPEARS FROM THE ATTACHED CERTIFIED COPIES OF INFORMATION FILED JUDGMENT AND SENTENCE, AND FELONY DISPOSITION AND SENTENCE DATA FROM WHICH ARE HEREBY MADE PARTS HEROF;

NOW THEREFORE, THIS TO COMMAND YOU, THE SAID SHERIFF, TO TAKE AND KEEP, AND, WITHIN A REASONABLE TIME AFTER RECEIVING THIS COMMITMENT, SAFELY DELIVER THE SAID DEFENDANT, TOGETHER WITH ANY PERTINENT INVESTIGATION REPORT PREPARED IN THIS CASE, INTO THE CUSTODY OF THE DEPARTMENT OF CORRECTIONS OF THE STATE OF XXXXX: AND THIS IS TO COMMAND YOU, THE SAID DEPARTMENT OF CORRECTIONS, BY AND THROUGH YOUR SECRETARY, REGIONAL DIRECTORS, SUPERINTENDANTS, AND OTHER OFFICIALS, TO KEEP AND SAFELY IMPRISON THE SAID DEFENDANT FRO THE TERM OF SAID SENTENCE IN THE INSTITUTION IN THE STATE CORRECTIONAL SYSTEM TO WHICH YOU, THE SAID DEPARTMENT OF CORRECTIONS, MAY CAUSE THE SAID DEFENDANT TO BE CONVEYED OR THEREAFTER TRANSFERRED. AND THESE PRESENTS SHALL BE YOUR AUTHORITY FOR THE SAME. HEREIN NOT FAIL

WITNESS THE HONORABLE JEREMY PARKER
JUDGE OF THE SAID COURT, AS ALSO CONNIE EVANS
CLERK, AND THE SEAL THEREOF, THIS
24th DAY OF June 20XX-5

BY: *Margaret Mills*
DEPUTY CLERK

IN THE FIRST JUDICIAL CIRCUIT IN AND FOR
CALUSA COUNTY, STATE OF XXXXX

CIRCUIT CRIMINAL DIVISON

STATE OF XXXXX   DIVISION: D
v.
<u>CHARISSA WASHINGTON</u>   CASE NUMBER: 20XX(-6)2132
DEFENDANT

CERTIFICATE OF SERVICE

    I, Connie Evans, Clerk of the Circuit Court of the County of Calusa, State of XXXXX, having by law the custody of the seal and all records, books, documents and papers of or appertaining to the Circuit Court, do hereby certify that a true and correct copy of the Judgment and Sentence has been hand delivered to the State Attorney and mailed to the Defense Attorney.

    IN WITNESS WHEREOF, I have hereunto set my hand and seal of said Circuit Court, this 24th day of June A.D. 20XX-5.

CONNIE EVANS
As Clerk of Circuit Court

Margaret Mills

As Deputy Clerk
Circuit Criminal Division

IN THE CIRCUIT COURT, 1ST JUDICIAL CIRCUIT
IN AND FOR CALUSA COUNTY, XXXXX
DIVISION   : D
CASE NUMBER : 20XX(-6)2132

STATE OF XXXXX
VS
Charissa Washington
DEFENDANT

---JUDGMENT---

THE DEFENDANT, Charissa Washington,   BEING PERSONALLY BEFORE
THIS COURT REPRESENTED WITH
PRIVATE ATTORNEY
Angelia Solomon, Esquire
THE ATTORNEY OF RECORD AND THE STATE REPRESENTED BY ASSISTANT STATE ATTORNEY
George Peabody Smalley, AND HAVING

Been tried and found guilty by a jury of the following crime(s): 1

COUNT	CRIME	STATUTE	COURT ACTION	DATE
1	Possession of a Controlled Substance, to wit, MARIJUANA	80112	GUILTY	16 April 20XX-6

And no cause being shown why the defendant should not be adjudicated guilty, it is ordered that the defendant is hereby adjudicated guilty of the above crime(s).

DEFENDANT Charissa Washington

Division : D
Case Number : 20XX(-6)2132
OBTS Number : 97421119

------SENTENCE------

THE DEFENDANT, BEING PERSONALLY BEFORE THIS COURT, ACCOMPANIED BY THE DEFENDANT'S ATTORNEY OF RECORD, PRIVATE ATTORNEY Angelia Solomon, Esquire
AND HAVING BEEN ADJUDGED GUILTY HEREIN, AND THE COURT HAVING BEEN GIVEN THE DEFENDANT AN OPPORTUNITY TO BE HEARD AND TO OFFER MATTERS IN MITIGATION OF SENTENCE, AND TO SHOW CAUSE WHY THE DEFENDANT SHOULD NOT BE SENTENCED AS PROVIDED BY LAW AND NO CAUSE BEING SHOWN

IT IS THE SENTENCE OF THIS COURT THAT THE DEFENDANT:

Pay a fine of $2000.00, pursuant to appropriate XXXXX Statutes.
Is hereby committed to the custody of the Department of Corrections for a term of: 3 Years, sentence to be suspended pending successful completion of 6 years probation.

------OTHER PROVISIONS------

AS TO COUNT(S) : 1
THE FOLLOWING MANDATORY/MINIMUM PROVISIONS APPLY TO THE SENTENCE IMPOSED :

DEFENDANT Charissa Washington

Division : D

Case Number : 20XX(-6)2132
OBTS Number : 97421119

------OTHER PROVISIONS------

Sentencing guidelines filed.

IN THE EVENT THE ABOVE SENTENCE IS TO THE DEPARTMENT OF CORRECTIONS, THE SHERIFF OF CALUSA COUNTY, XXXXX, IS HEREBY ORDERED AND DIRECTED TO DELIVER THE DEFENDANT TO THE DEPARTMENT OF CORRECTIONS AT THE FACILITY DESIGNATED BY THE DEPARTMENT TOGETHER WITH A COPY OF THIS JUDGMENT AND SENTENCE AND ANY OTHER DOCUMENTS SPECIFIED BY XXXXX STATUTE
THE DEFENDANT IN OPEN COURT WAS ADVISED OF THE RIGHT TO APPEAL FROM THIS SENTENCE BY FILING NOTICE OF APPEAL WITHIN 30 DAYS FROM THIS DATE WITH THE CLERK OF THIS COURT AND THE DEFENDANT'S RIGHT TO THE ASSISTANCE OF COUNSEL IN TAKING THE APPEAL AT THE EXPENSE OF THE STATE SHOWIN OF INDIGENCY.
DONE AND ORDERED IN CALUSA COUNTY, XXXXX, THIS 24TH DAY OF June 20XX-5

Evidence in Context:
Evidentiary Problems and Exercises

Chapter 6
Advocacy Assignments

1st Assignment – Introduction to Trial Advocacy	Professor_____ Trial Advocacy
Reading: Assigned Casebook "Fundamental Trial Advocacy," West Publishing (hereinafter FTA)	

1st Assignment:	Come to class prepared to actively participate in any of the introductory advocacy drills assigned by your instructor.
Process:	During classroom exercises you will begin to develop the fundamental skills of a competent advocate.
Outcome:	You will: • Leave class with an understanding of what is expected this semester. • Participate in all drills. • Leave class energized for the task before you.

In order for you to thoroughly understand and benefit from this course you must put aside your concerns about performance anxiety and "live in the moment." Consider this:

"Be yourself. All the other ones have been taken."

-Oscar Wilde-

These words make a great deal of sense to a new advocate. This process requires you to take the skills that you learn in class, through study and practice and then apply them in a persuasive fashion. True persuasiveness comes when you speak from a place of comfort and acceptance. That happens when you are most closely in tune with who you are and what you care about.

As you perform the introductory drills and exercises presented by your instructor take the time to center yourself and participate fully - Doing so now will pay huge dividends down the road.

2nd Assignment – Cases Analysis	Professor
	Trial Advocacy
Reading:	FTA – Asking Questions, Case Analysis

2nd Assignment:	Prepare a written case analysis for the assigned cases. Practice the Basic Questioning Techniques prior to coming to class.
Process:	During classroom exercises you will share your case analysis as requested by the instructor.
Outcome:	You will: • Leave class with an understanding of how case analysis works. • Prepare case analysis for the assigned cases. • Participate in all drills.

In order for you to thoroughly understand and benefit from the follow on advocacy exercises in this course you must first properly develop a thorough case analysis. Do this now; it pays of huge down the line. You must be prepared to provide your advocacy professor with a 3-6 minute oral presentation on the results of your case analysis. At a minimum this presentation should include:

- Your factual theory - the good facts that mean you win, the bad facts you must neutralize and the facts you expect your opponent to use.

- Your legal theory – the law that allows your facts to prevail.

- Moral Theme – that sense of injustice that makes the jury want to vote in your favor. It is the wrong that they can right by deciding the case your way.

In addition to the oral presentation your advocacy professor has the ability to test, push, challenge you as he or she sees fit during this period. Expect the unexpected in this second class session. You should be on your feet and talking, even if you aren't quite sure what you are saying yet. This is a chance to get your feet wet in a relatively unstructured exercise – take advantage of it. You may see other drills that your advocacy professor decides to use to make certain teaching points. Learn from them. It is important that you begin to lay the foundation now for preparation, preparation and preparation. Read the chapter on case analysis and ask questions about them during class.

3rd Assignment – Opening Statements	Professor_____
	Trial Advocacy
Reading: FTA – Opening Statements	

3rd Assignment:	Prepare a written diagram/outline of your opening statement. This document should be sufficient to show your instructor that you have taken the time to prepare but not be so over written that all you can use it for is to just read it.
Process:	During classroom exercises you present your opening statement to the rest of the class while they are acting as jurors.
Outcome:	You will: • Present an opening statement. • Understand how to prepare an opening. • Take away one critique point to make you better the next time you perform an opening statement

Opening Statements should be 5 to 6 minutes in length. In planning your opening statement, think carefully about your theory of the case and the most effective structure for the organization of your opening statement. **REMEMBER TO TELL THE STORY OF THE FACTS!** Use the storytelling techniques outlined in the text and the advocacy presentation lectures. Methods of delivering the story of the facts might include a narrative, "flashback," witness by witness, or some combination of these styles. The preferred methodology is a persuasive story of the facts told in the first person using the present tense verbs to set the jury in the middle of the action.

Remember to emphasize the major factual points which support your theory of the case. How will you address the weaknesses in your case?

In addition to the content of your opening statement, you must also plan its presentation. You may not "read" the opening statement and you should avoid the obvious use of notes. If you wish, you may have a single sheet of paper on the lectern which contains a "key word" outline of the opening statement - to be used only as necessary. Whether or not you decide to take the outline to the lectern with you, you must prepare one to be turned in at the end of the class on the date you make your opening statement. You will be recorded for this exercise.

All students must prepare opening statements as assigned by your instructor based upon the case files of State v. Alexander and Washington v. Hartwell.

Your trial advocacy professor will determine the order in which you will perform. Advanced students should be prepared to provide the opening statement for the opposing side if asked.

4th Assignment – Direct Examination	Professor_____
	Trial Advocacy
Reading:	FTA – Basic Questioning Techniques, Direct Examination

4th Assignment:	Prepare a written diagram/outline of your direct examination. This document should be sufficient to show your instructor that you have taken the time to prepare but not be so over written that all you can use it for is to just read the questions to the witness.
Process:	During classroom exercises conduct direct examination of witnesses as assigned by the instructor.
Outcome:	You will: • Conduct a direct examination. • Understand how to prepare a direct. • Take away one critique point to make you better the next time you conduct a direct examination.

For this assignment, the emphasis will be on proper direct examination techniques. We will perform Direct Exams over two class periods. Despite the fact that we will take two class periods to learn direct examination every student must be prepared to conduct direct examinations each class period. Remember there is no such thing as a "pass rule" in the courtroom.

The key points you wish to discuss in each Direct Examination are to be **prepared in writing and are to be handed in at the end of the class in which you conduct your direct examination.** When preparing your examination plan be sure to incorporate the principles of direct examination outlined in the text and discussed in the ARC presentations.

You should not necessarily write out the questions you intend to ask each witness. Be prepared to play the role of any witness who may be called that day. Remember to think about your theory of the case when preparing direct examination. Also, employ a logical structure for the direct (ex., personal background of witness, then scene description, action, etc...). Use proper **non-leading, open-ended questions** which begin with: who, what, when, where, why, how, describe, explain, tell us. Avoid the "What happened next?" question and the use of questions beginning with "did, do, was, and were." While not technically "leading," these questions are not an effective way to have the witness do the testifying instead of the advocate.

Your advocacy instructor will assign which witnesses you will use during your direct examinations.

5th Assignment – Cross Examination	**Professor**_____ **Trial Advocacy**
Reading:	FTA – Basic Questioning Techniques, Cross Examination

5th Assignment:	Prepare a written diagram/outline of your cross examination. This document should be sufficient to show your instructor that you have taken the time to prepare but not be so over written that all you can use it for is to just read the questions to the witness.
Process:	During classroom exercises conduct cross examination of witnesses as assigned by the instructor.
Outcome:	You will: • Conduct a cross examination. • Understand how to prepare a cross examination. • Use the one fact leading to a conclusion method of cross examination discussed in the text and ARC presentations.

For this assignment, the emphasis will be on proper cross-examination technique. Cross Exams will be spread out over 2 class days and everyone in the class should be prepared to do a cross exam of all the witnesses identified by your instructor. The key points you wish to discuss in Cross Examination are to be **prepared in writing and handed in at the end of the class in which you conduct your cross examination.**

You must be prepared to play any of the assigned witnesses.

When preparing for cross-examination you may assume that the witness testified on direct examination consistently with their previous statements contained within the case file. For cross-examination you MUST use short, incremental, one fact questions that lead inexorably to your goal question. You must be able to explain to your advocacy professor the moral theme, legal theory or factual theory that is supported by your cross examination questions.

Your advocacy instructor will assign which witnesses you will use during your cross examinations.

6th Assignment – Diagrams	Professor_____
	Trial Advocacy
Reading:	FTA – Basic Questioning Techniques, Direct Examinations, Exhibits

6th Assignment:	Prepare your plan to admit a diagram. Use the principles outlined in the materials on exhibits. You should also prepare a written plan of presentation. This document should be sufficient to show your instructor that you have taken the time to prepare but not over produced.
Process:	During classroom exercises conduct a direct examination of a witness designed to admit and use a diagram. The witness will be assigned by the instructor.
Outcome:	You will: • Conduct a direct examination to admit a diagram. • Lay the proper foundation for a diagram. • Use the techniques provided in the text for persuasive use of a diagram after it has been admitted.

You will perform a direct-examination with diagrams. The diagrams will be introduced in the direct examination but may also be used during the cross examination. Diagrams are best used to *reinforce* and clarify testimony. Structure the direct accordingly. Similarly, cross examination using the diagram often deteriorates into a repeat of the direct exam. Try to avoid this pitfall. **Limit your direct and cross examinations to the use of the diagram**, i.e. for the direct, begin with questions which "set up" the use/need for the diagram, then ask questions of the witness utilizing the diagram. You should construct your direct examination to have the witness actually "step down" to utilize the diagram. You may have the witness simply point and describe what he/she is pointing to or mark on the diagram itself. Remember - whatever is gestured to or marked must be done in such a manner that it is accurately recorded in the trial record.

Even though each person is assigned only a direct, everyone should come prepared to "jump-in" and follow up with a cross-examination of the listed witnesses. The cross examination should focus on questions related to the diagram, the witness' ability to perceive or know about the diagram, etc.

NOTE: If available, the elmo may be used to enlarge your diagrams. You need to bring your own markers. Think "color" for the record. Don't forget to prepare your witness for this assignment.

Your advocacy instructor will assign which witnesses you will use for admitting diagrams.

7th Assignment – Exhibits	Professor_____
	Trial Advocacy
Reading:	FTA – Basic Questioning Techniques, Direct Examinations, Exhibits

7th Assignment:	Prepare your plan to admit exhibits from your assigned case file. Your analysis should focus on the foundational requirements for each exhibit and the advocacy skills required to lay that foundation. Use the principles outlined in the materials on exhibits. You should also prepare a written plan of presentation.
Process:	During classroom exercises conduct a direct examination of a witness designed to admit and use the exhibit assigned by the instructor.
Outcome:	You will: • Conduct a direct examination to admit exhibits. • Lay the proper foundation for the exhibit. • Use the techniques provided in the text for persuasive use of an exhibit after it has been admitted.

In this assignment, our goal is to learn the foundational questions that are required for different types of exhibits. Concentrate on preparing an examination which includes questions that logically lead to the introduction of the assigned exhibit, the necessary foundational questions for the exhibit, and follow-up questions regarding the exhibit. As the advocate attempting to introduce the exhibit, you may need more than one witness for each exhibit (even though only one witness is listed). If you need more than the listed witness, then you must be prepared to call the additional witness. **All advocates should be prepared to play the witness role for any exhibit identified by your instructor.** Remember: if you are examining a witness, it is acceptable and encouraged that you get with your witness in advance to prepare for the examination. Note that some assignments require the cross-examiner to introduce the exhibit - so no advance preparation can be done with the witness. Opposing advocates should be prepared to make all possible objections to the admissibility of the exhibits. You may also ask to conduct a limited voir dire if you believe you can establish that the witness is not qualified to authenticate the exhibit. Assume there are no stipulations regarding the admissibility of the exhibits.

Any exhibits not provided in the cases must be provided by the advocate.

8th Assignment – Impeachment with a Prior Conviction	Professor_____ Trial Advocacy
Reading:	FTA – Impeachment

8th Assignment:	Prepare your plan to impeach your assigned witness(es) with a prior conviction. Your analysis should focus on the proper means of impeachment with a conviction, focusing on the evidentiary requirements. Use the principles outlined in the materials on impeachment. You should also prepare a written plan of presentation.
Process:	During classroom exercises conduct a cross examination of a witness based upon an admissible conviction.
Outcome:	You will: • Conduct a cross examination to impeach with a prior conviction. • Lay the proper foundation for impeachment. • Be prepared to argue the admissibility of the conviction based upon objection by opposing counsel.

The witness identified by your instructor will be assumed to have testified on direct. You are to impeach that witness with the applicable record of conviction. Apply the federal rules of evidence when introducing the prior conviction.

The impeaching counsel should perform the part of the cross-examination dealing with prior convictions. Opposing counsel should be prepared to make objections to the admissibility of the convictions and to redirect the witness as to the prior conviction if appropriate. All students must turn in written copies of their planned examinations.

Students should prepare to perform any of these impeachments as assigned by their instructor.

9th Assignment – Impeachment with Character Evidence	Professor_____ Trial Advocacy
Reading:	FTA – Impeachment

9th Assignment:	Prepare your plan to impeach your assigned witness(es) with relevant character evidence. You must analyze your case file and identify the character evidence you wish to use in impeachment. It must be relevant and admitted in the proper format as required by the rules of evidence. Your analysis should focus on the proper means of impeachment with character evidence. Use the principles outlined in the materials on impeachment. You should also prepare a written plan of presentation.
Process:	During classroom exercises conduct a cross examination of a witness based upon an both relevant and admissible character evidence.
Outcome:	You will: • Conduct a cross examination to impeach with character evidence. • Lay the proper foundation for impeachment. • Be prepared to offer specific instances of conduct as allowed under the rules on re-direct examination of the witness.

The witness identified by your instructor will be assumed to have testified on direct. You are to impeach that witness with the relevant character evidence. Apply the federal rules of evidence when introducing the admissible character evidence. You should be capable of dealing with any objections from the bench or opposing counsel.

The impeaching counsel should perform the part of the cross-examination dealing with the relevant character evidence. Opposing counsel should be prepared to make objections to the admissibility of the character evidence and to conduct a re-direct to rehabilitate the opinion or reputation testimony with specific instances of good conduct.

Students should prepare to perform any of these impeachments as assigned by their instructor and to conduct redirect.

10th Assignment – Impeachment with a Prior Inconsistent Statement	Professor _____ Trial Advocacy
Reading:	FTA – Impeachment

10th Assignment:	Prepare your plan to impeach your assigned witness(es) with a prior inconsistent statement. You must analyze the prior statement of the witness so that you can identify the inconsistency and perform the impeachment. Your analysis should focus on both the proper means of impeachment with a prior inconsistent statement and the proper substantive inconsistency. Use the principles outlined in the materials on impeachment. You should also prepare a written plan of presentation.
Process:	During classroom exercises conduct a cross examination of a witness based upon a prior inconsistent statement.
Outcome:	You will: • Conduct a cross examination to impeach with a prior inconsistent statement. • Lay the proper foundation for impeachment. Use the 3 C's of Commit, Credit and Confront • Be prepared to conduct a short re-direct to rehabilitate the impeached witness.

Trial advocacy is an art, and perhaps no part of trial advocacy illustrates this more than impeachment by a prior inconsistent statement. There are many subtle impeachment techniques and trial lawyers sometimes differ on which are the most effective. Much depends upon the lawyer's analysis of the significance of the inconsistency, the experience of the witness being examined and the lawyer doing the examination, whether the witness is a party or a disinterested outsider, and what the trial judge will permit. Should the impeaching evidence be shown to the witness or read to the witness? What questions, if any, may be asked of the witness after the witness admits the inconsistency to make the greatest impact on the jury?

In this exercise you should focus on the basic method of impeachment referred to as the 3 C's as outlined in the trial advocacy text. We will expect you to showcase the fundamental concepts of impeachment with a prior inconsistent statement. You may differ from the suggested method, but only if you can explain to your advocacy instructor the reason for your modification. That modification should be based upon your analysis of the case with particular attention paid to your theories of the case.

11th Assignment – Advanced Direct & Cross of Experts	Professor_____ Trial Advocacy
Reading:	FTA – Experts

11th Assignment:	Prepare a direct examination and cross examination of an expert utilizing the principles outlined in the text.
Process:	During classroom exercises direct an expert as required by your case analysis. Pay attention to the purpose of the expert witness testimony and develop that testimony in light of the additional weight given to expert testimony under the rules of evidence. Be prepared to explain how your direct examination is tied to your case analysis. Prepare written materials of your planned direct and cross for review by your instructor.
Outcome:	You will: • Conduct Direct Examination of an expert witness • Conduct Cross Examination of an expert witness • Argue the qualifications and admissibility of Expert Witness Testimony as required by Daubert and the F.R.E.

In this assignment, we will practice a combination of several of the skills we have been learning throughout this semester. You must display a greater development of your direct and cross-examination skills, both in terms of performance and in the content of the examination. You will perform these skills within the context of a direct and cross-examination of an expert witness. Included in the direct examination should be (1) the establishment of the necessary foundation to qualify the witness to give expert testimony and (2) **the use of some sort of demonstrative exhibit** which fits within the scope of the expert's testimony. **You are to prepare and perform a <u>complete</u> direct examination of the assigned witness. Furthermore, each student should be prepared to be called on to cross-examine or play the witness role of each of the three experts.**

Cross-examiners should be prepared to **voir dire** the witness to challenge the witness' qualification as an expert, if appropriate, and also to conduct a full cross examination, which will be limited to the scope of the direct examination. This will help you focus on your listening skills.

Students playing the experts may not change or add to their qualifications (with the exception of providing dates missing from the resume if necessary), but are free to invent testimony and research methodology. <u>**You must prepare thoroughly for your expert witness roles in order to make the examinations effective. I strongly encourage you to work with a partner in class for this exercise, in your advocate and expert witness roles.**</u>

11th Assignment – Refreshing Recollection & Past Recollection Recorded	Professor_____ Trial Advocacy
Reading:	FTA – Recollections

11th Assignment:	Refresh the Recollection of a witness on direct examination after they have forgotten something that they had written down previously. You should review the relevant rules of evidence concerning refreshing recollection and past recollection recorded in preparation for this assignment.
Process:	During classroom exercises refresh the recollection of a witness on direct examination. When necessary transition from refreshing recollection to past recollection recorded as required.
Outcome:	You will: • Refresh a witness's recollection during direct examination. • Use Past Recollection Recorded to assist the witness in testifying. • Lay the proper foundation for refreshing recollection and past recollection recorded.

You will each conduct a *limited* **direct examination** of a witness on the topic indicated. Do not show your witness any documents or prior testimony unless needed to refresh his/her recollection. During the examination, the witness will (of course) have difficulty remembering some relevant piece(s) of information. (If the witness does not experience this difficulty—in this instance—you're not asking enough questions about your topic.)

To prepare for this assignment, think about another source of that information you might show the witness to refresh their recollection (deposition transcript, document, etc.) regardless of whether that item would otherwise be admissible. You will need to utilize *at least* one such document to practice refreshing the witness' recollection. As a last resort, you might get away with asking the witness a leading question. If the question calls for detail(s) that the witness is still incapable of remembering, even after being shown a document, you might try to read the pertinent contents of the document into evidence under Rule 803(5) of the Federal Rules of Evidence.

12th Assignment – Closing Arguments	Professor_____
	Trial Advocacy
Reading:	FTA – Closing Arguments

12th Assignment:	Present a closing argument utilizing the principles of closing arguments outlined in the text.
Process:	During classroom exercises deliver a closing argument that combines your legal theory, factual theory and moral theme in a persuasive fashion utilizing appropriate rhetorical techniques. You should prepare written materials supporting your argument. Do not forget to use exhibits where appropriate.
Outcome:	You will: • Present a closing argument • Utilize exhibits and rhetorical methods of persuasion • ARGUE

Closing arguments are to be approximately 6 to 8 minutes in length. You must not "read" the closing argument. While you may use a ONE PAGE "key word" outline or a checklist of points to be covered, you must not rely on your notes except to refresh your memory--in the <u>unlikely</u> case they are needed. Remember that eye contact is essential to an effective closing argument. Use of notes detracts from your presentation. You should also not stand behind the podium while giving your closing argument.

Note that a keyword in your assignment is *"argument."* This is not an opening statement, so do not merely rehash the facts (after all, the jury was also in the courtroom). Use the *law* -- the jury instructions -- to support your argument. Weave the evidence (proven facts) into the law to persuade the jury of your argument. In a criminal case, the defense counsel should show how the evidence -- or lack of evidence -- or conflict in the evidence -- creates reasonable doubt. Similarly, the prosecution/plaintiff will use the evidence to show how it has proved each necessary element of proof (tell the jury what you *must* prove, so the jury will not be misled to believe because you did not prove some immaterial matter you have not proved your case beyond a reasonable doubt or by the preponderance of the evidence, whichever standard is applicable in your case). You are to assume that all relevant and admissible evidence was presented and admitted. **Please prepare closing arguments for both cases as assigned by your advocacy professor.**

14th Assignment – Voir Dire	Professor _____
	Trial Advocacy
Reading:	FTA – Jury Selection

12th Assignment:	Prepare and conduct jury selection utilizing the principles of jury selection outlined in the text.
Process:	During classroom exercises perform a Voir Dire designed to identify challenges for cause. You should prepare written materials supporting your approach. Do not forget to request individual voir dire when appropriate.
Outcome:	You will: <ul><li>Identify issues that result in a challenge for cause based upon your theory of the case</li><li>Prepare voir dire designed to identify bias that supports a challenge for cause</li><li>Conduct voir dire to support a challenge for cause</li></ul>

Voir dire is one of the most difficult skills for an advocate to learn because it requires the advocate to ask questions to which they do not know the answer. Not only must they ask, they ask them in the presence of a group of people who may all be as affected by the answer. The only way to master this skill is to practice it. You should also review every presentation on jury selection in the ARC, paying particular attention to the one by Judge Habas.

In this exercise the instructor will ask you to perform jury selection based upon the issues in your assigned case. All other members of the class will serve as jurors. Each juror must choose an issue that they believe creates bias. They should feel free to be creative. Each juror should write the bias issue on a piece of paper before the exercise begins.

As each participant conducts voir dire they are searching for the issue on the piece of paper. When they find it a challenge for cause is granted and the participant conducting voir dire becomes a juror. The individual whose bias was discovered is the next participant to conduct voir dire.

Supplemental Assignment – Pre-trial Motion in Limine	**Professor**_____ **Trial Advocacy**
Reading:	FTA – Motions Practice

Supplemental Assignment:	a motion in limine is used to exclude evidence you don't want to come in at trial. The format is fairly simple for your written portion (do not fret about the written aspect– just be clear in your reasoning for why you want the evidence excluded and tie it to the federal rules of evidence). Format is really unimportant other than you need 3 things: 1. State the evidence you wish to exclude/introduce 2. Give the federal rule(s) of evidence that you think tie to the piece of evidence and what the rule means 3. Tie the rule to the facts of the case that you think bolster your side. Be prepared to call a witness or witnesses to present evidence on the factual issue that you find through your legal analysis is important.
Process:	During classroom exercises argue your motion in limine to the court.
Outcome:	You will: • Argue your motion • Engage the judge • Listen to opposing counsel and respond to the arguments made

Here's the script:

Judge: *Are the Parties ready to proceed?*

Both sides: *Yes, Your Honor*

Judge: *Are there any preliminary matters?*

Defense: *Yes, Your Honor, we have 1 motion in limine...*

The evidence: **Past reckless driving conviction of Rebecca Hartwell**

On July 4th, 20XX-11 Rebecca Hartwell was driving home from a party she had attended celebrating the 4th of July. At the party she drank three wine coolers. She drove to the party and also drove home. While driving home late that night, around 11 PM she was driving north on 87th street when a homeless man stepped out in front of vehicle. She struck the man, injuring him severely. She stopped her car immediately and went out to help the homeless man. While she was assisting him the police arrived. Smelling alcohol on Ms. Hartwell they conducted Field Sobriety Test (FST) which she failed. She later gave a breathalyzer sample that registered .016, twice the legal limit. She was charged with DUI which h she plead down to the offense of Reckless Driving.

Provide a copy of your motion to opposing counsel, the judge and one to turn in to your TA.

Evidence in Context: Evidentiary Problems and Exercises
Chapter 7
Foundations

The following are sample foundations for common evidentiary offerings. You should adapt these as necessary when preparing to lay the foundation for an evidentiary offering, or to ensure that opposing counsel has fully laid the foundation for their evidence.[1] The sample foundations provided include:

- A. DIAGRAM 280
- B. PHOTOGRAPH 281
- C. FUNGIBLE EVIDENCE 282
- D. NON-FUNGIBLE EVIDENCE 283
- E. CHAIN-OF-CUSTODY DOCUMENT (CoCD) 284
- F. CHAIN-OF-CUSTODY DOCUMENT (CoCD) (Hearsay) 284
- G. CHILD WITNESS 286
- H. SPOUSE WITNESS 287
- I. LAY WITNESS WITH PERSONAL KNOWLEDGE 288
- J. LAY OPINIONS 288
- K. EXPERT OPINION 289
- L. BIAS 291
- M. HABIT 291
- N. REPUTATION 292
- O. PRIOR BAD ACTS RESULTING IN CONVICTION 293
- P. PRIOR BAD ACTS *NOT* RESULTING IN CONVICTION 294
- Q. OTHER CRIMES/UNCHARGED MISCONDUCT 294
- R. CHARACTER TRAIT OF UNTRUTHFULNESS 295
- S. CHARACTER TRAIT OF TRUTHFULNESS 296
- T. PRIOR INCONSISTENT STATEMENT 297
- U. PRIOR CONSISTENT STATEMENT 297

---

[1] Some portions of this section were adapted from the seminal text on this topic: EDWARD J. IMWINKELREID, *EVIDENTIARY FOUNDATIONS* (7th ed., LexisNexis 2008). In addition to sample foundations, Professor Imwinkelreid also provides limiting instructions and closing arguments for certain kinds of evidence to assist students in understanding what can be said about evidence *after* a foundation has been laid.

Each example identifies the type of evidence offered and the steps necessary admit it into evidence. These are examples of the minimum required information the attorney needs to elicit from the witness to authenticate the evidence or, in the case of the witness, to validate their competency to testify. The questions are intentionally written to be less detailed than expected in court. When preparing your own foundations, make your questions as specific as necessary to ensure each element is thoroughly met.

I. DIAGRAM

1. Mark the exhibit (ideally, this is done before the trial starts...).
2. Show opposing counsel the exhibit:
3. Ask the judge for permission to approach the witness with the exhibit:
4. Show the exhibit to the witness:
5. Lay the foundation for the evidence. Establish the following:
6. Retrieve the exhibit from the witness and offer to admit it into evidence:
   - What it is:
   - What the diagram depicts, the certain area or object in the diagram:
   - That the witness is familiar with that area or object:
   - The witness's basis for their knowledge of the area or object:
   - The witness affirm the accuracy of the diagram:

Q: "Your Honor, I am now showing opposing counsel what has been previously been marked as PE-1 for I.D. for their inspection and objection."

Q: "Your Honor, may I have permission to approach the witness?"

Q: "Your Honor, I am showing the witness what has been previously marked as PE-1 for ID."

Q: "Do you recognize this?"

Q: "What is it?"

Q: "What is in the diagram?

Q: "Are you familiar with it?"

Q: "How is it that you are familiar with it?"

Q: "Is the diagram reasonably accurate?"

Q: "Is the diagram drawn to scale?"

Q: "Your Honor, I offer into evidence what has been previously marked as PE-1 for ID as PE-1."

II. PHOTOGRAPH

1. Mark the exhibit (ideally, this is done before the trial starts...).

2. Show opposing counsel the exhibit:

    "Your Honor, I am now showing opposing counsel what has been previously been marked as PE-1 for I.D. for their inspection and objection."

3. Ask the judge for permission to approach the witness with the exhibit:

    "Your Honor, may I have permission to approach the witness?"

4. Show the exhibit to the witness:

    "Your Honor, I am showing the witness what has been previously marked as PE-1 for ID."

5. Lay the Foundation.

    - Establish what it is:

        "Do you recognize this?"

        "What is it?"

    - Establish that the witness is familiar with the object or scene:

        "Are you familiar with it?"

    - Have the witness explain the basis for his familiarity with the object or scene:

        "How is it that you are familiar with it?"

    - Establish that the witness recognizes the object or scene in the photograph:

        "How is it that you recognize this?

    - Verify that, to the witness, the photograph is a "fair & accurate" or "true" or "correct" depiction of the object or scene at the relevant time:

        "Is this photograph a fair and accurate representation of the [object or scene] at the [relevant time]?"

        ~or~

        "Is this photograph a true representation of the [object or scene] at the [relevant time]?"

        ~or~

        "Is this photograph an accurate representation of the [object or scene] at the [relevant time]?"

6. Retrieve the exhibit from the witness and offer to admit it into evidence:

    "Your Honor, I offer into evidence what has been previously marked as PE-1 for ID as PE-1."

III. FUNGIBLE EVIDENCE

1. Mark the exhibit (ideally, this is done before the trial starts...).
2. Show opposing counsel the exhibit:

   "Your Honor, I am now showing opposing counsel what has been previously been marked as PE-1 for I.D. for their inspection and objection."

3. Ask the judge for permission to approach the witness with the exhibit:

   "Your Honor, may I have permission to approach the witness?"

4. Show the exhibit to the witness:

   "Your Honor, I am showing the witness what has been previously marked as PE-1 for ID."

5. Lay the Foundation:

   - Establish what it is:

   "Do you recognize this?"

   "What is it?"

   - Establish that the witness is familiar with the item:

   "And you are familiar with this particular [item]?"

   - Establish that the witness acquired this familiarity by obtaining the item:

   "How did you come to be familiar with this particular [item]?"

   - Establish that the witness uniquely marked the item of evidence to enable him to identify it later:

   "Did you mark the [item] in anyway?"

   "Why did you do this?"

   - Establish that the witness properly safeguarded the item to prevent it from being lost or altered:

   "What did you do with the [item] after you [acquired] it?"

   "Why did you do that?"

   - Establish that the witness ultimately disposed of the item:

   "When you were finished collecting and marking the [item], what did you do with it?"

   - Establish that, to the best of his knowledge, Witness can positively identify the item as that which he previously had:

   "Can you positively identity this [item] as the one you collected and marked on [the relevant date and time]?"

   - Establish that the item is in the same condition as it was when he had the item previously:

   Is the [item] in substantially the same condition as when you had it last?"

6. Retrieve the exhibit from the witness and offer to admit it into evidence:

   "Your Honor, I offer into evidence what has been previously marked as PE-1 for ID as PE-1."

IV. NON-FUNGIBLE EVIDENCE

1. Mark the exhibit (ideally, this is done before the trial starts...).
2. Show opposing counsel the exhibit:

   "Your Honor, I am now showing opposing counsel what has been previously been marked as PE-1 for I.D. for their inspection and objection."

3. Ask the judge for permission to approach the witness with the exhibit:

   "Your Honor, may I have permission to approach the witness?"

4. Show the exhibit to the witness:

   "Your Honor, I am showing the witness what has been previously marked as PE-1 for ID."

5. Lay the foundation:

   - Establish what it is:

   "Do you recognize this?"

   "What is it?"

   - Establish that the object has a unique characteristic:

   "Does it have any unique characteristics?"

   - Establish that the witness observed the characteristic on a previous occasion:

   "Was this [unique characteristic] present on the [item] before?"

   - Establish that the witness identifies the exhibit as the object:

   "Do you recognize this [item] as the [item] from the [incident] on [relevant date]?"

   - Establish that the witness rests the identification on his present recognition of the characteristic:

   "And you know this is that [item] because you recognize here the [unique characteristic] on the [item]

   - Establish that to the best of the witness' knowledge, the exhibit is in the same condition as it was when the witness initially saw or received the object:

   Is the [item] in substantially the same condition as it was when you initially [saw or received] it?

6. Retrieve the exhibit from the witness and offer to admit it into evidence:

   "Your Honor, I offer into evidence what has been previously marked as PE-1 for ID as PE-1."

V. CHAIN-OF-CUSTODY DOCUMENT (CoCD)

1. Mark the exhibit (ideally, this is done before the trial starts...).

2. Show opposing counsel the exhibit:

    "Your Honor, I am now showing opposing counsel what has been previously been marked as PE-1 for I.D. for their inspection and objection."

3. Ask the judge for permission to approach the witness with the exhibit:

    "Your Honor, may I have permission to approach the witness?"

4. Show the exhibit to the witness:

    "Your Honor, I am showing the witness what has been previously marked as PE-1 for ID."

5. Lay the foundation:

    - Establish what it is:

    "Do you recognize this?"

    "What is it?"

    - Establish that the witness has personal knowledge of the business' filing or records system:

    "Does the [entity or organization in question] have a [filing or records system]?"

    "And you are personally familiar with their [filing or records system]?"

    - Establish that the witness removed the record (CoCD) in question from a certain file:

    "Did you remove this [CoCD] from a file in that system?"

    "And from what file in that system did you remove it?"

    - Establish that the record (CoCD) in question was a proper file entry:

    "Was this [CoCD] a proper file entry in the system?"

    - Establish that the Witness recognizes the exhibit as the record (CoCD) he removed from the file:

    "Do you recognize this [CoCD] as the record you removed from the file?"

    - Witness specifies the basis on which he recognized the exhibit:

    "How do you recognize this [CoCD] as the record you removed from the file?"

6. Retrieve the exhibit from the witness and offer to admit it into evidence:

    "Your Honor, I offer into evidence what has been previously marked as PE-1 for ID as PE-1."

VI. CHAIN-OF-CUSTODY DOCUMENT (CoCD) (Hearsay)

1. Mark the exhibit (ideally, this is done before the trial starts...).

2. Show opposing counsel the exhibit:

   "Your Honor, I am now showing opposing counsel what has been previously been marked as PE-1 for I.D. for their inspection and objection."

3. Ask the judge for permission to approach the witness with the exhibit:

   "Your Honor, may I have permission to approach the witness?"

4. Show the exhibit to the witness:

   "Your Honor, I am showing the witness what has been previously marked as PE-1 for ID."

5. Lay the foundation:

   - Establish what it is:

   "Do you recognize this?"

   "What is it?"

   - The CoCD was prepared by a person having a relationship with the agency preparing the CoCD:

   "Who prepared this [CoCD]"?

   "Does [name] have a relationship with [the agency preparing the CoCD]?"

   - The person had a duty to record the information on the CoCD:

   "Whose responsibility was it to complete this [CoCD]?"

   "So, it was [name]'s duty to fill in the [CoCD]?"

   - The person had personal knowledge of the facts or events recorded in the CoCD:

   From where did [name] get the information they used to fill in the [CoCD]?"

   - The CoCD was prepared contemporaneously with the events:

   "When did [name] complete the [CoCD]?"

   "And this was at the same time as [the event in question]?"

   - It was a routine practice of the business to prepare CoCD:

   "When are the [CoCD]s normally completed?"

   "And this was the routine practice of [the agency preparing the CoCD]?"

   - The CoCD was reduced to written form:

   "After the [CoCD] is completed, what happens to it next?"

   "So, this is when it is [reduced to written form]?"

   - The CoCD was made in the regular course of business:

   "And this particular [CoCD] was completed in the normal or regular course of business of [the agency preparing the CoCD]?"

6. Retrieve the exhibit from the witness and offer to admit it into evidence:

"Your Honor, I offer into evidence what has been previously marked as PE-1 for ID as PE-1."

VII. CHILD WITNESS

Depending on the jurisdiction, children below a certain age may be presumed incompetent. This rebuttable presumption may be overcome if the side offering the child as a witness can demonstrate the child possesses the requisite abilities to testify: the capacity to observe, remember, relate, and a recognition of the need to tell the truth.

In other jurisdictions there is no presumption of incompetence and it is simply a question of fact decided by the trial judge whether the child witness possesses the requisite abilities. In either jurisdiction, the side offering the witness should lay an adequate foundation for those abilities.

1. Call the witness. If opposing counsel objects to the child as an incompetent witness, offer to voir dire the child.

2. Lay the foundation by showing the four capacities:

    - Show the child has the capacity to observe:

   "How well do you see?"

   "Do you wear glasses?"

   "How well do you hear?"

    - Show the child has the capacity to remember:

   "How old are you?"

   "When is your birthday?"

   "What is your address?"

    - Show the child has the capacity to relate:

   "What school do you go to?"

   "What grade are you in?"

   "What classes do you have?"

   "What do you learn in [topic] class?

    - Show the child has a recognition of a duty to tell the truth:

   "What does it mean to tell the truth?"

   "Why should you tell the truth?"

   "What happens when you don't tell the truth?"

3. Offer the witness as competent:

   "Your Honor, I have no further questions about his competency. The child's answers demonstrate the capacities to observe, remember, and relate, and his recognition of a duty to tell the truth."

VIII. SPOUSE WITNESS

The spouse as a witness is problematic depending on the jurisdiction. The common-law view is that if the marriage exists when the spouse is called, the accused has the power to prevent the spouse from testifying. The majority trend, adopted by the U.S. Supreme Court in *Trammel v. U.S.*,[2] is the spouse witness holds the power to choose to testify at their discretion and the accused may not object. Other jurisdictions provide that both the accused and the spouse witness may invoke privilege independently and prevent the testimony. Finally, some jurisdictions do not hold any spousal privilege and treat spouses like any other witness. Ensure you research the requirements in your jurisdiction before proceeding.

Two exceptions may apply to disqualifying a spouse witness: the injured spouse doctrine, and pre-marital facts. If the spouse is the victim of the accused's charged offense, the accused cannot invoke the privilege to prevent the victim from testifying. In some jurisdictions, if the facts to which the spouse will testify occurred before the marriage, the jurisdiction may bar the accused from preventing the testimony.

1. Call the witness. Opposing counsel may object to the spouse as incompetent and seek to voir dire.
2. The opposing party will seek to show the witness has married the accused and the marriage still exists.

    - Show the witness married the accused:

    "Mr. Gordon, isn't it true that on July, 14, 1984, you married the accused, Margaret Gordon?"

    "Isn't it also true that Margaret Gordon is the accused in this case?"

    - Show the witness is still married to the accused:

    "Mr. Gordon, isn't it true that there have been no divorce proceedings since the marriage?"

    "And, further, that there haven't been any annulment proceedings since the marriage?"

3. The proponent of the witness will need to show the witness is the victim of the accused, or that the facts to be presented preceded the marriage.

    - Show the witness is the victim of the accused:

    "Mr. Gordon, I see you are missing your left arm. Is the person who cut off your arm in the courtroom today?"

    - Show the facts about which the spouse witness is to testify occurred before the marriage:

    "Mr. Gordon, when did Mrs. Gordon cut off your arm?"

    "And this was before your wedding to Mrs. Gordon on July 14, 1984?"

---

[2] 445 U.S. 40 (1980)

IX. LAY WITNESS WITH PERSONAL KNOWLEDGE

Common-law and the Federal Rules require that non-expert witnesses have first-hand knowledge of the facts or events about which they will testify. Although the bar set by FRE 104(b) is rather low, the side offering the witness may want to far exceed the minimal showing needed. The jury's consideration of what the witness testifies to is often tempered by how convinced the jury was that the witness actually observed the facts or events in the testimony. Persuasively showing the personal knowledge of the witness is key to the fact-finder's acceptance of the testimony as offered.

1. Call the witness.

2. Lay the foundation for the competency of the witness to testify by showing the witness was in a location to perceive the event, that they did perceive the event, and that they remember the perceived event.

- Show the witness was in such a position as to be able to perceive the event (normally, observation is by sight, but any sense may have been used):

"Mr. Gordon, you testified that at 7:00 p.m. on the night of June 22, 2008, you were standing on the corner of 5th Avenue and Main Street. Could you see the entire intersection from where you were standing?"

"What direction were you facing?"

"Was there any other traffic present other than the two vehicles that were involved in the collision?"

- Show the witness did perceive the event in question:

"Did you see the collision?"

"What did you see?"

"Could you hear anything?"

- Show the witness remembers what they perceived (why they remember it so well, how it is significant to them):

"Mr. Gordon, how well do you remember seeing the collision?"

"Why do you remember the collision so well?"

X. LAY OPINIONS

Two types of lay opinions commonly accepted in courts are the collective fact opinion and the skilled lay observer opinion. The collective fact opinion, also known as a shorthand rendition opinion, is based on the concept that lay persons commonly and reliably draw inferences from perceived facts and form an opinion on subjects such as height, distance, speed, color and identity by virtue of common human experience.

1. Call the witness.

2. Lay the foundation for the opinion of the lay witness by showing the witness was in a location to observe, that they did observe, that they observed enough to form a reliable opinion, and that the witness can state the opinion.

- Show the witness was in a position to observe the event about which they formed an opinion:

"Mr. Gordon, where were you standing at the intersection of 5th Avenue and Main Street?"

"What direction were you facing?"

- Show the witness did observe the event about which they formed an opinion:

"And from this position, Mr. Gordon, what could you see?"

- Show the witness observed enough of the event to form a reliable opinion:

"How long were you able to see the truck as it approached the intersection?"

- Have the witness state their opinion:

"Do you have an opinion of the truck's speed?"

"In your opinion, what was the speed of the truck as it approached the intersection?"

The other type of lay opinion is the skilled lay observer opinion and includes lay opinions about someone's handwriting style, the sound of that person's, or that person's sanity. All of these opinions require intimate familiarity with the particular subject by the witness through their repeated exposure and observation.

1. Call the witness.
2. Lay the foundation for the skilled lay opinion by showing the witness is familiar with the subject, the subject's voice, or the subject's handwriting through repeated prior opportunities for observation.

- Show the witness is familiar with the subject:

"Mr. Gordon, how long have you known Ned Miller?"

"How did you come to meet Mr. Miller?"

"In the time Mr. Miller has been your neighbor, have you had occasion to spend time with him?"

"Are you familiar with the sound of Mr. Miller's voice?"

"Have you ever heard Mr. Miller speak?"

"How often have you spoken with Mr. Miller?"

"Under what circumstances have you heard Mr. Miller speak?"

"How well do you know Mr. Miller's handwriting style?"

"How did you become familiar with Mr. Miller's handwriting?"

XI. EXPERT OPINION

The Federal Rules allow an expert to testify when the trier of fact requires assistance in understanding "scientific, technical, or other specialized knowledge ... to determine a fact in issue."[3] While the standard in the Federal rules is simply that the expert just possess more knowledge than the trier of fact, in *Daubert v. Merrell Dow Pharmaceuticals, Inc.*, the U.S. Supreme Court held that the trial judge must ensure the expert's testimony "rests on a reliable foundation and is relevant to the task at hand."[4]

The burden is on the side presenting the witness to show the witness is an expert. Reliable foundations for an expert's knowledge may include presenting information on:

- Academic degrees earned by the witness in their field
- Specialized training in their field
- Professional licenses held by the witness in their field
- Length of time spent by the witness in their field.
- Publications by the witness in their field.
- Membership in professional organizations in the field.
- Honors or prizes presented to the witness.
- Previous experience as an expert witness on this topic.

Some or all of these areas may be touched on when laying the foundation for your expert, depending on the specific nature of their expertise and the needs of your case. Your case analysis will identify these needs.

1. Call the witness.

- Show the witness has specialized knowledge:

"Mr. Gordon, please introduce yourself to the jury."

"Where did you go to school?"

"Do you have a degree?"

"What is your degree in?"

- Show the witness has specialized training:

"Do you have any technical training?"

"Where did you receive this training?"

"When did you complete this training?

- Show the witness has specialized experience:

"After your technical training, did you work in this field?"

"How long have you been the operations safety officer for the Calusa County Nuclear Power Plant?"

"What are your duties as the operations safety officer at the Calusa County Nuclear Power Plant?"

---

[3] FRE 702.
[4] 509 U.S. 579, 597 (1993).

"Your honor, I tender Mr. Gordon to this court as an expert in nuclear power plant operations."

These are sample questions; design your foundation questions with the specific expert witness and subject matter in mind.

XII. BIAS

The bias a witness holds is a potential means of impeachment. There are no particular requirements for laying a foundation for bias evidence; the side seeking to show bias may prove any fact or event that logically shows the bias.

1. Call the witness.
2. Lay the foundation by proving an event that indicates bias.

   - Show when and where the event occurred:

   "Mr. Gordon, isn't it true that at 7:00 p.m. on the night of June 22, 2008, you were present at O'Neil's Irish Pub?"

   - Show who was present at the event:

   "Mr. Gordon, isn't it also true that the defendants, Nicholas Cox and James Thaler, were both there with you at O'Neil's Irish Pub that night?"

   - Show what occurred at the event:

   "And, Mr. Gordon, finally, isn't it true that you, and Nick, and James, were all drinking beer at O'Neil's Irish Pub that night?"

Note: it is probably not necessary to get the witness to concede their bias. It is unlikely the witness would actually admit to it, and trying to force it may make counsel appear argumentative. It is often better to simply prove the fact or event showing bias and then later invite the jury to make the inference during closing arguments.

XIII. HABIT

Habit evidence may be used as circumstantial proof of conduct. Unlike character evidence, which is usually only admissible if the accused first raises the issue, habit evidence may be admitted by either side. The elements of the foundation for habit evidence are:

- The witness is familiar with the person or business.
- The witness has been with the person or business for a substantial length of time.
- The witness has an opinion about a specific behavioral pattern of the person or business.
- The witness has observed the conformity of the person or business with the specific behavioral pattern on numerous occasions.

Some jurisdictions may additionally require that there be either no eyewitnesses to the specific conduct involved in the case, or that the specific conduct be corroborated by an eyewitness that described the conduct as consistent with the habit.

1. Call the witness.

- Show the witness is familiar with the person or business:

"Mr. Gordon, are you familiar with the UtoteEm in Calusa County?"

"How is it you are familiar with the UtoteEm?"

- Show the witness has been with the person or business for a substantial length of time:

"How long have you been shopping at the UtoteEm?"

"How often do you shop at the UtoteEm?"

- Show the witness has an opinion about a specific behavioral pattern of the person or business:

"When shopping at the UtoteEm did you ever observe the attendant use the cash register?"

"How did the attendant use the cash register when you shopped at the UtoteEm?"

"How consistently did the attendant use the cash register when you shopped at the UtoteEm?"

- The witness has observed the conformity of the person or business with the specific behavioral pattern on numerous occasions

"How often did you see the attendant use the cash register at the UtoteEm?"

"Have you ever seen the attendant at the UtoteEm fail to use the cash register?"

"Have you ever seen the attendant at the UtoteEm use the cash register in any other way?"

Don't seek to have the witness actually state their opinion; that would be improper. Instead, similar to bias evidence, during closing arguments argue in favor of the inference you want the jury to make.

XIV. REPUTATION

In most jurisdictions, the character of the accused does not become an issue unless the accused presents character evidence, that is, something more than simply testifying on their own behalf. Character evidence presented by the prosecution is normally only allowed in rebuttal.

1. Call the witness.

- Show the witness is a member of the same community as the accused (home, work, or social):

"Mr. Gordon, who is Marlin Fischer?"

"How do you know Marlin Fischer?"

"Where does Mr. Fischer live?"

"Where do you live, Mr. Gordon?"

"And how close do you live to Mr. Fischer?"

- Show the witness has been a member of that community for a substantial period:

"Mr. Gordon, how long have you lived in your current residence?"

"How long has Mr. Fischer lived next door to you?"

"How long have you known Marlin Fischer?"

- Show the accused has a reputation in that community, either a general reputation or a reputation for a specific character trait:

"Mr. Gordon, does Mr. Fischer have a particular reputation in your neighborhood?"

- Show the witness knows the reputation:

"Do you know that reputation?"

- Have the witness state the reputation:

"What is that reputation?"

XV. PRIOR BAD ACTS RESULTING IN CONVICTION

Proof a witness other than the accused has suffered a past conviction can be a telling blow during impeachment and the Federal Rules allow these facts to be admitted under certain circumstances, especially if one of the elements of the crime of conviction involved dishonesty or false statements.[5] While all courts allow this method of impeachment, they differ on what offenses may be used. Ensure you check your jurisdiction's standards as you plan your cross-examination.

1. Begin cross-examining the witness.

    - Show the witness is the person who suffered the prior conviction:

"Isn't it true, Mr. Gordon, that you are the same Bufford Gordon who was once convicted of a felony?"

- Show the conviction is for a crime the jurisdiction considers impeaching:

"Isn't it a fact, Mr. Gordon, that felony was smuggling prescription drugs?"

- Show the conviction was entered in a particular jurisdiction:

"Isn't it correct that you were convicted of that crime in Calusa County?"

- Show the conviction was entered in a particular year:

"And isn't it also correct that you were convicted of that crime in 2005?"

- Show the witness received a particular sentence:

"And, Mr. Gordon, isn't it also a fact that as a result of that conviction, you were sentenced to 10 years in prison for smuggling?"

---

[5] FRE 609(a).

If you are using a copy of the judgment, there is an additional element to the foundation:

- Show the copy of the judgment is authentic:

"Your Honor, may this be marked as D.E. 1 for I.D.?

"Please let the record show I am showing what has been marked as D.E. 1 for I.D. to opposing counsel."

"I now offer D.E. 1 for I.D. into evidence as D.E. 1., a copy of the judgment including a properly executed attesting certificate, making this exhibit self-authenticating under Rule 902."

XVI. PRIOR BAD ACTS *NOT* RESULTING IN CONVICTION

Most jurisdictions allow impeaching a witness on cross-examination with proof the witness has committed untruthful acts. However, there is a risk: because extrinsic evidence of the untruthful act may not be admitted,[6] opposing counsel must accept whatever answer the witness gives.

1. Begin cross-examining the witness.

    - Show when the witness committed the untruthful act:

    "Mr. Gordon, isn't it a fact that in 1998 you filed a false tax return?"

    - Show where the witness committed the untruthful act:

    "Mr. Gordon, isn't it also true that you submitted this false tax return to the IRS from Calusa County?"

    - Show the nature of the act reflects against the character of the witness for truthfulness:

    "Mr. Gordon, in this tax return, you claimed that your wife requires 24-hour care. That wasn't true, was it?"

    "You also claimed, Mr. Gordon, in this 1998 return, that your 10-year-old son had been wounded in Vietnam. This wasn't true, was it?"

    "And, Mr. Gordon, when you tried to claim nine children as dependents, including one who was a member of the clergy, you were not telling the truth, were you?"

XVII. OTHER CRIMES/UNCHARGED MISCONDUCT

The Federal Rules allow the prosecution to introduce evidence of other crimes or of uncharged misconduct, not to show the accused is a law-breaking immoral person, but to show other things, such as motive, intent, opportunity, knowledge, etc.[7] If the evidence of the uncharged act is logically relevant to a fact in issue other than character, it may be admitted. The trier of fact will decide whether the logical relevance of the evidence outweighs its prejudicial

---

[6] FRE 608(b)(1), a remnant of the common-law collateral fact rule which limits the impeaching counsel to intrinsic impeachment when the issue relates only to the credibility of the witness.
[7] FRE 404(b).

nature.

1. Call the witness (assume the defendant has been charged with possession of stolen goods).

- Show where the other criminal act or uncharged misconduct occurred:

"Mr. Gordon, please tell the jury where you were when you first encountered the defendant, Snake Berman."

- Show when the other criminal act or uncharged misconduct occurred:

And, Mr. Gordon, when was it that you first came into contact with Mr. Berman?"

- Show the nature of the other criminal act or uncharged misconduct:

"Mr. Gordon, please describe to the jury what happened when the defendant entered your home."

"Mr. Gordon, when Mr. Berman left your house, was he carrying anything?"

- Show the accused committed the other criminal act or uncharged misconduct:

"How well did you see Mr. Berman when he left carrying your television?"

"How close were you to Mr. Berman when he took your television?"

"Is Snake Berman in this court room right now?"

- Show the relevance of the other criminal act or uncharged misconduct to the charged offense:

"Mr. Gordon, did Mr. Berman have permission to take your TV set?"

"Did you give anyone permission to take your television?"

"Did you report the theft to the police?"

"After you reported your television as stolen, did you get a police report number?"

The defense will have the right to seek a limiting instruction, under FRE 105, where the judge will inform the jury they may not use this evidence as general character evidence but only use it to decide the existence of the fact the evidence was admitted to prove (the accused's motive, intent, opportunity, knowledge, etc).

XVIII. CHARACTER TRAIT OF UNTRUTHFULNESS

Extrinsic evidence, usually a second witness, may be used to impeach the credibility of a witness. This is usually in the form of a second witness, who testifies to the trait in the witness being impeached.

1. Call the second witness.

- Show the second witness is a member of the same community (home or social) as the witness being impeached:

"Mr. Gordon, who is Marlin Fischer?"

"How do you know Marlin Fischer?"

- Show the second witness has been a member of that community for a substantial period of time:

"How long have you been a next-door neighbor of Marlin Fischer?"

"How long have you lived in Calusa County?"

"How long have you attended the same church with Marlin Fischer?"

- Show the witness being impeached has a reputation for untruthfulness in the community:

"Mr. Gordon, does Marlin Fischer have a reputation for truthfulness or untruthfulness in Calusa County?"

- Show the second witness knows of the reputation for untruthfulness of the witness being impeached:

"What is that reputation?"

"Given Mr. Fischer's reputation, would you believe him under oath?"

Note: some jurisdictions allow the second witness to add that, considering the reputation of the witness being impeached, the second witness would not believe him or her under oath.

XIX. CHARACTER TRAIT OF TRUTHFULNESS

Proving the character trait of truthfulness in a witness is necessary after the opposing side has attempted to impeach the witness and rehabilitation is necessary. Typically after the second witness impeaches the first witness, the court will allow the proponent of the impeached witness to call a third witness, to testify to the reputation for truthfulness of the impeached witness.

The elements of the foundation are the same as the Character Trait for Untruthfulness (above).

1. Call the third witness.

    - Show the third witness is a member of the same community (home or social) as the witness being impeached:

"Reverend Miller, who is Marlin Fischer?"

"How do you know Mr. Fischer?"

- Show the third witness has been a member of that community for a substantial period of time:

"How long has Marlin Fischer been a member of your church?"

- Show the witness being impeached has a reputation for truthfulness in the community:

"Reverend Miller, does Marlin Fischer have a reputation for truthfulness or untruthfulness in Calusa County?"

- Show the third witness knows of the reputation for truthfulness of the witness being impeached:

"What is that reputation?"

"Given Mr. Fischer's reputation, Reverend Miller, would you believe him under oath?"

XX. PRIOR INCONSISTENT STATEMENT

Another means of impeaching the credibility of a witness is to show they made prior statements that are inconsistent with their current testimony. The fact of these inconsistencies calls into question the ability of the witness to recall and relate what was observed.

1. Begin to cross-examine the witness.

- Get the witness to commit to the testimony given during direct examination:

"Mr. Hightower, you just testified that Mr. Gordon was not at your Planet Calusa County restaurant the night of the incident, correct?"

- Show the witness made an earlier statement at a certain place (if the earlier statement was in writing, where it was written is not essential):

"Mr. Hightower, isn't it true that after the incident you were present during a meeting at the Calusa County Town Hall to discuss what had happened?"

- Show the witness made an earlier statement at a certain time:

And, Mr. Hightower, that meeting at Town Hall was at 11:00 p.m., immediately after the incident occurred?"

- Show that certain persons were present when the witness made the earlier statement:

Mr. Hightower, weren't Doctor Jones and Mayor Stevens both present with you at this meeting?

- Show the earlier statement made by the witness was of a certain tenor:

"In that meeting with Doctor Jones and Mayor Stevens, didn't you say that Mr. Gordon was present and participating in the all-you-can-eat buffet, and you were concerned about your losses?"

- Show the earlier statement made by the witness is more likely reliable than the present testimony:

"Isn't it a fact, Mr. Hightower, in that point of time, that conversation was closer to the incident than your testimony today?"

"Isn't it a fact your memory was fresher then?"

Note: it may be preferable to not force the final concession from the witness. Merely elicit the facts of the statement's timing and then argue the relative reliability of the earlier statement compared to the testimony during your closing arguments. Indeed, the judge may find these final questions are objectionably argumentative.

XXI. PRIOR CONSISTENT STATEMENT

Similar to recovering from an impeachment for untruthfulness, when a witness has been impeached for making prior inconsistent statements, it may be necessary to rehabilitate them by showing past statements that are consistent with their testimony. For procedural reasons, many jurisdictions impose a requirement that the prior consistent statement precede the prior inconsistent statement or that the prior consistent statement have been made before the witness had any motive to lie.

1. Call the witness.

    - Show where the prior consistent statement was made:

    "Mr. Hightower, after the incident at your Planet Calusa County restaurant, did you speak to anyone there?"

    - Show when the prior consistent statement was made:

    "And this interview took place immediately after the incident?"

    - Show who was present when the prior consistent statement was made:

    "Was anyone with Brad Bradley during the interview?"

    - Show the tenor of the prior consistent statement:

    "During that interview, did you tell Mr. Bradley who was present in the restaurant?"

    "During that interview, what did you say to Mr. Bradley about Mr. Gordon?"

    - If a temporal requirement must be met, show the prior consistent statement preceded (1) the prior inconsistent statement or (2) any motive on the part of the witness to lie:

    "Was this interview with Brad Bradley before or after the meeting at the Town Hall with Doctor Jones and Mayor Stevens?"

    "Was this interview with Brad Bradley before or after you had been contacted by attorneys regarding this legal action?"

Typically the judge will be asked to give the jury a limiting instruction, that although the jurors could consider the testimony for credibility purposes, they should not treat the prior statement as proof "Mr. Gordon" was (or was not) present during the incident.